Black Becomes A Rainbow

AGI L. BAUER

'BLACK'
Becomes a
Rainbow

The mother of
a baal teshuvah
tells her story

FELDHEIM PUBLISHERS *Jerusalem ☐ New York*

This story is true but the names of certain individuals have been changed in order to protect their privacy.

A glossary of foreign words and phrases appears at the back of this book.

First published 1991
ISBN 0-87306-572-7 hardcover
ISBN 0-87306-573-5 paperback

Copyright © 1991 by Agi L. Bauer

Edited by Marsi Tabak

Philipp Feldheim Inc.
200 Airport Executive Park
Spring Valley, NY 10977

Feldheim Publishers Ltd.
POB 35002
Jerusalem, Israel

Library of Congress Cataloging-in-Publication Data

Bauer, Agi L.
Black becomes a rainbow / by Agi L. Bauer.
320 p. 24cm.
ISBN 0-87306-572-7. — ISBN 0-87306-573-5 (pbk.)
1. Orthodox Judaism—Israel. 2. Jews—Israel—Return to Orthodox Judaism.
3. Bauer. Agi L. 4. Jews. Hungarians—Australia—Biography. 5. Mothers and daughters—Israel—Biography.
I. Title.
BM390.B36   1991
296.8'32'092—dc20   91-21165
[B]   CIP
                                                           r91

10 9 8 7 6 5 4

Printed in Israel

Contents

Publisher's Foreword

The Jewish People has faced many threats to its existence throughout history but perhaps none so great as the ever-increasing rate of Jewish intermarriage and assimilation, and the concomitant decreasing Jewish birthrate. The frightening statistics point to a widespread failure to inculcate Torah values in Jewish youth, values that would remain with them beyond their scholastic and academic years and enable them to live meaningful, productive lives as religious adults and to pass on the Tradition to the next generation. Our spiritual leaders and educators are engaged in a life-and-death struggle against the temptations of a secular world that draw so many away from their Jewish heritage. But clearly if the battle is to be won, more creative and more effective educational means must be employed.

The worldwide "Teshuvah Movement" has provided a partial answer to the question of Jewish survival, and the successes of its *kiruv* ("outreach") programs should be applauded. However, those involved professionally in *kiruv* do not view their relatively small gains as true success. While they manage to painstakingly cast a few additional stitches onto the fabric of Jewish existence, our beautiful tapestry continues to unravel at an alarming pace.

It is apparent, therefore, that the burden of *kiruv* cannot be borne by a dedicated few alone; it is the obligation of every Jew to reach out and bring others closer to *Yiddishkeit*.

Those of us who were fortunate to have been born and raised

in Orthodox homes and who possess a genuine love for Judaism have an even greater obligation. We know that

> The Torah is a tree of life for those who
> grasp it, and its supporters are praiseworthy.
> Its ways are ways of pleasantness and all its
> pathways are peace. (*Mishlei* 3:18)

By emulating the Torah's "ways of pleasantness" we can be most effective in helping to spread its light.

Many of our regular readers may wonder why we chose to publish a book by an author who professes to be "secular." The answer is simple: She represents a very large part of our nation, Jews deprived of any Jewish education who live their lives in spiritual darkness, their vision dimmed by ignorance of their own heritage. When they are exposed to the light of Torah, they may be blinded by its brilliance, and, like the author, try to shield their eyes from it. But with patience and understanding — "ways of pleasantness" — we can help to bring the wondrous light even to those who have grown to love the dark.

Yaakov Feldheim

The beginning of wisdom is: get wisdom;
therefore use all your means to acquire understanding.
PROVERBS 4:7

Blessed are You, Hashem our God, King of the universe,
Who remembers the covenant
and keeps His promise faithfully.
BLESSING RECITED ON SEEING A RAINBOW

ברוך אתה ד' אלקינו מלך העולם
זוכר הברית ונאמן בבריתו
וקים במאמרו

Preface

The Urge to Write this Book

I must tell you that although I had a great urge, desire, and enthusiasm to write this book, a small book on a very large subject, I seriously doubted that it would ever be written. You may well ask, What would make an author start off by doubting that his or her book will ever be written? The answer is simple: sheer lack of time and complete exhaustion. Like many mothers of *Baal Teshuvah* children living in Israel (which, to me, is the most logical place for a *Baal Teshuvah* to be), I travel from the opposite end of the world to visit my family and am immediately catapulted into a totally alien lifestyle — and there I stay till the day of my return home. All in all, it is very tiring and debilitating, and not particularly conducive to book writing.

Nevertheless, this book finally did get written, almost twelve years after my becoming the mother of a *Baal Teshuvah*, ten years after my becoming the mother of a married *Baal Teshuvah*, and eight years after my becoming the grandmother of the first of several gorgeous little geniuses (which without any shadow of a doubt, each one of them is. But we will not enlarge on that — yet!). Now if this does not make me an expert on *Baalei Teshuvah*, what does? And being a good observer, and a great lover of writing, what better pastime could I find for myself in the wee hours between 2:00 and 4:00 A.M. when sleep eludes me, than to tell you what being the mother of a *Baal Teshuvah* has meant to me.

Over the years, I have had many conversations with other parents whose children chose a path so different from the one planned for them from birth. I know what that choice has meant to those suffering mothers and fathers. Almost without exception, they relate tales of estrangement from their children and grandchildren; most are bitter and resentful, angry and even repelled — emotions I could well identify with way back then. Today, their misery evokes in me only pity, because I know that to a great extent they have brought it on themselves, and the remedy is in their own hands. Maybe, in reading about my experiences, they will discover that there truly is another way.

Being with my *Baal Teshuvah* family for month after month during my annual pilgrimages to Jerusalem, I do see and hear almost daily the most interesting and fascinating things. To write about them all would take volumes, so I chose only those that really captured my heart and mind, filled me with a kind of awe, and moved me to write them down, to preserve them and share them with readers in similar circumstances who might be as ignorant and unbelieving as I was, in the hope that they might turn into people as cautious and tolerant as I am trying to be.

I have not added to the episodes I've recorded so as to make them seem funny, since for the most part they were quite hilarious on their own. Nor have I tried to color them, as they were colorful enough. In fact, it was that very point that inspired me to give my book its title. There was indeed a time when everything — *everything* — having to do with my daughter's newfound *Baal Teshuvah* life seemed as black and somber as the traditional attire of the very Orthodox Jew. I did not know then how much joy the future could hold. I did not know then how full and rich and vibrant my own life could be. I did not know then — but I most certainly do now — that "black" becomes a rainbow.

❋   ❋   ❋

To thank the countless people who have in one way or another provided me with renewed strength, continuous enthusiasm, and growing confidence to achieve what I had set my heart and mind to, would be impossible. But without any doubt, my gratitude goes first and foremost to my daughter, who was the catalyst as well as the inspiration for everything connected with this book.

Many individuals helped me to travel the rocky road from my "black" beginnings to my "rainbow" days. I am convinced that without these special people I would not have been able to make this transition. The kibbutz "parents" Moshe and Ruthi and their marvelous family, as well as Tova and Rafi, to name but a few of our kibbutz friends, provided a unique learning experience for both me and my husband.

I am grateful to the numerous members of the Israeli family who were often my only comfort when I was thousands of miles away, as I knew that at any time Esther or one of her children would be there to help and guide "Natalie" in some spiritual matter or in any other possible way.

Sometimes I simply *could not go on* without the wise advice of David Bar-Sela, and the always *helpful strong arm* of Agi Bar-Sela. The door to their home was always open to me, and I often took refuge there, at times when things seemed too overwhelming for me to cope with. I call them my Tel Aviv family, my "home-away-from-home."

I cannot imagine what the entire transition would have been like without the warmth that various members of one particular family extended to me. Neither can I think about "Natalie's" wedding without recalling the most unforgettable "gift" that the head of this family presented to us all when he not only danced but even somersaulted with his two sons, just to make us happy on our daughter's wedding day.

I must certainly mention Shlomo Dinur, a wise, sensitive man, a real friend who is very learned and spiritually rich, though not religiously observant. His always-ready attention to and patience with my problems and doubts were immeasurably helpful.

With sadness I must note the passing of my dear friend Atara Hasofer, who was a great inspiration back in Sydney. Her open house and warm friendship were often my only contact with Orthodoxy and learning. She will always serve me as an example to remember and to quote from.

Erwin Frenkel, former editor of *The Jerusalem Post*, provided the encouragement to write this book, at a time when I most needed it.

I am grateful to Doris Lankin, my treasured friend, for putting my messy tenses and spelling into proper English without changing a word in the manuscript. And who would be more suited to this task than the expert who wrote the legal column in *The Jerusalem Post* for over twenty years, covering, among other things, the Eichmann trial.

There are so many things that I should say a special thanks to my husband Steven for, that it almost seems ludicrous to mention this one. But I must thank him for persevering with the seemingly hopeless task of teaching me to use the computer. I also thank Deborah Siegel for always rescuing me whenever I got stuck with it, at times when Steven was not within reach.

And above all, I thank the Orthodox, "black," "glatt" families of "Givat Dat" who contributed to my growing awareness of and my newfound joy in being with and writing about Orthodox Jews, people whom I once knew nothing about, people with whom my daughter has chosen to live her life, people who I feel have since accepted me.

It is hard to choose one among the dozens of special

Orthodox families who mean so much to me, but the "Schoens" are the most special of all. They lived in the same building as "Natalie," and on my first visit I met their boys running down the steps. I rushed into my daughter's home, exclaiming: "How can you expect me to behave normally in your environment when I see boys as alien-looking as those super-Orthodox, 'black' children I just saw outside your door!"

I will never forget "Natalie's" quiet reply: "Mummy, how very wrong you are when you let your first impressions rule your emotions. A finer family, and finer boys than the ones you so mockingly described, would be hard to find." Today I can truthfully say that getting to know, growing close to, and eventually becoming personal friends with the "Schoen" family, and especially with Yosef, have in many wonderful ways only enlarged and enriched my life.

I take this opportunity to thank a very special person, Rabbi Ben Zion Sobel, a quiet, sensitive human being who taught me a great deal, both directly and indirectly.

With humility I must talk about the "Upper Hand" that guided me to Feldheim Publishers' bookstand at the impressive Book Fair in Jerusalem, the magical first contact with Feldheim's editor-in-chief, Marsi Tabak, and the subsequent meeting with Yaakov Feldheim, who — after his initial ambivalence towards a "secular" author — finally agreed to accept my manuscript. The tremendous enthusiasm that radiated from Marsi and other members of the editorial and production staff paved the way for publication of my book, and their skill and professionalism are evident throughout.

Finally, I would very much like to express my profound gratitude to Yaakov Feldheim personally. I wanted only Feldheim to publish my book because for me the Feldheim seal represents the highest standard in Jewish religious literature.

Agi L. Bauer
Jerusalem, Sivan 5751

Introduction

"Where Did I Go Wrong?"

It was a peaceful Thursday morning and I was in my kitchen in Jerusalem cooking a large pot of vegetable soup that contained everything good under the sun. I had spent a lot of time selecting, cleaning, cutting and chopping the vegetables for our Friday night dinner, and when the soup began to simmer, its fragrance filled the whole apartment. It smelled marvelous.

Now, I must tell you that I am a renowned soup-maker, so much so that my daughter Natalie once said to me: "You know, Mummy, you could run a soup kitchen in Jerusalem!" (to which I muttered under my breath: "I have higher aspirations").

On this particular Thursday, Natalie popped in unannounced, as she sometimes does when I am visiting. I am always happy to see her come through my door, as I think of all the times when I am simply dying to see her but can't, because we're thousands of miles apart. I greeted her with a warm smile.

"Something smells awfully good," she said. "I'm sure it's one of your famous soups that nobody else can make."

I confess that I love praise, especially when it comes from my daughter.

Natalie lifted the lid of the large soup pot and peeked in. "Yum! It *looks* delicious too," she said, and just as she said it, her face suddenly took on a stern expression and she began peering more closely at the soup.

I knew there was trouble looming. I knew something was not quite kosher for Her Highness. "Mum, what did you put into this soup?" she demanded, the change in her voice quite startling. She almost put her head into the big pot, so closely did she examine its contents.

Wordlessly I protested my innocence, but to no avail. Natalie's gray eyes flashed with anger, and for a fleeting moment I thought she was going to lift up the heavy pot and dump it down the drain! (Maybe a less sensitive *Baal Teshuvah* would have done just that.) She tried to control her rage and spat the words out: "Mum, you may do whatever you like with this soup, but *we* will not *touch* it, as it is full of the very thing I have repeatedly asked you to avoid using."

I stood there like an idiot as she went on with her "sermon," delivered to me, her mother, who had been standing over the hot stove all morning cooking the very best soup for Natalie's family for Friday night dinner. "You forgot the rule, Mum: PARSLEY — NEVER. You know you cannot clean it the way we need to have it cleaned. I have told you many times, NO PARSLEY!"

I did vaguely remember her asking me to avoid using fresh parsley, but what am I to do when I simply love having it in a soup, both for the taste and the appearance. A good friend of mine used to say, "Parsley gives it the professional touch."

"Don't even bother to cool it down and pour it into the container for us," Natalie concluded. "I meant what I said: WE'LL HAVE NONE OF THIS SOUP!"

I was livid. I knew only one thing: that my daughter was crazy. I stalked out of the kitchen and into my bedroom, slamming the door behind me.

❋   ❋   ❋

I am the mother of a *Chozeret B'teshuvah*, a daughter who recently discovered the religion of her ancestors and embraced it in its strictest form. If you too have such children, then you know what their newfound faith means to them. It gives them a sense of identity (which we apparently failed to provide?), a feeling of belonging (I suppose we failed there too?), and a purpose to their lives (score one more failure for us!). What it means to us secular or non-religious parents, however, is pain, shock, and annihilation of everything we have tried to raise our child to be. That same child who was up until now *our* child, has suddenly become the child of a *Rav* — a Rabbi we have never even met; a junior member of the "Circle"* — a support group of veteran *Baalei Teshuvah* and their mentors; and altogether an integral part of the "black" world of Orthodox Jews.

As you will read in this book, I was born in Budapest into a traditional, Hungarian Jewish family. At the early age of 12 or 13, I realized that no matter how sophisticated, cultured and assimilated we thought ourselves to be, we were regarded in so many words by our fellow Hungarians as "filthy Jews."

I survived the Holocaust (by a sheer miracle) and in 1949 I married and emigrated to far-off Australia, carefree sunny Australia, where if you were prepared to work (as my husband was) the result was tremendous. We achieved all we could hope for materially, and were able to give our two children everything that we thought constituted the good life.

Almost at the peak of this "good life" my daughter, then 18 years old and entering Sydney University, became something that words could hardly describe — a *Chozeret B'teshuvah*. She not only abandoned everything she had loved up until then, but with a swift and sharp turn began to move farther

---

*I must stress that this is my own term for the *Baal Teshuvah*'s circle of friends and teachers and *not* some cultish phenomenon.

and farther away from us, her parents, and her entire family.

Eagerly and wholeheartedly, she embarked on a learning process which to us, her parents, was alien and incomprehensible. I, her own mother, could not even ask questions, as she had no time for my questions: she wanted first and foremost to find answers to all *her* questions which we, obviously, could not supply.

This process of alienation has many shades, many moods. There is the always pressing guilt in the mother of a *Baalat Teshuvah* (henceforth, for the sake of brevity, B.T.); she will keep on asking herself: "Where did I go wrong?" With each passing day our child distanced herself farther from us, and we asked ourselves this same question over and over again, without ever finding the real answer. The hurt, shock and humiliation of losing our child to the "black" world of Orthodox Judaism was hard to bear.

It is possible that this loss affected me so deeply because of my own personal background as a Holocaust survivor and because I have only two children. Perhaps others are more able to let their child go her own way, although I have not yet met such a person, regardless of his personal history or number of children, who has done so without feeling that a part of his heart has been cut out. I became utterly determined to deal with the enormous problem of my B.T. daughter, knowing that if I were to fail, I would lose her completely, and this I was not prepared to do under any circumstances.

I started — with an iron will and a great deal of LOVE — to try to observe Natalie's total change and alienation, jotting down each time I found some new, unbelievable (to me) thing my B.T. child was doing. I somehow found solace in taking notes and made it my business always to carry a notebook with me; instead of losing my temper, I would write down everything she did, every new "crazy" thing she found under the heading: *Being a B.T.*

I am not a recorder of statistics; I did no research, as I feel there is no research that is better than real life experience — the "here and now." All I needed was a keen power of observation, good eyesight and hearing, and — above all — *strength*.

After the first couple of years of anger, I noticed something interesting. I carried the little notebook with me and whenever my daughter did or said something that was new to me, I tried to write it down *without* anger, with more tolerance and even humor, as what was there to gain from killing myself with anger??

I kept these notebooks and they became my source of entertainment and at the same time my own learning material. I took them home and read extracts from them to my family and friends to acquaint them with all the new knowledge I had gained from my religious daughter.

At the same time, I began to notice that other young women her age that I was acquainted with were having various problems that made my B.T. daughter appear to be a much happier, more well-adjusted person than any of them were. And I slowly became aware that my anger had changed to amazement and, eventually, to straightforward enjoyment!

I often found myself boasting about what my daughter does, in obvious positive contrast to what *we* do. I started to admire instead of to oppose her way of life, and actually discovered beauty in it instead of hardship.

That was when I realized that instead of asking myself: "Where did I go wrong?" what I should have been asking was: "Where did I go *right*?"

And that was when I said to myself: enough of the notebooks. You are ready to tell the world about the newfound joy in your life.

And so the notebooks became a book.

❄ ❄ ❄

I must add a P.S. to this Introduction. Seven years after the soup incident described above, Natalie presented me with a very special gift. I was once again cooking one of my famous soups when she once again popped in unannounced, this time with a bouquet wrapped in cellophane and tied with a big yellow ribbon. A mischievous smile lit up my daughter's face — this daughter with whom I've gone through so many hard times and with whom I've finally achieved such a marvelous relationship — as she triumphantly handed me the present.

"Mummy," she said, "it's your dream-come-true. They've developed it JUST FOR YOU!"

The "bouquet" was a large bunch of greens with a label attached certifying that they were one-hundred-percent kosher *bug-free parsley*.

I stood there with my beautiful bouquet of "just for me" parsley, inhaling its scent and happier than I would have been over sweet-smelling lilacs, and said: "Natalie, I have EARNED this!" And we laughed together.

1   *Metamorphosis*

The *Chozer*, or *Baal Teshuvah* is a person who has been metamorphosed, often straight after finishing university. Just when the parent has arrived at a happy and contented stage of life, thinking: "Well, now my son has finished law school and soon he will be a successful lawyer and I can think of retiring," or "Now my daughter has finished architecture with a Master's degree, is working on her Ph.D. thesis and has acquired every-thing she's yearned for," just then this child, with his or her fabulous education, suddenly decides that what he or she has studied is really unnecessary.

B.T.s readily turn their backs on the prospect of getting good positions or excellent starts towards successful careers. At an age when others begin making a very good living in their chosen professions, B.T.s abandon theirs and commence with renewed strength and vigor a second and altogether different learning period of their lives.

This is what happened to our Natalie. She made a turn as sharp and abrupt as is humanly possible, back into what we thought of as the dark, black world of the Orthodox Jew, the world of our ancestors.

Orthodox Jews live with strict and rigid rules in an easy and comfortable way from birth. They do not question these rules; they are God's rules, handed down from Sinai. The Orthodox know the rules well and apply them to themselves and to their children, just as countless generations of Jews before them have done.

For *Baalei Teshuvah* it is very different. They were born into Jewish families, ranging from the totally non-observant of any Jewish laws to the partially observant. And then, suddenly, for reasons from the sublime to the ridiculous, at some point in their lives comes a moment of truth, a moment of decision-making, when they decide to return to the ancient and Orthodox way of life...of which they know nothing.

This is not an everyday occurrence. This is not something we can minimize in any way, as it demands a complete change from all the rules which B.T.s thought fitting until then, to new ones they will have to fit their lives to in the future. There's so much for them to learn!

But learn they must, and learn they will, all the intricate and stringent laws that our forefathers clarified and codified over thousands of years of scholarly research. As they need and want to know them as quickly as possible, they eagerly sit in yeshivas and study almost night and day. Orthodox Jewish men and women all over the world today subject themselves to this incredible discipline, as they find this the only way in which to cope with a world that is too fast, too unjust, too promiscuous, and in fact, too everything.

But why look for more adjectives to describe our troubled world of today? We thinking people have only to open a newspaper in any country or listen to the news on the radio, and we come face to face with stories so horrific and horrendous that it is not surprising at all that some of our youth should want to change their way of life completely.

I will tell you what my own child said, as a perfect example: "I like waking up in the morning, knowing what God expects of me." This she can do only by adhering to a most rigorous set of Laws and Customs. In a world in which "anything goes" and the rule of law seems to have collapsed, it is understandable that people should seek to put some order in their lives. Strictly Orthodox Judaism, where every rule is carefully spelled out and life is neat and orderly, was apparently what Natalie wanted.

For B.T.s, Torah study, learning Jewish Law, is the *sine qua non* of their existence. So much time must be devoted to learning that the *Baal Teshuvah* has little or none left for employment. Consequently he often cannot support his wife and family at all in the beginning, and sometimes even later on. It must not be assumed that he is avoiding work or shirking his responsibilities, as he actually is working very hard: LEARNING IS A FORMIDABLE TASK NOT TO BE UNDER-ESTIMATED!

They are in a hurry, these B.T. yeshiva students, and at the same time they are scared of doing something wrong. I must stress the word "scared." They want to do the right thing as their forefathers did, and their forefathers' forefathers before them. They are ever so careful to do the right thing at all times — something which the born-Orthodox seemingly absorb with their mother's milk — but which these adult, mostly highly-educated men must master within the space of only a few years, and this they accomplish by concentrating intensively and exclusively on learning.

It is a tantalizingly interesting, yet heart-rending process which does not allow an inch of tolerance for error. (This is not, strictly speaking, true, as God is Just and He forgives those who err out of ignorance, but B.T.s are much harder on themselves.) B.T.s become totally absorbed in their learning, and I would go as far as to say that their entire outward appearance and their attitude towards everything, not only religion, consequently changes.

As a result of the secular parents' feelings of resentment and anger over these changes, almost every word uttered by their B.T. child is heard by them as though through a special "Declaration of Rejection" filter, since by his actions he has demonstratively rejected the parents' entire value system. His voice, perhaps unintentionally, seems to take on a superior tone. Therefore, many of his utterances may sound like denigrating and belittling remarks, which serve only to exacerbate the parents' feelings of hostility towards him, his new lifestyle, and those responsible for "turning him away from them."

At the same time, the recent B.T. himself, despite his learning, is often still ignorant and unsure of the reasons for everything he does, or is incapable of explaining himself in what is likely to become a confrontation situation with his secular parents, but he cannot admit to ignorance. Consequently he may resort to a firm, dictatorial manner of speech that brooks no argument.

It is difficult enough for two newlyweds to start to build a new life together; imagine how hard it must be for a young couple who hardly know one another (as happens in most B.T. cases) and rely primarily on the fact that their union was "bashert" — Divinely predetermined. Such young couples, besides getting used to the peculiarities of a normal existence, have to cope with the rigorous routine that entails not only learning from dawn to dusk, but everything that is part and parcel of their Orthodox Jewish life. From the time of their wedding, their lives move at the speed of a Concorde and they hardly have breathing space between Festivals and Holidays and Fast Days and giving birth — the ultimate goal and fulfillment of the B.T. couple.

If they are lucky, young and healthy, their children will arrive into this turbulent world in a yearly procession — beautiful, healthy, clever little wunderkinds one after another (just as in our case!).

In the beginning of our daughter's metamorphosis, I must

admit that we were thoroughly bewildered. We had no idea how to handle the situation. With each passing day, it seemed, Natalie was changing before our eyes into something un-recognizable.

Very often, when my husband or I came across yet another strangeness in our daughter's behavior, we would wait until we were alone together to try to reason it out for ourselves. We never failed to appreciate our good fortune in that we were able to cry on each other's shoulders, to explain the new strange things to one another.

Sometimes we were so shocked that it took us days to regain the inner strength to be together with Natalie, as we just could not confront her until we'd let our anger subside. We had to wait sometimes for days or weeks to face her again, in person or on the phone, until we felt in full control of ourselves.

Everything she did seemed to be aimed at upsetting us, her parents. We had the feeling she was testing how far she could go with us before we would break with her completely. This was something that stayed with us for many years, this threatening fear of our own child.

We even sought Rabbinical advice, so disturbed were we about our daughter's new lifestyle. (Do not ignore this last but by far not least venue for finding out more about what to you are threatening, yet in reality are only unfamiliar, laws which your child has chosen to obey.)

In a number of incidents, we discovered, the basis for Natalie's apparently outrageous behavior was not the Law (*halachah*) per se, but custom (*minhag*) or stringency (*chumrah*). The newly-religious B.T. is unable to distinguish between Law, custom, and stringency; being as fearful as he is of the slightest transgression, he simply emulates his mentors or takes upon himself the most extreme stringencies.

[I will always remember my Natalie's utter surprise when, in what I call "My Enlightenment Years," we were having a rather brisk, feverish argument about something she stood unshakably firm about, and suddenly I turned to her and exploded: "Okay, but tell me one thing, Natalie. Is this *halachah* or *minhag*?" Natalie stopped, dumbfounded, and just stared at me. Eventually gathering her composure, she asked me in return, with, I thought at the time, a definite mixture of surprise and pride in my growing inquisitiveness towards her religious standing: "And since when do *you* know the difference, Mummy?"]

I would like to tell you about our own Rabbi in Sydney, Australia. He was a parting gift our daughter left us before she immigrated to Israel. She said: "I know this will sound crazy to you today, but if you ever encounter some totally unacceptable problem, please go and talk to him."

We did think the idea crazy, at the time. But, as we did indeed encounter some totally unacceptable problems (repeatedly), I did go, alone, to the Rabbi one day and I found him most helpful. Later on I persuaded my husband to join me for some highly educational sessions with this *Rav*. His advice was invaluable. He told us something that has become a sort of maxim for us, one that has helped us at times when we simply did not know how to keep the peace with our daughter.

At those times, we would look at one another and repeat what the *Rav* had taught us: "When you don't know what to do anymore, then simply do the following: LOVE HER MORE!"

We did have a choice: to accept Natalie's new way of life, or not to accept it — to let her go to live her chosen life in her chosen way with our acceptance, love and support, or without it.

We chose the easier path — and I am convinced that this *was* the easier one — and decided to accept her way of life, no matter how hard this would be for us, no matter how strange it would seem to us.

In the intervening years, we have had occasion to reconsider this decision, but it always came down to the same choice: Did we want to lose our child, or win her back *on her terms?* Under no circumstances were we prepared to lose our child.

You may be faced with the same difficult choice. But as you read on, you will discover that it is not so difficult after all, or it won't be if you learn from my mistakes. In fact, you may find, as I did, that it can be truly rewarding.

2   *It's What Matters*

Until now, I have only hinted at my personal background, but I believe that in order for you to gain a better understanding of what we did about Natalie and why, it is important for you to know more about me and my husband, Steven.

I was born in January 1929 in Budapest, during what they say was one of the coldest winters ever. I was the second of my parents' two children (I have an older brother) and for a bourgeois Hungarian Jewish family, this was the right number of children to have. For the first three years of my life, I spoke German, taught to me by a carefully chosen German *Fräulein*, who cared for me and loved me.

We had two homes, in which we lived according to the seasons. In winter we lived in Pest, in a huge apartment on Andrassy Ut. I loved looking out the window, watching kings and queens go by. Something wonderful was always happening on Andrassy Ut. I still remember the corner where we would stop to buy hot, roasted chestnuts on our way home from skating, in the twilight of a winter's afternoon.

In late spring we packed our large wicker baskets and moved to our summer villa in Svabhegy. I adored our beautiful garden there with the fruit trees blossoming, the lilacs filling the air with their sweet fragrance. Each summer I helped the gardener to water the dahlias or pick the juicy cherries, and watched the servants preserve the fruit under the strict scrutiny and supervision of my mother.

I had my winter life and my summer life. It was a wonderful childhood. Together with other Jewish girls like me, I attended a fine Evangelical girls' school from the first grade on, but I knew that we were Jewish, because we celebrated the Jewish festivals — and I loved them. We went to Synagogue on Rosh Hashanah, and on Yom Kippur everyone in our family fasted.

Passover was a marvelous holiday, and we would always spend *Seder* night at my maternal grandparents' home. I particularly liked Passover, as I ate only matzah for the entire eight days. The gentile children in my school always admired my "play-lunch" and I gave most of it away so they might taste this tasteless, exotic "bread."

I don't think I ever saw a *sukkah* in Budapest, or even knew what one was. But I did know that each December brought the Chanukah festival, as we lit the silver Chanukah *menorah* and even played *"tremdedli"* — *dreidl*. Xmas, although widely celebrated, was a non-event in my life; I thought it belonged only to the "other people."

I grew taller and years passed in uneventful ease, until I noticed that my parents were staying home more in the evenings and my father was listening to some noisy radio every single night. I was aware of the tension building up in our home and I too started to listen to the voices on the radio.

My childhood from around 1940 onward was disturbed greatly by those radio voices, barking and harsh in German and faintly quiet in English. The news occupied my father's life and I was told to be still. I think it was then that my carefree existence ended.

On the 19th of March, 1944, when the Germans marched

into Budapest, my father gathered the family around him and told us: "The world has come to an end." Although I did not understand what he meant, I knew that it was so.

In the summer of 1944 my father took ill and was operated on. The diagnosis was cancer. The world around us was tumbling over, but for me nothing mattered. I hardly noticed anything; I only knew that my father would die soon.

I never looked out onto Andrassy Ut anymore; I hated everybody and everything. I suddenly grew up and I felt a terrible sadness.

My father told us one day in September that we had gotten Swedish protection and we would be moving into a house where we would be safe. He told us the address of the "Swedish House," but I did not know this part of Budapest at all; I had never been on Pozsonyi Ut before.

In May, my brother Pista, who had been called up to go to *munkatabor* (labor camp), was taken "somewhere" (I did not know where) and so it was only the three of us who were to move to the Swedish House the following day. But that night the Nazis assembled all able-bodied people from Andrassy Ut 9 and, it seemed, from all over the city, and suddenly my mother and I were among the thousands of people being herded down the streets of Budapest towards an unknown destination.

My father was too weak to even cry as we waved good-bye to him. I decided then that I would find a way to return to him somehow. A few days later, after gathering us all in the brick factory, the Nazis decided to chase us further.

We were crossing a bridge, a bridge spanning the Danube from Buda to Pest, when I turned to my mother and said: "Now we will quietly walk away and escape." My mother thought I had lost my mind and hushed me urgently but I was deadly serious and determined. "If they see us they will kill us now; if we stay on, they will kill us later. But if we escape, we can be with Father again!" I grabbed my mother's hand and pulled her with me... towards survival.

I will never know how I found the Swedish House on Pozsonyi Ut, but I am sure I was led by an Upper Hand.

A few days later, a wonderful gentile acquaintance of my beloved bachelor uncle, Eugene, sent for us all — Father too — and she hid us in a cold, empty apartment. From that moment on, our very lives depended on her as she alone knew of our existence. I hardly noticed the bombs falling after that; my poor ailing father said: "Let them come," and that was good enough for me.

And they came. We were nearly killed as the room next to ours was struck by a bomb. I decided that we had to go down to the public bomb shelter, in spite of the risk that involved, as Father was cold. At the age of 15, I had somehow taken command of our lives.

We survived. The Russians liberated us on an icy day in January of 1945 — maybe it was my birthday — who cared? WE WERE ALIVE, and that was all that mattered.

I walked with my very sick father to Andrassy Ut 9. Drained of all emotion, we looked at that building that was now nothing but an empty facade with a great big hole in the middle. My beloved piano was hanging in mid-air. I saw my father's ashen face and quickly pulled him away from this ugly sight.

We moved into my grandparents' home and Father was in great pain most of the time. The only wish he had was to see his son once more.

And he arrived, one beautiful day, in some kind of American uniform with a bag full of delicacies and he looked like a movie star and my father was happy.

On the 13th of July, 1945, my father died.

In 1949 I married my brother's best friend, my childhood sweetheart. Somehow I knew that he would always take care of me. Steven was very clever and he could fix anything and everything, and, equally important, my father had known and liked him, so he really was the perfect choice for me.

We did not like the mood of the country; we could not see ourselves progressing there in post-war Hungary. So my mother in her loving wisdom encouraged us to leave, to start a new life somewhere else, and we followed her good advice. In 1949, together with my brother, we left Hungary and headed for Vienna, the city my father had loved so very much.

We had no plans to remain in Austria. It was only our first stopover on our way to Freedom, but we had not yet decided where that was to be. Since my only cousin had emigrated to Australia one year previously and had sent us landing permits, we knew that at least we had something, somewhere to go. But we were in no hurry to decide. We had plenty of time to think about the future.

We were walking the streets of Vienna one day, in a very lighthearted mood (despite the fact that we were broke and as usual, hungry), discussing the various options. We were like children, taking the globe in our hands and circling our fingers around it, tossing up countries like footballs when Steven suddenly stopped and asked me: "Agi, should we go to Israel?" And I stopped too and answered in horror: "Oh no, that really would be impossible," and the subject was closed.

We boarded ship in Genoa and arrived in Fremantle, our first port of call in Australia. We had a few hours to spare, so we strolled down the streets of this faraway country and I broke down and cried bitter tears. "Steven," I sobbed, "let's turn back now. This is as far and as strange as the moon!"

Steven smiled at me. "It will be okay," he assured me. But in my heart of hearts, I knew it would never be "okay."

Sydney was a big, beautiful city, a metropolis, and there were some friends of ours already waiting for us. Steven started to work immediately and I started to look out the window, to the blue Pacific Ocean. I knew that what my eyes saw was beautiful, but I also knew that what my heart felt was sorrow. I felt so far away, I don't know from what; but I felt I had come to the wrong place.

It was September when we arrived and I remember it was pouring rain. Steven wanted to know where he would be able to go to pray, as the High Holidays were approaching. I was very impressed with him. And on Yom Kippur, he walked to the synagogue. I was sick in bed that day, or I would have joined him. I suppose the die was cast: we were going to be proud and practicing Jews in this beautiful, faraway place called Australia.

Within a year my mother joined us, and it was wonderful that we were all together once more and starting our new life. Steven established his own business and I became pregnant. We had a little girl, and later a little boy, and we began to save money and we spoke "that funny English." We built a brand new home and I suppose we really were a very happy family.

Back in Budapest, my husband's family had been "sort of kosher." This was a very common phenomenon among Budapest Jews: kosher at home but *treif* (non-kosher) out of the home. Steven's mother had died when he was 13 and from then on there had been no really religious festivities in his home. But he never forgot about his quasi-kosherness. In my family, on the other hand, we were never kosher, so it seemed quite normal for me to continue in that way.

At the age of 20, starting our new immigrant life in Australia with many problems, Jewishness was not one of them. We decided to join an Orthodox synagogue as this was what we had belonged to in the past, and we took our Jewishness quite seriously. We lived in a nice neighborhood surrounded by Australian non-Jews and a few fellow Hungarian Jewish immigrants. Among our friends, we were considered the most "religious," as some were "nothing" — that was what they called themselves (as in: "Are you Jewish?" "No, we're nothing.").

We observed all of the "important" Festivals (or so we

thought!). We went to synagogue on Rosh Hashanah and Yom Kippur, and maybe Passover. We could never make up our minds whether or not to keep *Pesach* fully, or just *Seder* night, and whether to keep the children home from their secular school or not. But *Seder* night, with my husband conducting the proceedings very seriously, was a beautiful yearly event.

As to the children's schooling, it was a choice between a secular public or a secular private school, and so at first they attended the nearby excellent public school. We also sent them to Sunday School at our synagogue and they learned a little bit of Hebrew. When a high school was to be chosen for Natalie, we decided to send her to the prestigious Church of England Ladies College.

I must stop for one moment and alert you to the fact that this could easily have been the making of my daughter's Jewish awareness. For it was in this school, where she was the only Jewish girl in her class, that our daughter became aware of a void in her life, as attending prayers in class or in the Church of England chapel was a regular daily event. We never discussed this, thinking that it was not something to cause us concern.

Natalie loved going to the Jewish Sunday School, and frequently brought home information about traditions which she encouraged us to start practicing in our home. Often she suggested that we light Friday-night candles. She was very diplomatic about it, always asking me first: "Are you staying home this Friday night, or are you going out?" If we were staying home, Natalie suggested we light candles, and I did. If we were going out, we did not light them. She never ever pressed me to do so, and somehow I never noticed how important this was for her.

In all other respects, we did not observe the Sabbath, and we merrily ignored most of the "minor" Festivals. Yom Kippur we observed more or less strictly, but Saturdays were the most sports-oriented days for both the children.

In Australia where Xmas is celebrated with frenzy, we did not *really* celebrate it, but we did throw a big party on Xmas Day, with an enormous exchange of presents between us and our friends. And at Easter time the children ate themselves silly feasting on chocolate Easter eggs.

And so, despite our Orthodox synagogue affiliation and our reputation as being "religious," we lived a secular, non-observant Jewish life. We did read a lot of books on Jewish subjects, listened to some records of Hebrew songs, and even decided once to send our son, then aged 12, to a Jewish camp. There was one particular young Australian counselor at the camp who wore a *kippah* all the time, and I thought very well of him for doing so.

There was never any doubt about our son's having a Bar Mitzvah. We gave him an unforgettable Bar Mitzvah, and he read his portion of the Torah very well. After the synagogue service, we drove to the most elegant reception hall, where a feast of a lunch was served. I will not tell you what was on the menu, as it might disgust you, but suffice it to say that it was not kosher.

One evening in 1969, we saw a film entitled, "The Shoes of the Fishermen," and I said to Steven: "Italy looks beautiful. Let's go and see it." And we went to see the world.

Our first stop was exciting, pounding, crazy New York. Then we crossed the Atlantic and toured England, and realized how badly we spoke our adopted tongue. We were enchanted with Paris, and in clean, civilized Switzerland I envied the people who had never known the meaning of *angst*.

We revisited Vienna and ate huge portions of food to make up for the hunger we still remembered. And I flew to Budapest alone, only to visit my father's grave, and I felt empty and homeless.

Then we went to Rome and its beauty captivated me. In

Florence the exquisite doors alone drove me wild with excitement, while in Venice my heart almost stood still. We ran through the world, spending three or four days in each place. But we left ten days for our final stop: Israel.

As the plane landed and we walked down the steps I rubbed my eyes — was I seeing right or was I in a synagogue? The Hebrew lettering on the signs spoke to me. I was mesmerized. I felt faint. And I felt *something I had never felt before.*

It was as if I had finally arrived. As the taxi drove us up the winding road to Jerusalem, again I felt that faintness coming over me. I realized we were actually traveling *upwards.*

I did not sleep at all that night, and at dawn I stood on the small balcony of our room in the King David Hotel and only then I burst into tears, the happiest tears I had ever shed. I knew for the first time in my life that *yes*, I had reached my goal at last. I had found what I had thought no longer existed anywhere in the world: I WAS HOME.

I did not write to my children, but sent them tapes and I told them that if I were 20 years old I would not move from this Land. My children did not understand what I meant.

We took a guided tour of Jerusalem and when the guide said: "This neighborhood is Rehavia," and told us about all the famous people who lived there, I whispered: "Steven, this is where I would like to live one day." Steven smiled, and thought I was joking.

We returned to Sydney and while Steven spoke about our fabulous trip, I only spoke about Jerusalem. We subsequently brought our children twice to Israel, and they were memorable holidays. The first visit was part of a long trip, our only family trip to Europe, when we took them to Hungary and visited my father's grave in the Jewish cemetery. The second trip was only to Israel, as we all somehow yearned to go back there together.

Then a small miracle happened. Natalie, my 18-year-old

daughter, started to share my love for Israel, and in my heart I knew that if she ever decided to make *aliyah*, we would have to let her go.

In Australia it was customary to send Jewish boys and girls to spend six weeks in Israel, on a program called "Academy." In 1971 we were very interested in sending Natalie on Academy, as she had just finished high school and had started attending Sydney University where, to our distress, she was exposed to all sorts of radical influences that were incompatible with our life.

Before she left Sydney, I instructed her to call us upon reaching Jerusalem, which was meant to be a week or so after her arrival in Israel. But the phone rang on the first Friday after she'd left, and Natalie said: "I just *had* to call you today, before *Shabbat* comes in in Jerusalem, and I want you to know that I feel something so exciting, that I cannot put it into words." And I understood her so well!

In Israel our daughter became friendly with a group of American, Canadian and Israeli Orthodox boys and girls. Her curiosity about all that she had seen and heard and liked so much about them remained with her when she returned to Australia.

As she could not very well come to me for much information about religious observance, she decided to go to the "ultimate" source of learning, none other than the Lubavitcher Rabbi in Sydney. She started to attend lessons with the *Rebbetzin* (the Rabbi's wife) and spent a great deal of time researching what she was studying.

Natalie liked going to the ultra-Orthodox home of this young, dynamic Rabbi (who at a later stage became a real family friend of us all), and while we viewed her attachment to these people with growing dismay, we did not as yet feel threatened by it. Even "sophisticated" parents can be blind when they choose to be, and we in our blindness assumed that our daughter was going through a phase. It was a little "bug" she'd picked up on Academy, something she'd soon get out of her system.

In 1978, after finishing her university studies in Sydney, Natalie said to me: "Do you remember what you said on the tape about your visit to Jerusalem?" I remembered it well. She tried to persuade us that being Jewish was easiest and best in Jerusalem, and she yearned to return there. I was not at all surprised at this love for a place I myself was devoted to, *but what parents would want their child to go from Australia to Israel??*

To cut a long story short, when after her years of university studies and receiving her Social Work degree, our daughter decided to immigrate to Israel, I wrote an article for the *Sydney Jewish Times* called: "And Now Your Child Wants to Go on *Aliyah.*" It was an open, unequivocal confession that I agreed with and supported my child, who wanted to leave comfortable Australia for the rugged, hard life of Israel, just because she wanted to be part of the great miracle called *Eretz Yisrael*. In my heart of hearts I envied her.

I think I was a bit stunned when I heard that she had chosen a religious kibbutz on which to spend her first six months in Israel, but even more shocked that she had become a so-called "child" of a foster family there. No parents like to have competition for their natural roles, so we decided to go and see this kibbutz, and the so-called "parents" and our daughter.

To our amazement, we had the most unforgettable experience. Suddenly we were confronted with the lifestyle of the *genuinely* Orthodox, as the kibbutz was indeed an observant one. A finer place and finer people would be hard to find. We found ourselves enjoying all the religious customs, and we decided, upon returning from our visit to Israel, that we would apply some of the practices we had seen and heard of at the kibbutz in our everyday lives.

And so it was that we in our own strange way, knowing that our daughter was living and learning a new and, to her, exciting religious Jewishness 12,000 miles away, joined Natalie in solidarity.

From Friday evening until Saturday night, I did not light a cigarette. We stopped eating any kind of "obviously *treif*" food. We even occasionally went to synagogue on Saturday mornings, and last, but not least, I did something that still amazes me: I started attending a Hebrew class, just in case my daughter should really decide to stay in Israel, forever....

The years passed quickly and our trips to Israel became regular and frequent. We enjoyed Israel more with each visit, and our life began to take on a new shape alternating between the "in between" times, and the "being there" times. And each time I left Jerusalem my heart grew heavier. With each departure, I was not only leaving Natalie behind, I was leaving Jerusalem. I felt that Jerusalem had become my home and Australia my exile.

Natalie was changing before our eyes and I felt an over-whelming need to be with her, although I had no idea how, or if, I would be able to do anything about it.

Back in Sydney we established a regular *leil Shabbat* (Friday night), with my mother and son always staying with us, with candles, blessings, challah and all, and we enjoyed something that we could have had so many years previously but did not, and we tried to make up for lost time.

When Natalie, now a serious, well-versed and learned religious young woman (it had not been just a phase after all), working and living in Jerusalem, became of an age when living in a nice place rather than in rented rooms was important for her social status, I made one of my visits to Israel, alone, to spend some time with her. On this visit my old dream became a reality: we purchased an apartment in Rehavia, and Natalie moved into this very nice neighborhood.

From then on, whenever Steven and I visited, we stayed in

our "quaint" Rehavia apartment with Natalie, until she married and moved to her own place (more about that later). The apartment is small and lacking in most of the conveniences I have in Sydney, and yet whenever our visits draw to an end, I feel terribly torn. Leaving Jerusalem has become very difficult for me. I know how lucky I am to have the best of both worlds — but who wants *two* worlds, when I have found my one and *only* world?

I love Israel because here everything that matters to me, matters. And everything that matters, matters to me.

I have become a familiar figure by now in Rehavia. Recently, when I was buying stamps in my beloved Chopin Street post office shortly after my arrival, the usual, dark-complected, fiery-eyed clerk greeted me. "How long is your stay this time, *Savta*?" (as I have become known locally). I told him I'd be staying until just before *Pesach*.

Five days before my departure, I made another stamp-buying excursion to Chopin Street. It was a hot day and the post office was packed, with a long queue waiting. Just as I was leaving the cashier's window, my fiery-eyed friend called after me: "*Nesiah tovah, Savta* — have a good trip and a happy Holiday!" I almost walked away, when suddenly it hit me: How did he know?

Although the line that had formed behind me was quite long, the customers allowed me to put my head in the window to ask, "How do you know that I'm leaving?"

The fiery eyes smiled back at me as he replied: "Why, I remember what you said when you arrived."

I was quite taken aback. I thought to myself: This busy young man, this wonderful human being, actually cares, *it matters to him*, enough so that he should remember something I told him in passing *weeks* ago! And despite the press of the crowd and the pressure of his work, he cares enough to wish me a good journey and a happy *Pesach!*

This is what I meant when I said that in Israel, *what matters to me, matters.* You see, the things that are important to me personally, are important to everyone else as well.

I love traveling on the bus when I'm in Israel. I find it a never-ending fascinating and elating experience. The driver, who seems to me to be almost the equivalent of an army general, not only drives the bus, but also looks after us, his passengers. He turns the radio up especially on the hour, so that we may all hear the news.

Often the driver is one who wears a knitted *kippah* and when this occurs, I find the sight joyous. What can I do, I find joy in the smallest, everyday sight. But of course this is not an everyday sight in Sydney or anywhere else in the world. Only here, where being Jewish is so normal, does one see normal policemen, postmen, taxi and bus drivers wearing a *kippah*.

Gazing out the bus window at an intersection one day, I saw in the car alongside us a handsome officer in a pilot's uniform. You know how one just gazes out the window of a bus, with no special interest, just passing the time. Well, what caught my eye was the *kippah* on this pilot's blonde head.

Suddenly I felt an inexplicable warmth, this unique feeling reserved for seeing things that one can only see in Israel. On the parcel shelf in the back window of his car there was a clear plastic bag, containing his *tallit* and prayer book. Just as in Australia, we would have a box of tissues.

To me this meant: Here, *that's what matters.* And clearly, *it matters to me.*

3

Bashert?! —
What Does It Mean??

When I first heard this (to me) ugly-sounding Yiddish word, "*bashert*," I tried to blot it out of my mind as I simply could not stand those "black" words which were constantly cropping up in my daughter's new vocabulary. As a young girl, she had made it her business not to speak the "uncultured" Australian dialect, and had always spoken proper English. For her immigrant parents, this had been a source of pride.

I, on the other hand, with my pronounced Hungarian accent, cannot *ever* open my mouth and utter one word in any language without being kindly reminded that I must come from Hungary (as if I did not know it myself!). Still, it was my aim to learn to speak a good, articulate, educated English. Although I realized I would never become fully assimilated in Australia, I would at least be able to communicate intelligently with my adopted fellow countrymen in my adopted tongue.

And then along comes my daughter, who was born with and educated in the English language, but who, since joining our Sydney *Rav*'s class in Torah study, had acquired a new Yiddish vocabulary, which she now sprinkled liberally throughout her once-proper English.

As long as this annoying habit of hers did not interfere with our lives, I could not reasonably raise any objections. But then, when did reason ever govern my behavior?

On several occasions, in the early stages of her metamorphosis, I indicated my abhorrence of those expressions she had begun using, particularly the term "*bashert.*" Whenever I would try to dissuade Natalie from doing something I disliked, that is, taking on some new religious observance, she would inevitably recite her magic formula: "Mummy, there's no use talking about it any further, as you know it is all *bashert.*"

Well, frankly, I did *not* know! In fact I hated this word and its connotation. After weeks of hearing it — and still not knowing what it meant, as I was not going to give her the satisfaction of my showing any curiosity towards her "black words" — I finally exploded. "I don't know this word," I said angrily, "I don't want to know it or what it means. I have lived this long without knowing, and I can go on living without knowing what *bashert* means."

The *Rav's* wife, the *Rebbetzin*, gave classes for young women on Judaism, and Natalie began to attend these in the evenings. She always came home in a wonderful mood after one of these *shiurim*, and occasionally she would want to tell me about some marvelous thing she had learned. But I turned a deaf ear to her. I closed myself to all her "learning," and especially her teaching sessions.

One day, towards the second year of attending these classes, Natalie decided to press on me her newfound knowledge in connection with just this one word. "Mummy," she said, "I understand that you don't care to be educated by your daughter about things you never knew about and never missed, but I would so love for you to understand the meaning of this word, *bashert*, as really without it we just about cannot exist."

"Come on Natalie," I scoffed, "don't make me laugh. Do I look to you like somebody who does not exist, simply because I don't know one of your ultra-Orthodox Yiddish words?"

Natalie, who — had she been *that* kind of a person — might have rudely replied that I did sometimes look like somebody who could do with a bit of deeper understanding, said only: "Mummy, you're doing fine, you're a wonderful mother and everything. But you are missing the point completely if you think that by trying to force your own will on others you will achieve anything..." She paused for a moment and then continued in a warm loving voice, "...as everything is really *bashert.*"

That was the limit. I just could not listen to this anymore. I turned to my daughter and almost shouted the words: "What does it mean, for heaven's sake?"

She sat there, looking calm, very composed and understanding of my frustration. "Mummy, *bashert* means that it is all written Up There," she said, affectionately pointing heavenwards and meaning that which I often sensed was the Upper Hand, a Hand that guides us mortals in trying times.

Natalie went on: "It means it is all from Hashem, God. He has the final say in whatever decision we try to make. We need His help at all times to be able to make the right decisions, and to do that, we must know Torah and we must understand in human terms exactly what Hashem expects of us. *Bashert* simply means: *it is all written Up There.*"

I was amazed at how peacefully I sat there listening to my daughter's explanations. It was one of those rare moments when her didactic tone of voice did not irritate me. It was almost as though I were listening to something I had wanted to know for a long time but had never taken the opportunity to find out.

Actually it was strange hearing about this "*bashert* thing." I had always thought, in my simple way of reasoning, that the less discipline we subjected ourselves to, the easier it would be for us to manage our lives. Why had I closed my ears so vehemently to all the "black" religious learning in which my daughter found so much pleasure? Because I could clearly see how much discipline went with it and how many sacrifices one had to make to adhere to it.

Oh, no, I had told myself, I certainly was not prepared to obey any ancient Laws that had been written thousands of years ago, before there was technology. Surely those rules written so long ago could not apply to us today, in an era when people walk on the moon and machines think for us. Was my daughter trying to tell me that the Jewish dietary Laws known as *kashrut* were anything more than a way to keep healthy and avoid contaminated food, laws instituted by our forefathers in an age when they could not have foreseen the technological advances that would make these things possible for everyone?

I had my own *"shiur"* for every one Natalie gave to me. I was a modern woman, I said, a *thinking* woman, in the almost-twenty-first century, who enjoyed and *used* the benefits of this modern high-tech era. I would not crawl back to the ancient, benighted world of our ancestors.

My poor daughter had to sit there and listen to my laudation of electronic computers (which I used to hate but have learned to appreciate), of refrigeration (about which I really knew a lot as it is Steven's area of expertise), and of modernity at large.

Natalie had to admit that I was a thoroughly modern woman and she realized I thought she was not so anymore. "Whatever modern means," she added quietly.

"I can't fight you anymore," she went on. "You must try to find out for yourself, in your own life, what *bashert* really means. But I think that today, for the first time you have understood the fundamental meaning of the word."

Years later when Natalie was already living in Israel, I (still at a very negative stage) decided to visit her *Rav* in Sydney in the hope that he might help unravel some of the mysteries that my own flesh-and-blood daughter could not. It was one of many such visits, as I found the Rabbi to be surprisingly warm and understanding.

This young *Rav* had successfully turned the new day school in Sydney into a flourishing institution of education that was very popular among Jewish parents who wanted their children to be educated in that special "old fashioned" way. The waiting list for enrollment grew each year — an altogether new phenomenon for Sydney in the 1980s.

Although he was very busy, this *Rav* always found the time to talk to me whenever he heard my S.O.S. distress signal. On this occasion, I was seated in his office wondering at his ability to answer calls on four lines at once, and deal with a diverse assortment of persons seeking his advice — including me. When he had satisfied his callers, he turned to me and asked with genuine friendship: "What can I help you with today, Mrs. Bauer, as I sincerely hope I can?"

I explained that Natalie was now studying in a religious institute for adults in Jerusalem instead of going out into the big world and working in her profession. I told him how disconcerted we were over this, as we had thought that now at last she would work and mingle in a modern world and find a nice modern young man, somebody we would like for her and as our son-in-law — a lawyer, perhaps, or a doctor, or a good businessman, Jewish, naturally, and a "mensch," just as she was. I went on at great length to say that in the world in which she had placed herself, she would never find a suitable match; she was moving in the wrong circles (i.e., not ours).

My dear friend, this ultra-Orthodox *Rav*, listened with great concern. He did not interrupt me once. In the end, he looked at me and said, "Mrs. Bauer, you must understand: no matter what you want, do, or suggest, ultimately it is all *bashert.*"

I sat there a bit stunned. Had he said "that" word? The one I did not want to know about but did know nevertheless? "But surely one cannot just sit and wait for the baked pigeon to fly into one's mouth," I insisted. This is a well-known Hungarian saying that means one cannot, should not, sit idly, just waiting for things to happen.

"Oh, no," he replied, "you cannot simply sit and wait for whatever you said — it's a good example. But you must try to help things to happen in a *learned* way. Then it will all be *bashert*. In other words, Hashem will help you if you try to help yourself."

And suddenly I understood it all clearly. I walked out of the Yeshiva School lighthearted, feeling like a new person, a mother who realized that it was not *our own* suggestions and good ideas that would enable us to reach our ultimate goal, but if we would walk the road shown to us by the Upper Hand we might find the way to all that we aim for, all that we want.

I wrote a letter to my daughter that afternoon and told her about my visit to the Yeshiva. I conveyed the *Rav's* best regards to her, and I also mentioned, quite casually, that although I would love for her to get a job in the *real* world and not bury herself in the religious world of learning, I would nevertheless not object if she chose to follow her own conscience in this matter, because after all, "everything is *bashert*."

4   *From Saturday to Shabbos*

Saturdays were always the best day in the week, at least in our family's week. With our growing children, from the time they were toddlers until they were teenagers, there was simply nothing better to look forward to in sunny Australia than Saturday, as it signaled the beginning of a rather exciting "package deal" comprised of Saturday and Sunday and known to us (and others, I suppose) as the *Weekend*.

Friday night was rarely included in this celebration of the *Weekend*, as Friday night was nothing special; Steven and I either went out and left the children with babysitters or with my mother, or later on, when they were of an age to go out themselves, they merrily did so on their own, to their own various destinations.

We had several means of transportation arranged for them: either we would drive them to their destinations and have friends of ours bring them home, or vice versa. Regardless, they were safely transported to and from at all times, especially on late Friday nights out. As soon as they qualified for their driving licenses, they were permitted to borrow my car, until around their 20th birthdays, when they each received their very own small car. At last they could drive themselves everywhere on Friday nights, sparing us the constant pick-up-and-delivery service.

On Saturday, the *Weekend* activities reached their peak: our family became the "sportiest" family on the block, or so it seemed to me. Saturday morning was reserved for tennis, golf, cricket — you name it, we did it. After all, was this not the purpose of our life — to give our children as much joy as possible?

The desire to give as much joy as is humanly possible to one's children is not an unusual phenomenon, especially among Jewish parents, and even more so among parents who were Holocaust survivors, as we both were. It is the most natural thing that such parents should want to provide their children with as much as they are able to since they themselves were so deprived in their own youth.

We wanted to give our children *everything* we thought that mattered, to make a wonderful life for the offspring of hard-working Jewish immigrants in Australia. (Please keep this word "everything" in a special memory bank of your brain, as it is the key to our whole philosophical debate over religion. It was on this point that we differed: what Steven and I called *everything*, versus what Natalie called *everything*. No more and no less.)

It's odd, but I don't remember Saturdays being such "fun days" back in Budapest in my young school years. I remember them more like ordinary weekdays, as the shops were open all day and my father worked as usual the whole of Saturday. When my brother and I were old enough to go out alone, we went skating together. I remember we had a *berlet* — a pass that was good for Tuesdays, Thursdays and Saturdays. On those days we traveled from Andrassy Ut by the *foldalatti* — the subway which took us door-to-door right out to the skating rink. Those afternoons are some of my happiest memories, as it was then that we would meet all our friends and fool around together. What lovely days those were! But Saturday was no different from Tuesday or Thursday.

Before we had children, the weekend consisted of two separate parts, one for my husband and one for me. My husband worked all day Saturday and, when he opened his own business in 1954, he often worked late into Saturday evening as well. For me, Saturday was mainly the cleaning-, shopping-, and all-the-special-chores-day. We made the most of the day, but not only with work, as we often set aside time for outings to the country and sightseeing trips as well. On long weekends, we arranged excursions to faraway places and explored this vast country, Australia.

From the time that our children arrived four-and-a-half years apart, the weekends became devoted exclusively to enjoying ourselves. Our days, weeks, months and years were spent in the sunshine of the Australian summer and winter with as many outdoor activities and sporting pursuits as possible, and a lot was possible.

We had numerous birthday parties each year to attend and to give. They were celebrated mostly on Saturdays, or occasionally on Sundays. I don't think it ever happened that a child could not attend a birthday party for religious reasons.

As I mentioned earlier, we even drove to our own son's Bar Mitzvah party on Saturday, from the synagogue which was located on one side of Sydney to the catering hall on the other side of town, and we celebrated it with live music and microphones. It never occurred to us to do any differently. This was our world, ours and our children's.

This is what our Saturday was, as distinct from what is known in Orthodox circles as *Shabbat*, and in certain "black" circles as *Shabbos*.

[Let me be honest and call a spade a spade: I have always disliked the word "*Shabbos*." The very sound of it irritated me. "*Shabbat*," I felt, was all right. It is what Israelis call Saturday, so naturally it was fine with me. But "*Shabbos*" was the bitter end for me. The word gave me goose-pimples, especially when preceded by "*Goot.*" It must be my personal aversion to Yiddish, perhaps a holdover from my youth. But whatever the reason, when I would hear the expression "*Goot Shabbos*" with which the "black" Jews greet one another with almost automatic repetitiveness — a greeting that to them sounds beautiful — I would feel as though it was something they had brought back from the dark ages.

Over and over I have openly demonstrated to Natalie my refusal to use this greeting. Whenever her friends would say it to me, I would make a point of replying loudly and clearly: "*Shabbat Shalom.*" This is what I considered a civilized greeting on *Shabbat*, whether in Israel or anywhere else that I found myself in religious circles.

It is quite strange how just one word could evoke in me such anger, such opposition, to that "black" world my daughter was trying to melt into. It seemed to me sometimes that this was really what she was trying to do: go the absolute opposite way of my world, away from the things we have always done, and away from whatever we brought her up to do. But I must not let one "black" word distract me from my systematic account of the how and why of our almost losing our daughter.]

Just as Saturdays meant little to us from a religious point of view, so did the "minor" Jewish Festivals. Whenever we traveled overseas, we naturally did not make any allowances for Saturdays or "minor" Jewish holidays since we never celebrated these at home. We flew, rode, sailed, to wherever was on our itinerary, on Saturdays just as on weekdays.

On one occasion I was flying alone from Zurich to Tel Aviv for the birth of one of my grandchildren. This was already in the days of what might be called "My Enlightenment Years"; still my ignorance of things religious was profound.

I knew that usually on this short European hop to Israel, the plane was full of the black-garbed ultra-Orthodox flying back home. It always amused me how they would carry on in the plane or, worse still, at the airport before boarding. Undeterred by their surroundings, they would put on their prayer shawls and, no matter where they might find themselves, disregard the rest of the world and start praying wildly, swaying back and forth. Sometimes I would see them wrapping black straps around one arm, and positioning a little black box on their foreheads. I know now that those religious articles are called *tefillin*, but nobody in our family had ever worn anything like that (I think).

I usually felt embarrassed at such public demonstrations of Jewishness. But on this particular day, as I settled down in the plane I couldn't help noticing the total absence of all those "black" Jews. I did not want to admit it to myself, but I almost missed them and the strange excitement they generate around themselves. I suppose I'd become acclimatized to their strangeness.

About an hour into the flight, I asked a young stewardess, "Could you tell me please, where are all those very religious, darkly-clad, Orthodox Jews today?"

The stewardess looked me over and, somewhat surprised replied: "Oh, don't you know? Today is *Shavuot*, a major Jewish Festival." No more and no less than the Festival of the Giving of the Torah, one of those Festivals we never observed at home, as it did not belong to our "major" Festivals.

For Steven and me, the slow, painstaking, and often aggravating transition from Saturday to *Shabbat* started as Natalie's religiosity grew. I must stress the point that our inability to adjust to our daughter's complete obsession with the observance of *Shabbat* became the main source of conflict between us. The battle over our totally different approach towards Saturday and her approach towards *Shabbat* often seemed hopeless.

We really came face-to-face with what it means to be a *Shomer Shabbat* (a Sabbath observer) the first time our newly-religious daughter came back to Australia for a short visit, three years after her immigration to Israel. She was still single at the time, but fully immersed and well-versed in religious life.

During one of our numerous phone calls prior to her visit I asked, just for the record, "Natalie, you will naturally want to stay at home with your family, won't you?" I was stunned and hurt when I heard the answer. In her new (to me), self-assured, and rather authoritarian voice, she said: "Mum, let me warn you, it will not be easy for you." Little did I know *how* "not easy"!

Before her arrival, she had inundated us with lists of instructions of what to do, how to prepare, what to acquire, who to inquire from, etc., etc., just to get us acquainted with what was in store for us. But no notes, no lists, no contacts, could have prepared us for the conflicts that awaited us upon receiving our beloved daughter back in the circle of her family, in her own, old home.

At first glance, Natalie looked as if she were still our own daughter. (How deceptive looks can be!) She still had her long, lovely, dark, straight hair, hanging shoulder length. But at second glance, we realized that that was about all that remained of her old self. She looked *religious* — you know what I mean.

She now wore dresses with necklines high up to her chin, buttoned all the way up. She now wore stockings even on the hottest summer day. Her blouses all had long sleeves. She would not go to the beach anymore. Not to the beach or, for that matter, even to our own swimming pool. In our own home! *Home* — we couldn't imagine what this meant to her by now.

And then there was the matter of being kosher. Not just kosher, mind you, but *glatt*-kosher — super-kosher.

As far as our kitchen went, we were in a lucky position. We had a very small "butler's pantry" just off the kitchen which we had transformed into a kosher kitchen with all the necessary equipment, for our daughter to cook her own meals.

Her very own microwave oven, dishes, cutlery — the works — all carefully arrayed to make Natalie feel welcome in our *treif* (non-kosher) household.

On her recommendation I had acquired a "book of knowledge" in which were listed the kosher products available in Australia. I shopped for days with this little booklet in hand. I did my homework diligently, but despite all my efforts, it seemed I was not to be awarded the prize for the Mother of the Year.

On the morning of Natalie's arrival, I began showing off about all the preparations I had made. She followed my guided tour (of her own home) as if she had never been there before. She inspected everything with a gracious nodding of her head. Triumphantly, I sat down in our family room for our first cup of coffee together.

Natalie's eyes followed my every move. Just as I was about to pour a drop of milk into her own (brand-new) cup of (kosher) coffee, she asked in a tone of voice that to my ears sounded slightly shrill: "Have you got the 'yeshiva milk' I asked you for?"

I must admit I had been found out. I was found guilty in the first hour. I had not done my homework diligently enough. "No problem," said this new Natalie in her new superior tone of voice, "I just won't drink any milk until I've fetched some of my own from the yeshiva."

Suddenly all my good humor vanished. I was like a bull who saw red. I could not help raising my voice: "Surely you don't think anything will happen to you if you have a drop of our 'contaminated' milk?" I looked squarely into her gray eyes.

"Mummy," I heard *that* voice say, "you don't think I want to have an argument over such a little thing, and in the first hour that I'm at home?"

"*Who* is arguing and *who* is making a mountain out of a molehill?" I bellowed.

I could not believe my ears when I heard my *Rebbetzin-*

daughter's super-calm voice admonishing me: "Mummy, please don't talk in such an ugly way. Let us not lose our heads over a drop of milk. Can't you see, to me it does not matter at all."

Maybe I was going crazy already, but I thought: How dare she stand there, so calm and so pious. And in the first hour of our being together! I can still see it clearly before my eyes: a child who would not have a drop of my milk in her coffee, but had to run to her *Rebbe* to ask for *his* milk. In my book, *this* was crazy!

I don't know why it is, but my husband and I always differ on the question of the "craziness" of our daughter. He sometimes thinks she is crazy, when I might see her point. Then again, when I sometimes think she is *really* crazy, he will come to her rescue. That infuriates me the most, when they — the two of them — are against me, and I stand there alone, totally alone. I, who after all went to the most trouble to do my very best for her.

I had made the first of thousands of foolish remarks that ruined the whole of the three-week visit that followed. In retrospect, how sorry I am; I should have shut up, and just let her be. I should not have argued, not wasted our precious time together with trying to change a person who was changed already.

I realized, too late, that I was trying to "throw peas at the wall" — an old Hungarian saying meaning: peas thrown at the wall will only roll down, no matter what. With a B.T., and especially one who was herself a beginner, this could never work. She would certainly reject and resent anything I would say, advise or suggest. (Please take note. I learned the hard way.) The tone was set for the next three weeks. She was different; we were our old selves. She, like all B.T.s, was of course on a higher spiritual level than we were, or ever could be. She knew about something we knew nothing about, that is, about religious practices, which we had managed quite well to live without until now. Suddenly we were the outsiders, the ignoramuses — we, her parents; I, her mother, the one who had brought her into the world.

The next morning there was yeshiva milk sitting in our refrigerator.

The following day, Thursday, I knew would be a busy one as Natalie had prepared us well for the forthcoming "hurdle" of *Shabbat* arriving on Friday afternoon.

I thought I knew quite a lot by this time about *Shabbat*. We had been in Israel and had spent *Shabbat* in the religious kibbutz where our daughter had lived for six months. We had also spent *Shabbats* in hotels in Jerusalem and, I might add, we had always loved them. We had walked to the nearby synagogue and we had walked back for a marvelous lunch in the hotel. We had slept in the afternoon, as one does on a lazy *Shabbat* afternoon in Israel, and we thought we had observed *Shabbat* quite nicely.

That was on our first three or four visits. In the luxury of the really nice hotels in Israel, where *Shabbat* was observed by everybody around us, it had been very easy for us to fit in. We were able to pick and choose our religious practices, and reject those that did not suit us. We observed the parts of *Shabbat* which we enjoyed observing and we naturally also did all the marvelous things one does on a free day, such as swimming in the hotel pool or the sea. Sometimes we were fetched by our secular friends in their cars, and went with them on lovely excursions.

We had the best of both worlds when in Israel on *Shabbat*: we loved the *Shabbat* atmosphere that surrounded us and we loved the lifestyle we chose for ourselves.

This routine worked perfectly as long as we were separated from our daughter, as on *Shabbat* she would disappear to her numerous religious friends. I almost felt that she was escaping from us, her parents. We had become, especially on *Shabbat*, a kind of embarrassment to her. It was definitely better for all of us to separate from Friday afternoon until the following Sunday morning.

But that was in Israel, where we could be physically separate from Natalie for the duration of *Shabbat*. How was I to know the hardship that would come from being physically together with my daughter in Australia?

Thinking back on that first *Shabbat* with Natalie as a visitor, it seems as though there was no way to overcome the hurdles. I certainly tried but, just as certainly, failed.

Before our first Friday evening, Natalie cooked her own dinner and set the table for us all in the dining room. Naturally, I had everything prepared: wine and candles and challah — "yeshiva challah," not the normal kind one could buy anywhere. Actually, I had bought the challah from a place called "Grandma Moses," a shop that sold only *glatt*. Up until then, I had thought that kosher was kosher, but I was wrong. For our daughter it had to be *glatt* kosher.

I had done (or at least I thought so) everything that was necessary for the preparation of our first peaceful Friday night and *Shabbat* with our B.T. daughter at home. But the hurdles, the stumbling blocks, were beginning to appear.

It was almost time for us to light the candles. Suddenly, Natalie gasped. She ran to the kitchen and opened the refrigerator door. I watched her in amazement as she put her head right into the refrigerator and started to search for something. She finally found what she must have been looking for, as I heard her say: "Aha!" And then, with a quick movement, she turned the light bulb off. Consequently darkness fell in the refrigerator.

I just looked at her in total astonishment and asked: "Tell me, why did you do that, my darling?"

She looked back at me with blazing eyes and answered: "Please Mum, don't call me 'Darling' when you really don't mean it."

I was so antagonized by then, watching her do strange

things the whole day without explaining any of them to me, that I turned to her and said with anger and provocation: "You know that a lot of what you do is nonsense. I have been watching you the whole day, without saying a word. But now you have done the strangest thing of all. So what next, our darling religious daughter? Maybe you want to turn all the lights off in the house, not just the one in the refrigerator?"

With these words we stood opposite one another, mother and daughter, non-observant mother and religious daughter. Two different worlds, most marked on the peaceful day called *Shabbat*. And I was ready for battle.

"So what else is not to your satisfaction, my wonderful, loving, respectful, easy-to-get-along-with daughter? What else would you like us to suddenly turn upside-down for you? Maybe you would like me to wear a *sheitel* for your famous *Shabbos*?" I was furious. I was fuming.

Then I heard her say something quietly, almost to herself: "No, not a *sheitel*, Mummy. But you would make me very happy if you would cover your hair with a scarf for the candle-lighting."

Natalie stood there, calm and quiet, with an air of superiority that drove me wild. She just looked me over, top to bottom, up and down. Her stare made me feel uncomfortable. Though I am almost a head taller than my daughter, suddenly I felt it was the other way around. I felt almost threatened.

And then, very softly, she said, "Mummy, I feel sorry for you."

That was all I needed at this point. I started yelling loudly, "Don't *you* feel sorry for *me*, you who are trying to complicate your life so much that you will *never* be able to untangle yourself."

Suddenly I remembered all the terrible stories I had heard from other B.T.s' parents. I had not believed them. I had hoped my relationship with my daughter was stronger and better than their relationships with their children. It could *never* come to anything like what they were talking about.

I had even tried to defend the B.T.s when I heard their parents use words such as "cult" and worse. Whenever someone heard that my daughter had become religious, in fact a super-religious B.T., they would look at me with a sort of faint, sad smile and say, "Oh well, it's still not as bad as if she were a drug addict."

I hated it every time somebody made this idiotic statement. I grew wild and told them off. I told them they had no idea what they were talking about, as how could they compare a terrible, horrible addiction to a meaningful return to religion. I had always defended the B.T.s when people spoke badly about "those fanatic, religious freaks."

Now I closed my eyes, and pushed the bad thoughts away. I hated myself for thinking about them just now, in my sudden, terrible anger. But I did manage to say to Natalie: "In all your famous 'learning,' have you ever come across something called the Ten Commandments? And if so, do you know by any chance the Fifth Commandment which says 'Honor thy father and thy mother'? Or have they made you wipe out the words 'father' and 'mother' and exchange them for 'Rebbe,' as it seems to me you have forgotten all about your parents. Well, let me bring your memory up to date: we are your parents, and I am your mother, the woman who gave you life."

With that, I stormed out of my own kitchen, and slammed the door.

Natalie did not come after me; she made no move towards reconciliation. I felt totally alone, certainly daughterless, and I was certain Natalie and I would never be able to reestablish the love and friendship that we once had had. The pain of that was terrible.

What was I to do, I wondered, ruin the rest of our first Friday evening, or go out and pretend all was well? It was a miserably hard choice for me. I returned to the dining room and the evening proceeded in an uncomfortable, unnatural but more or less controlled way.

In the end, I even had a bitter argument with my husband, who (annoyingly) seemed to get on better with Natalie. He did fix the time-clock so that it switched the electricity off at a certain hour, but the house was only in semi-darkness, as I refused to succumb to all her craziness. I insisted on having light in my bedroom. It was about this that Steven and I had our disagreement.

He said, "What's wrong with having an early Friday night for the next three weeks just for the sake of peace?" And I said, "No, I will not let myself be ruled by her!"

Shabbat morning started bright and early. We ate our breakfast, she on her own private end of the table, on a special mat, with a special cup, a special everything; we just as we always did. We had bagels (naturally from Grandma Moses) and cream cheese and salmon, all of us eating the same kosher breakfast. Nevertheless there was tension in the air.

Towards the end of breakfast our son came down, in his "all whites," ready to go for his usual Saturday morning tennis. He had been a member of the same tennis club on the North Shore since his primary school days; now he was almost a qualified lawyer of twenty-three, who did as he pleased, and he did very nicely indeed.

Natalie sat and ate slowly and we all felt a certain tightness in our stomachs (I did, for sure). Danny grabbed a bagel and was almost out the door when Natalie called after him. "And what would happen if you did not play tennis for once?" she asked, pleadingly, I thought.

Had I asked him the day before to cancel his tennis, I believe he would have done so without a word, but truthfully, neither of us had thought of it.

Although Danny and Natalie now lived in different countries, they were still very, very close. They have always had a great love and respect for one another. Natalie adored and mothered her younger brother. In fact, through her motherly, affectionate ways with him, we realized long ago that she was a natural-born mother. When they were still teenagers I had often heard him say to her, "I can't wait for you to have your own children to boss around instead of me." Despite the distance and totally different religious attitudes that separated them, they corresponded regularly and their love had prevailed. This morning was the first time that they had ever clashed with each other as adults. I knew this was an issue between brother and sister, and it required no comment from parents.

Danny came back to the table and in a most respectful and serious voice said, "Natalie, please, let me make this clear to you once and for all. We are brother and sister, from the same home and parents. You went your way; nobody stopped you. We are happy to see you at home with us. We are willing to go out of our way to please you in your new religious awareness. But please don't try to change me. I live and I do as I please. Do not try to make me conform to your newfound laws." And with these firm but well-spoken words he walked out to his car, and on to his usual tennis session on Saturday, on *Shabbat*.

We were to have visitors for lunch, acquaintances of Natalie's, and she prepared all the food. This was our arrangement. Our guests were actually a young religious couple who walked to our house from their own place nearby.

Natalie was looking pale, so I suggested she put on a little make-up before our guests arrived. We were all suntanned (it was summer in our part of the world) and she looked so white coming from winter and all. She smiled her special *Shabbat* smile and said, "Mummy, we don't use make-up on *Shabbat*." And then she went on, in that preaching voice that had irritated me from the start: "You must learn that *Shabbat* is a day of special meanings, special observances. We don't fritter it away...."

I bit my lip to restrain myself from saying anything, determined not to get into another argument. I knew better this time. But I was fuming inside. Her kind of *Shabbat* was certainly not my kind — this much was already clear.

Danny came home happy and tanned from his usual tennis game, just as we, or rather Natalie and her guests, were "*bentching*," reciting Grace after the meal. (Okay, I confess: we never *bentched*. We never *bentched* in my childhood not in my parents' house or in our own home in Australia. I personally did not know how to *bentch*. Consequently, on this first, religious *Shabbat* with our daughter back home, Steven and I sat rather stupidly at our own table. We mumbled along, while the young couple and Natalie speedily recited the whole prayer, by heart.)

Danny sat down just as they reached the end of the lengthy blessing and said "Amen." Steven and I did too. The three of us seemed to share the same uncomfortable feeling of being very outnumbered, and very ignorant. After a brief, strained moment, the conversation reverted to "normal," or what was passing for normal on that strange day.

There was one more significant event on this infamous first *Shabbat*: our first *Havdalah*.

I had first seen the *Havdalah* ceremony (the special prayer recited at the close of *Shabbat* to separate the Day of Rest from the ordinary days of the week) at the religious kibbutz where Natalie had stayed and we had visited. My mother knew nothing about *Havdalah*, so how could I? Or, for that matter, my children? In the kibbutz I had sniffed the sweet-smelling spices in the quaint box, and I had rather liked it. Maybe, if for nothing else, because it signified for me (then) the end of *Shabbat*.

When Natalie entered our dining room that *Shabbat* night, clutching her very own blue-and-white braided *Havdalah* candle and wooden scent box, I could not help but cry out in utter surprise: "Surely you are not going to go through this *alone*?" (It seemed to me that this prayer was meant to be recited by the father or husband for the benefit of his family, and totally inappropriate for a young single girl to do on her own.)

Natalie replied, "Why, who else will do it *for* me?"

Steven and I looked at each other. Despite all that had transpired up until then, we both felt belittled, and terribly hurt. We felt that she was really trying to show us up, that she was "out to get us."

Without further ado, Natalie went through the whole of the actually beautiful process of lighting the *Havdalah* candle, chanting the sing-song prayer, reciting the blessings, doing the peculiar little movements with her hands towards the light. She passed the scent box to each of us to smell, and then she extinguished the flame of the candle in a puddle of wine she had poured for this purpose. With an exuberant glow on her face, she looked around at her family and said, "*Shavua tov* — have a good week!"

Ever since her arrival, as she had gone from one peculiar religious observance to the next, each time meeting either our silent or loudly voiced disapproval, our totally transformed daughter had looked at us with pity, as though she felt sorry for us for not sharing her newfound joy. But at this moment, I felt the situation was completely reversed. I thought, but did not say: "It is *I* who feel sorry for *you*, my daughter. Not because you have become religious, really not because of that, not at all, although it is pretty hard on us. But as I watch you perform all these things alone, I feel sorry for you for *being* alone. So very much alone."

I prayed that night to God, with all my heart, to send a partner, a good man, for my daughter to share her new "religiousness" with. I prayed there would be a husband standing next to her to light the *Havdalah* candle, to say the blessings, to drink the wine, as there should be.

And God heard my prayers.

5   *The Wedding*

I have always maintained that the only time a traditional Jewish parent has the right to be anything but joyful over her child's marriage is when the child marries "out." My child did not marry "out"; on the contrary, Natalie married "*in*," a new concept I have just invented. Why, then, was I somewhat less than joyful? To answer that, I must give expression to some of the *pain* and *sacrifice* which I suffered and which you must suffer if you decide as I did to stand by your B.T. children, no matter what!

Because of this I am warning you in advance that if you are not prepared to read a harsh and even painful chapter, please skip this one, as it contains several very harsh and painful episodes. The memory of them still causes me heartache today. Some wounds may never heal; some may never fail to raise a little inner voice scolding me: "Why did you succumb? Why did you not fight to have things your own way?" But this was not to be. There was something so urgent, so emphatic about the couple's desire to have things their own way, that Steven and I were simply powerless to insist on anything at all. We had to capitulate entirely to their demands.

I know those are very strong words — "capitulate" and

"demands" — but there are no soft words for dealing with a recent B.T. Not when it comes to her having a *"glatt"* wedding in Jerusalem, despite the feelings of her parents who, in their desire to remain loving, agreed to comply — without having the faintest idea what having a *glatt* wedding entailed.

I must pause for a moment and let you in on a secret: I really have a terrible nature. I love nothing more than to have things turn out the way I want them to — that is, my way. I am sure this is not a unique fault; lots of people like things to turn out their way. But I doubt that they all have as vivid an imagination as I have, and can foresee, in theory, every minute detail of a future event. I pre-plan it, I pre-color it, and finally, I pre-live it. Then I sit back and wait for it to happen, just the way I imagined it would be.

Knowing this about me, you can now try to understand my disappointments as the mother of a daughter who was raised in a wonderful, middle-class, traditional Jewish way. As she grew up and approached marriageable age, I started to form a certain idea of what kind of wedding we would make for her, although the world was changing and many new avenues were opening for young people as far as the institution of marriage was concerned. Few if any of these options appeal to the older, tradition-oriented generation.

Consider the worst possibility: that your child chooses not to marry at all, a sadly common phenomenon today. She opts instead for a "life partner" or no partner at all — I don't know which is worse. There is very little a parent can do, except hope that the child will eventually change her mind.

Or take the possibly less extreme but equally aggravating case: your child will agree to have a wedding, but certainly not a big Jewish wedding. A small wedding held, let us say, at the end of a quaint street in a suburb of Sydney, at the edge of the water, on the sand barefoot... and officiated by a Reform rabbi.

If you are really lucky, your child might agree to please you and accept your old-fashioned way, adding just a little touch of her own. She will have a synagogue wedding in the synagogue to which you all belong, with the Rabbi you know. She might want to limit the guests, which could create a problem for the parents, but you would be prepared to reconcile yourself at least to that.

There are still many other variations, some so "far out" as to be almost unimaginable and incomprehensible for us "oldies." For us, at least in Sydney, a "normal" wedding would be one that takes place in the Central Synagogue, at four or five o'clock on a Sunday, preferably in the late spring or early summer. The bride would wear white but the wedding dress would be semi-formal, allowing the possibility of wearing it again for some other occasion after the wedding.

This is what I planned in my imagination for my daughter. I did not get as far planning the reception, as that was looking too far ahead, even for me, particularly as there was as yet no groom on the horizon. But I did decide on something for my own peace of mind, something that had grown within me as the years passed by. I would at last put right a big wrong-doing: unlike my son's Bar Mitzvah party, my daughter's wedding reception would be a kosher one.

So much for fantasy. Now, back to reality, in which only a small part of my dream came true: the bride did indeed wear white. But Natalie did not have merely a kosher wedding; she had a *glatt*-kosher wedding, a kind that I did not even know existed until the day of the affair.

I will try to be as honest as is humanly possible. From the very first, Natalie's wedding was, for me, a great disappointment. My plans, my dreams, were cut down, one by one, as if with an ax, until nothing was left of them except for the bride, and the groom, and us, the bride's bewildered parents.

No stone is left unturned in searching for a suitable groom for a girl in the Circle (as I call the religious milieu in which

Natalie has placed herself). The Circle looks after the introductions, one way or another. You can leave everything to them; they will find a *shidduch* for an unmarried young woman or man. Someone who meets all their requirements, as distinguished from all *your* requirements.

Now, don't misunderstand. I think there is nothing wrong with making a *shidduch* — an arranged marital match. In fact just the other day, in 1989 (not 1889), I read the following in the English-language daily newspaper *The Jerusalem Post*: "A London Rabbi, anxious to reverse Anglo-Jewry's declining marriage and birth rates, has inspired a revival in *shadchanut* (matchmaking) in the community here." The idea has considerable merit.

I know that my daughter was not all that young when she became a B.T. at the age of 24, but she certainly was not old either. However, when she turned 26, I started to worry just a little, even though there was still plenty of time and I knew that the Circle would come up with somebody suitable in the not too distant future. I also knew that Natalie had high standards and I agreed that it was better that she wait, rather than rushing into anything less than perfect. Eventually, a friend of hers introduced her to a student at a prestigious Yeshiva, a B.T. like herself whom he considered to be a suitable *shidduch* for her. And then began what I call "going out on walkabouts," a form of courtship peculiar to religious circles. This is how it works:

A young man and a young woman who are deemed appropriate for one another are introduced and they start getting to know each other. They will first start to climb the hilly streets of Jerusalem, as in the case of Natalie and her prospective bridegroom, at any given time of the day or night. And walk they will, for hours, walking and talking. They will walk side-by-side, not touching, nothing familiar, nothing twentieth-century style. They must never cross the line of the Orthodox ways and traditions. And they don't forget, I can assure you.

But we must not forget either that they are made of flesh and blood, so a long period of courtship is not ideal. Consequently, they must hurry up the getting-to-know-each-other phase.

This is how it was with Natalie and her prospective groom. They courted, they walked, and they talked, for about six weeks or more, and then the time of reckoning arrived. Steven and I were having our summer vacation in Jerusalem during this period, but after four weeks, Steven had to leave. I, in my motherly wisdom, stayed on. The B.T. is unlikely to talk to you about the young man she is going out with, so do not expect any intimate discussions. Intimate discussions? What am I talking about!

I was informed after three weeks of "walkabouts" that Natalie was going out with a young man whose background was not unlike hers: we were from Hungary; his parents were from Yugoslavia. Natalie's father is an engineer and businessman; his father is a physicist. We left Europe in 1949; his parents left in 1968. They went to America, just as we went to Australia. Perfect match, right?

In reality, the two families are like chalk and cheese, so different are we from one another. But to an eager mother of a 26-year-old B.T. daughter, everything looked rosy. All I needed to hear was that Natalie actually liked the "walkabouts" and I immediately decided that she had found Mr. Right. I started to get very excited.

I would have dearly loved to invite the young man my daughter was going out with to my home, but she said: "This is not done." I could not understand why, but I was too scared to make a move, a wrong move. I kept quiet.

After four weeks of courting, Natalie called me to her room (we shared our apartment in Rehavia at this stage) and said quite sternly, with an unsmiling face: "Mum, we are going to the Israel Museum today, between 4:00 and 6:00 P.M. If you would like to see him, you can sit outside the entrance, and we will walk by. I might bring him over to you, but I might not; it depends." This was all she told me.

There were thousands of things I would have liked to ask, like for instance: "Natalie my darling, why don't you say this with a happy face?" Or: "Darling, what will make you decide to introduce me to the young man you seem to like?" Or: "Is there something, anything, special you would like me to wear?" Or: "I would wear anything, do anything, *say* anything you would like me to, just, please will you let me talk to him for a moment, instead of just passing me by?"

But I said nothing.

Miracle of miracles! I will never know how I merited the unexpected joy of being the lucky chosen mother who would after all be introduced face-to-face, as one human being to another, on such an occasion. I could clearly hear Natalie saying those marvelous words I had waited to hear as I sat outside the museum entrance, as instructed, between 4:00 and 6:00 P.M.. Here is what she said:

"This is my mother."

And I, who usually knows what to say, arose and stood there quite speechless, wondering what to say, what to do, as something told me (my lucky sixth sense) that I must not say a word or move an inch. I must not stretch out my hand — this I must have heard or noticed before, otherwise how on earth could I have been so clever as to not shake the hand of my possible future son-in-law? I just stood there, with a frozen smile on my lips, and said only: "Hello." I knew his family name, but I had no idea what his first name was.

Like an idiot I continued to stand there and repeated my helpless "Hello" until at last I heard my daughter faintly mention his name — Avi. Oh, good, I thought, now we can have a conversation. But just as I was going to say... I really don't know *what*, Natalie's voice chimed in: "Mum, enjoy your concert, and I will see you in the evening." And the meeting came to an abrupt end, before it had even begun.

I looked after them as they walked away side-by-side, but neither of them turned to look back at me. I continued looking till they had disappeared. And a clever voice in my head told me: "Agi, my girl, this is all you are going to see of him before the engagement — like it or not." I felt certain this was true and, as it turned out, I was quite correct.

Natalie did not ask me that night or the next morning if I had liked him. It was obviously unnecessary for her to know whether I liked him or not. I could hardly believe it but I had to, as every time I wanted to talk about the young man I had met at the museum, Natalie cut me short or walked away. I felt terribly hurt, terribly frustrated. But this was only the beginning.

I managed to hide my disappointment. I did not even allow myself to cry to Steven on the phone, though I did mention to him that I felt I ought to remain in Jerusalem as something important was developing. But I did not dare to tell him how little I really knew.

Natalie tapped on my bedroom door late one night, or it might already have been dawn. It was after one of those very long walkabouts. She stood in the doorway, not quite in my room, but not out of it; sort of in-between. "Mum," she said, "I am engaged."

I looked at her and I knew exactly what my role was, what my lines for this part were. Something I had repeated over and over, every time I was in doubt as to what to say on a happy occasion. It's not hard to memorize as it is only two words: "Mazal tov." (I advise you to learn these two very useful words, as you will need them on many occasions — if you are lucky!)

Avi entered our house in Jerusalem for the first time at the engagement party, which I made for the young couple with all the love and expectations of a Jewish mother. There was naturally something missing, or rather a lot missing — like for instance Natalie's father, brother, grandmother, uncles and aunts, and my dozens of good friends, who all loved her.

But the B.T. does not look back, to the past and to past relationships. This is such an important statement that you would do well to memorize it, so that you might recite it to yourself by heart whenever you need reminding. B.T.s are very serious-minded people who know what is expected of them; they must not waste time with the everyday, mundane things with which we occupy ourselves, because they're in a hurry to get on with the really important things. The B.T. only looks ahead. This you must get into your thick skulls, you backward, romantic, sentimental parents of a B.T.!

Be happy and satisfied that your child is becoming a real Jew. Is this not enough for you?? You want more, you want trimmings and frills? Oh, no, you can't have those. Those are for the average person; they are all *schmontzes* (trivia). The B.T. has time only for things of value — in the religious sense, of course. The now, the today, and the tomorrow are for the B.T. Yesterday is gone, passé, obsolete.

That evening, alone in my room, I was deep in thought about something a very wise friend of mine once told me. "Agi," he said, "you must swallow the bitter pill and realize that as of today you have become superfluous to your daughter. She does not need you anymore; she has her Circle and her *Rav*."

I had listened, but my heart could not accept what my ears had heard. I looked up in my Concise Oxford English Dictionary the definition of this word *superfluous*: "more than enough, redundant, needless," and to this I now added my own interpretation: "useless, unwanted." Oh, yes, this was a very bitter pill to swallow!

After the engagement party, I noticed a new look on my daughter's face, one that she flashed at me with every glance. It seemed to me like one of those neon signs that go on and off with a thousand-and-one blazing colors vibrating, blinding, screaming: "You are *treif*, you are bareheaded, barelegged, you are unkosher. You are everything I want to change from. I want to be your opposite. There is nothing I can ask you, or talk to you about. Your whole world has become alien to me. I have my own world, my own 'family' now. You can stay, but you must be silent, as you cannot teach me anything anymore. I must live my own life according to my own laws. This is all I have to say to you now and in the future."

But I've already told you I have a vivid imagination.

I had cried bitter tears for nights, for weeks, before the engagement party, feeling lonely, rejected. My own flesh and blood, my child, had turned away from me. She treated me as a kind of embarrassment to her, somebody she could do without. But I, her mother, had stayed on to prepare the engagement party.

My real pain was that I knew that had I not been able to stay on for the engagement party, it would have been arranged very well without me. Though I had worked *so* hard, and I had done my Jewish-motherly best, I felt later that anybody in the Circle could have done it just as well with less fuss. And I had, in truth, made a bit of a fuss.

How could I not? After all, it was the engagement party for my one and only daughter that I was planning. No matter that it was not in my own home, in Sydney (as I had imagined it would be), not with my own family at our side and surrounded by our own circle of friends welcoming a new member of the family, a second son (as I had imagined my future son-in-law would be). Still, I did all I could on my own to welcome a total stranger, with all the love and warmth I could muster for this occasion.

Natalie did not discuss any details with me before the party. After all, what was there to discuss? She told me whom to invite. Some of them I knew; most of them I had never heard of. The handful of my own friends in Israel, about a dozen or so, were accepted. There was one uncle of Avi's who had been living in Israel for over twenty-odd years. I immediately drew my own conclusions: he must be secular. He was not mentioned with the same kind of élan as some of the new friends of the young couple. (My guess was right. But Uncle Laci turned out to be a lovely addition to our non-existent family in Israel.) "If only we had some Rabbinical ancestors," was something Natalie lamented over and over again. But no matter how much I wanted to please her, this I could not arrange for her.

I was asked to phone a certain *glatt* kosher place and order a few things. I even baked some cakes, and picked up some food the Circle had prepared for us. I was to buy lots and lots of fruit drinks, paper plates and cups. I was asked by Natalie to wear stockings and a modest dress for the party, and altogether to speak as little as possible.

On the day of the party Natalie was almost friendly towards me. "Mummy, it will be very nice," she said smiling, "if you do all that I ask you to do."

I did all that she asked me to do, more or less. Another aspect of my nature is my innate enthusiasm. One cannot help one's nature. And when one meets in one's own house (which after all bears one's family name on the door), the man who wants to marry one's daughter, one would like on such an occiasion to do what one's natural instincts dictate.

As Avi walked through the door, I went towards him, and yes, I confess, I was going to shake his hand, or do something, *anything*, to suggest an intimate contact. I was actually going to touch my future son-in-law. And I almost did. But my daughter, my clever B.T. daughter, foresaw her mother's stupidity. She stood next to him and, smilingly but firmly, warned me: "No hands, no touching, no kissing, Mum. You must learn, we don't do that."

I wished my husband had been there to hold me, as I thought I would faint, or attack my child — either/or. I wanted to do something demonstrative. If I was not allowed to do something affectionate, demonstratively affectionate, I was going to do something else, such as say: "Hey, come on, I'm your mother and you, my daughter, are getting engaged to this fellow. I want to do as I would see fit to do anywhere else in the whole world — I want to hug my future son-in-law and wish him *Mazal tov.*" Instead I stood there motionless, feeling empty and hurt. I did mutter "*Mazal tov,*" but my heart wasn't in it. How could it be, when I did not see or feel anything like *mazal* on my side, at all. I felt — what was this new word? Oh, yes: *superfluous.* I had better get this word right, I told myself, as this feeling was going to be my companion for many lonely years to come — or so I thought then, on the day of the engagement of my daughter, in Jerusalem, in 1981.

The High Holidays were approaching and I knew I had to fly back to Australia to be with my family. That was where I had to be. Yet I stayed on as long as I could stretch time, as I had the most peculiar sensation about leaving.

I knew that Natalie and I should talk about the wedding. I also knew that I was defenseless, alone, and feeling threatened by something much bigger than me. Somehow I knew that no matter what I would envisage or suggest, the final say would be the prerogative of a higher authority than a mere parent.

Naturally I considered the possibility of having the wedding in Sydney; that, as I mentioned earlier, seemed to be the most "normal" idea, since our whole family and our friends and our home were there. I wanted everything that might contribute to making Natalie's wedding as much like what I had always imagined as possible.

In Australia, summer was approaching, while in Israel it was winter. I fantasized, very logically I thought, that we could have the wedding sometime in early December, when it would more or less suit everybody, with the holiday season on our doorstep. One of my most important considerations was our son, Danny, who was taking his final law exams at the end of November. Under no circumstances could he be disturbed at so vitally important a time.

During sleepless nights, I rehearsed several talks to have

with my daughter in the mornings. They were just never to be. In the mornings she went to work, then returned in the afternoons and made several phone calls to people who were all unknown to me. She was happy and laughing on the phone; she had a lot in common with those people who were strangers to me. I felt as though I were the very last person she thought of talking to about the wedding. I seriously weighed which one of the burning issues I should raise with my daughter. I knew that every minute was precious to her, so I had to be exceedingly clever in choosing what to talk about first.

Oddly, I chose my son's approaching exams, and within this framework, the date of the pending wedding. "Natalie," I said, "I know how much this wedding means to you. Let's not minimize it: a wedding is the biggest event in a person's lifetime." She sat opposite me, motionless and unsmiling, the hostility oozing from her even before she knew what I was about to say. I felt that she was sure that whatever it was, it would not find favor in her eyes. "As you have not told me anything yet," I went on with my heart pounding painfully, "I would like to suggest that you have the wedding at home in Sydney, maybe early December, after Danny's examinations." I couldn't remember ever feeling more uncomfortable in my life than I felt at this moment.

My daughter continued to sit there motionless for a few seconds, seconds which seemed like hours to me. One could feel the silence in the room. And then a voice that did not sound at all like my daughter's voice said, "I was aware that you know very little about our way of life and how we function, but I still gave you some credit. The time of the wedding will certainly not be determined by my brother's law exams, or by summertime in Australia. There are much more important and vital factors to take into consideration, and it will be those that will determine the date of the wedding."

She hardly took time out to breathe before she continued.

"Mum, I thought you would cherish the idea of your child's marrying in Jerusalem," she said, her eyes positively blazing, "a dream of thousands of parents, but obviously not of mine. I am afraid there is no question about this. It is pointless to even suggest anything else. My wedding naturally will be in Jerusalem, and nowhere else."

I must confess that deep inside me, in my heart of hearts, I too could see no comparison between Jerusalem and faraway, alien Australia. But how were we to overcome the problem of the 12,000 miles, and of having everybody and everything in Australia, while the bride and groom were in Jerusalem?

I am sure I did not know then, but today, sitting and writing about it, I know exactly how: with Hashem's help! Even so, it was not easy, but we went to work.

There was one scene that symbolized the pain my daughter had to endure in order to stay strong and unbending in her newly acquired religious belief. I will try to describe it to you, so that you will understand that you are not the only one suffering; your B.T. child suffers too.

It took place in our apartment, the night that Natalie decided to call Australia and inform the family about the date of the wedding — the date she, her fiancé and her Circle had decided on. It was to be straight after *Sukkot* according to the Hebrew calendar they used exclusively. On our Gregorian calendar, it was to be mid-October.

Natalie wanted to speak to her brother, to her one and only brother whom she loved dearly. I was in the kitchen when I overheard the conversation. "Danny," she said excitedly, "I want you to be the first person to know when my wedding will be!" There was a brief silence, and I walked towards the room where Natalie knelt girlishly in the middle of my bed. She was clutching the phone tightly and I could see she was on the verge of tears. "But Danny," she pleaded, "you must make it to the wedding!"

The bent, stooped body of my daughter seemed to be in

agonizing pain, a sight I will never be able to erase from my memory. It was a desperate cry for her brother to do the impossible, and she knew it. But she also knew she would not bend for him.

She started to sob, still kneeling in that awful stooped position in the middle of the bed, with the phone pressed to her ear. "Danny," she cried, "Danny, please do come," and I had to walk away from the door, as I too felt like crying, for both of them. For both my children, I knew, were fighting for their own principles.

Mine was the hardest task. I understood my daughter, and I also understood my son. But I did not even attempt to argue with Natalie. I knew the date was fixed. I had to explain to my hurt and disappointed son that she simply could not wait the few weeks that would have enabled him to get on a plane and come for the wedding. That's all it was — a matter of a few weeks — yet to change the date apparently was impossible. I did not know exactly why, but the urgency was everything, from this moment on.

The following week was strangely beautiful, with Natalie choosing her white wedding gown and both of us organizing whatever we possibly could. I was familiarized with the weirdest of places, new (to me) customs, habits and rules. To my amazement, there really was an element of "fun" for someone as enjoyment-oriented as I am, and I allowed my sense of humor free rein.

I flew back to Australia for the High Holidays exhausted, rather disturbed, but not unhappy. There was only a short time and a lot to be done before Steven and I had to return to Jerusalem.

In no time we were on a plane to Israel once more, my husband, my best friend and I. We had to leave behind my mother who was not well enough for the long journey. She was not to witness her beloved granddaughter's wedding, something she had dreamed about many a year. Danny had been so immersed in his studies that we had spent no time discussing the imminent event. My old friend, whom I had known from Budapest and who was part of our close-knit Hungarian-Australian circle, had decided to join us and represent all of our other friends who were unable to come, as were my brother, his family, and my cousins.

It was the busiest time of the year in Australia, with everything at the peak of activity before the Xmas holidays. Schools, universities, shops, offices — every place was hectic. It was no time to leave; no one could just get up and fly to Israel. Australia was not like England, from where you could get on the plane and be back at work the next day.

Avi had had the most beautiful wedding invitations printed to send around the world, to his and our families and friends. We brought back with us a suitcase full of presents for the young couple from the many who could not attend the wedding. (This unique "special delivery service" was to be repeated at every succeeding joyous occasion, and we graciously transported the gifts to them no matter what.)

Upon our arrival in Israel, our own problems were immediately forgotten as we were met by two pale, thin, obviously tense young people, who must have had a tremendous load on their minds. Our aim was to relieve as much of their burden as we possibly could.

During the few days before the wedding, we were in a constant daze, plunged into a mysterious world about which we knew nothing. But I must stress that the Circle, with their long, helpful and powerful arm, guided us along.

After our brief encounter at the airport, Avi was not to be seen. He was in the Yeshiva, as after all, his learning was paramount. Natalie did take time off from her job, and the four of us (including our friend) walked our feet off and spoke ourselves hoarse in several languages. We booked the hall for the wedding, one that was large enough to accommodate at least 200-250 people, as this was the number of guests they expected to have.

"This must be a huge mistake, Natalie," Steven said with surprise when he was presented with the guest list. "We hardly know twenty people in the whole of Israel, let alone two hundred or more. What are you trying to do to us?"

She was indignant at first, but later on explained. "With Avi's family and ours and your friends, we will already be close to twenty-five," she said, "and we have not started to count my friends and, above all, Avi's friends. The whole of the Yeshiva will want to come — this is how weddings are in our circles. Avi would want all his *chevreh* [group] to be with him at our *chassunah*."

I winced at this Yiddish-sounding word for wedding; I never thought it would apply to *ours*. But there was no time for my stupid, empty reactions — there were big issues to talk about. After all, why should the hundred or so *bachurim* (yeshiva students) not join in our *simchah*? Who, if not them?

I will spare you the details, as there were hundreds of them, one more alien than the other. By the end of the week, we had just about finalized arrangements for the whole wedding, from the "*glattest*" caterer to the most elegant hotel roof-garden. We were really lucky as the weather was still warm and we could have the *chuppah* (wedding ceremony) outdoors as was customary, and we could have the *seudah* (festive meal) and the dancing and merrymaking in the hotel's ballroom.

Each night, we were so exhausted that much as we would have loved to talk things over with each other, Steven and I simply fell into bed and slept until morning, to commence with the new day's peculiarities.

We seemed to be carrying out the injunction in the Bible: for six days we worked, and on the seventh day we rested. I had never before appreciated and understood the meaning and the importance of the *Shabbat*. Without this *Shabbat* and its enforced rest, we were sure we would not have survived the trials that were yet to come.

By Sunday everything had to be finalized as the wedding was only two days off. (I found out, quite by accident, that to have the wedding on a Tuesday was considered an added good omen.) And so, on Sunday Steven sat down in the living room and started busily writing something. "Dad, what are you doing?" Natalie asked. "What's all this that you're writing?"

Her father replied with a shy smile, "I am just making a rough outline of my speech for my daughter's wedding."

Natalie put her arms around her father, and said, "Oh, Daddy, did I forget to tell you? Customarily, there are no speeches at a *frum* wedding like ours, except the *Rav*'s."

Now it was my turn to be "speechless." Did she mean that her father would not have a chance to greet her and everybody else at his one and only daughter's wedding? We were to have a speech by an unknown "black" Rabbi, whose words we would not even understand?

The wedding was too close to call the whole thing off — that was my first thought. Then I felt that strange sensation once more: what was that word? *Superfluous.* Yes, that was what I felt we were. Strictly speaking, they could have done without us, their parents, but never without the *Rav.* He was the one who was "giving our daughter away." We were really only there as a formality.

On that Sunday Avi's parents arrived, very nice easygoing, European-type people. They behaved as though they had come to a party, all ready for them. I consoled myself, smiling, "You'll see, my girl, your day will also come to attend a party readied for you by others — your *son*'s wedding."

The day of the "*chassunah*" finally arrived. Can you imagine being at your one and only daughter's wedding and taking part in it as if you were split right down the middle, as if you were two people? That was how I felt, like two people.

One was the loving Jewish mother, whose heart beat with every step her daughter took through the wedding. And the other was the observer, the spectator, at a most exotic, never-before-seen-or-heard spectacular: a Jewish Orthodox "*glatt*" wedding. I can only write about this wedding from the point of view of both these people.

I was not told anything beforehand; no one sat me down and prepared me in advance for what was to take place or what was expected of me. Oh, no, there was no time for that. I had to put the puzzle together from all the little pieces I had picked up here and there during the preceding ten days of preparations in Jerusalem. Still, Steven and I found ourselves pathetically unprepared for the role of parents of the bride at a *glatt*-kosher wedding.

I saw Natalie for the first time in her stunning, long-sleeved, high-necked wedding gown when I entered the beautifully decorated ballroom of the hotel. She was enthroned in a large chair and surrounded by Orthodox women, obviously her friends from the Circle. Natalie was glowing, shining with happiness. I did not know most of the women, but they all seemed to know me: I was the mother of this beautiful B.T. bride.

There is no use denying the fact that I could not have looked more different from all those Orthodox women, wearing their *sheitels* and so meticulously and properly dressed. Not that there was anything wrong with the way I was dressed. In Sydney I had had my gown made to measure — a cornflower blue, georgette dress, buttoned almost to my neck, with long sleeves and ankle-length skirt — along with a matching smart little hat. My long hair was done simply, curled nicely under my hat. Despite my very modest attire, I felt I stood out like a sore thumb.

There was a person specially designated to do nothing else but guide me, call me at the right time to the right place, through the whole of the wedding ceremony. There is no doubt about it: they had thought of everything. I was not going to get lost at my own daughter's wedding. I was guarded and advised all along.

I was first called to meet up with Steven in a private room downstairs where the groom, his parents and all the Rabbis were assembled. I did not have a chance to count them, but I think that without exaggeration there were at least seven of them. One of the Rabbis was busy completing the *ketubah*, the marriage contract, which is the most important paper to have. And this one, I thought to myself, was to be the most kosher one there ever was.

The mother of the groom and I grasped the ceremonial plate together and smashed it, amid loud shouting of "*Mazal tov!*" Then my personal guardian angel gave me a gentle reminder to go back up to the bride. I remember it all, but I know I was in a sort of trance. Everything whirled around me and with me. In a way it all seemed as if it were happening to someone else, and I was there only looking in....

Natalie and I went up some stairs, and suddenly we found ourselves outdoors, under the sky, under the stars on a huge open terrace, where everybody was already waiting for us. Sitting in neat rows, the men were on one side, and on the other side, the women. At the very end of the huge terrace was a raised platform and the wedding canopy, decorated with flowers.

I looked around me and what I saw was overwhelming, and what I felt was indescribable. I was very conscious of being in Jerusalem. Yes, this was my overriding feeling at that moment. I would have loved to stop and talk about this feeling of mine to someone close to me, like my husband or daughter, but I was gently nudged towards the stage where the main event was to take place. Steven and I were each handed a lit candle. We were to hold it with one hand, and with the other guide our daughter, who stood between us, towards the *chuppah*. But I felt that the reverse was happening. I felt more as if

Natalie were escorting us towards the chuppah, and it seemed to be miles and miles away from us. It almost looked beyond our reach, it was so far and so distant.

As we walked — the three of us, father, daughter and mother — holding the burning candles, our daughter taking us with her to her destination, hundreds of people around us stood and all were chanting, singing. But all I could see was the dark sky, the stars and the moon, and Jerusalem. It was exhilarating.

I knew at this moment that something wonderful was happening to us, but it was all happening too fast. Under the chuppah the groom was dressed in a long white shirt that reached almost to his knees. I was immediately told, in whispers of course, what this symbolized, as I had no idea about it.* (I realized by this time that my "guide" had been assigned to me not merely to prevent me from embarrassing the bride and groom, but to help me feel more at ease with the many unfamiliar procedures.) The groom's mother and I were instructed to walk the bride around the groom seven times with the burning candles in our hands. I felt a bit dizzy. I wondered what would happen if I fainted. But I did not.

I held the cup of wine for my daughter to sip, while lifting the veil over her head, and we actually smiled at each other, in this one, intimate moment between us.

There were all the Rabbis around us, each one of them singing, chanting blessings. A glass was placed on the ground and Avi stomped on it. Suddenly a thunderous roar broke out, and I realized the actual wedding ceremony was over.

"Mazal tov!" was on everybody's lips. My eyes filled with tears, and once more the sensation of being in Jerusalem moved me.

The band began to play immediately, lively, happy music,

* The long white shirt, known as a "kittel," symbolizes purity. On their wedding day, the bride and groom are absolved of all their previous transgressions.

as everyone clapped to the rhythm. The songs were not any that we knew, but it didn't matter. There was excitement in the air.

At the *seudah*, the dinner following the ceremony, the men and women were again seated separately, as I knew they would be, but I still had not imagined it would be SO separate: the men on one side, at large, round tables and the women beyond the *mechitzah*, a barrier set up along the middle of the huge room. When we entered, all the women were already dancing, holding hands, making one large circle and many smaller ones. On the other side of the barrier, the men also started dancing, singing, almost going into a frenzy. What a wild, happy bunch we all became.

The food was served, but it was unremarkable; it reminded me merely of a Friday night dinner. The emphasis at this affair was on the dancing, and the music, and the singing, and the blessings, unlike our passé affairs where the emphasis was on the wedding feast, and the champagne, and the five-layered white-iced wedding cake. All that, I noticed with great surprise, was of secondary importance to the merrymaking.

Though I sat next to my daughter at the head table (on the women's side), there was little opportunity for us to talk. She did manage, however, to ask me, her face glowing with happiness, "Well, Mummy, what do you say? Did you ever think it would be so big, so nice, so marvelous?"

I had to reply in all honesty, "No, I really never thought so."

We were then pushed to sit in the center of the ballroom, just we, the two sets of parents and the young couple. And there were these clever, athletic, talented yeshiva *bachurim*, entertaining only us, dancing and gyrating and juggling, making us laugh, making us clap and sing along with everybody. Natalie pulled me with her to the women's half of the dance floor, to dance with her and the others in a big circle. But I was very self-conscious, and not quite comfortable dancing with women.

Then, returning to our seats, Natalie looked at me and said, only to me, "Mummy, now comes a most important part of the wedding celebration. First, the *Rosh Yeshivah* [the dean of the yeshiva] will deliver his speech to us, and then our very best friends will each recite a special blessing."

We actually heard two long speeches by Rabbis, but unfortunately we did not understand one word of either of them. One was in Hebrew and one in Yiddish, but Natalie smiled at me, and I more or less guessed what was being said.

Towards the very end there was a bit of confusion, as I did overstep the *mechitzah*, but I am sure they understood. After all, there were a few of our own personal friends to whom I was dying to speak, even if only for a moment.

It was then, at that very moment, that my husband and I looked at one another, and touched each other, secretly, so no one should see us. Our hands clasped, we did not have to say anything, as we each knew what the other was thinking:

"If only *we* might have had such a wedding!"

6   *Just a Little "Black" Word*

I want to write about a word, a little "black" word that cannot be found anywhere else but in a Jewish heart.

In the past, the word *"naches"* meant for me something quite different from its real meaning. The very sound of the word irritated me as it sounded so Yiddish. And I, the blue-blooded Hungarian Jewish aristocrat (as I imagined myself to be), and later the assimilated but still aristocratic Australian Jew, had alienated myself from all low-class Yiddish-sounding words. They were just beneath my dignity.

"Naches," I had thought, was for other people. It was for the "black," ultra-Orthodox, funny-looking Jews whose children wore sidecurls, fringes and skullcaps and looked completely alien. I never, NEVER, mixed with the ultra-Orthodox who talked about something called *"naches."*

But that was eons ago. Gradually the word *naches* started to take on a different shape for me. I started to listen to its Yiddish connotation with a certain kind of envy, as it is always accompanied in the religious circles by absolute joy, by a profound sigh of pleasure, and by a kind of fulfillment that derives from something one hopes to get from one's children. But these children always appeared to be Orthodox children, the only ones that filled this funny-sounding word with meaning for their parents.

We sophisticated, assimilated Jews hoped, on the other hand, that our children would make us proud by becoming educated, clever, successful people — all the things that we had wanted to become ourselves — and this sometimes seemed to be quite a burdensome challenge for our children to meet. And often, we sophisticated, assimilated Jews could not ever attain genuine fulfillment and had to reconcile ourselves to something less.

Today the sound of the word *naches* makes me smile because I know that the little "black" word is *synonymous* with joy. I did not have to look in any dictionary, I did not have to search in libraries to find the real meaning of *naches*. It came to me only after a long and bumpy road after overcoming the period of conflicts, the so-called alienation syndrome — that trap we parents of B.T. children invariably fall into.

When you get to where I am, and you discover the real meaning of *naches* — with a capital N — you will have achieved something that you will never want to relinquish. Most of the time this unique feeling appears on your doorstep with the arrival of your Orthodox, observant children's own children — your grandchildren. They are your source of *naches*.

I wish you all to know this feeling, an emotion that can only be expressed by this little word, this little "black" word, with all its connotations. The most thrilling word in my life.

7   *The Birth of Our Bechor*

Steven flew in from Australia on a Wednesday afternoon in August 1982, and Natalie and I were waiting for him at the airport. He took one look at his daughter and very aptly asked, "Nu, Natalie, how about giving me a grandson for my birthday?" To which Natalie replied in her most obedient voice: "I will do my best."

She did!

Friday morning she was admitted to Hadassah Hospital and I, in all honesty, did something very strange and selfish. This was to be our first grandchild and our daughter's first child, and I knew by this time that to have a son first was the dream of most B.T. families because there are some very beautiful additional ceremonies associated with firstborn male children. (Some of these ceremonies I had never even heard of before, let alone participated in, but more about this later on.) What I did was go to the *Kotel* (Western Wall to us, "*Koisel*" to *them*) and there I prayed, begged Hashem to give us a grandson, a healthy firstborn son for our daughter.

Natalie was feeling quite well before the birth and she had time to come to the window of the hospital room she was occupying with other soon-to-be mothers. I was outside in the garden below her window, with a pen and paper to take last-minute notes of what to do. I was to go and buy all the *Shabbat* food Avi would need, as he was naturally staying with her. Since they only ate *glatt*-kosher, the regular kosher hospital food would not do.

They had been married for just under a year and they were still terribly anxious over their religious observances, guarding every step they took. Not that they are less particular today, but then they were always fearful of making even the slightest wrong move. We, on the other hand, were in what we would now call "The Ignorant Years," the totally un-accepting and even hostile years. But, once we had decided to remain good and loving parents, we were obliged to accept their ways and their demands — sometimes with clenched fists and tight lips, but accept we did!

It was a very hot day on this *erev Shabbat* morning, when all the duties of our B.T. family fell on my strong shoulders. I looked at my notes and read: "The only shop where you can buy *glatt*-kosher prepared food is in Meah She'arim." Little did I know what this short order meant. Let me enlighten you.

My good husband (who was in an even darker, hazier state than I was, as he had only arrived two days before) was to drive me to the Meah She'arim neighborhood — the ultimate "black" neighborhood of Jerusalem — and drop me off at the corner. He was then to proceed to purchase the challah and cakes in the nearby Hungarian-owned cake shop.

Close to midday, the temperature was near 40° centigrade (104° Fahrenheit) and I was dressed, at my daughter's insistence, in a modest high-necked summer shirtdress with elbow-length sleeves. Natalie knew I would be spending a lot of my time in Meah She'arim. As for me, I was so ignorant that I was happy to obey blindly. I constantly reminded myself of the vow my husband and I had made: "We are going to stick it out, rain or shine, and accept our child's strange transformation, regardless of what it entails."

The recommended *glatt* take-out shop was itself invisible, but the long queue outside its doors reached far out into the street. I took my place on line in the blazing sun. My Hebrew then was nonexistent, but as Yiddish was the primary language spoken here, I was able to use my German, disguising it to sound more like Yiddish and making myself understood, more or less.

In those days I did not even know enough to wear a hat to protect myself from the midday sun. I was far too busy learning the rules of the B.T. world to learn how to provide for my own comfort. I put myself and my needs very much in the background, desperately dedicating myself to helping Natalie and Avi.

When I looked around at the others on the queue, I realized that once again I stood out like a "sore thumb." I was the only bareheaded and barelegged person perhaps in the entire neighborhood. Still, I tried to melt into the crowd. (I was already melting from the heat!)

I was glancing at the note in my hand, worrying about what other things I needed to attend to, when I heard a voice behind me say: "Whatever the reason may be that you are standing here with *us* [the stressed word *us* sounded amiable coming from her lips] on this hot Friday morning will be acknowleged by Hashem."

I turned in the direction of that pleasant voice and found a smiling woman. She went on: "You must be doing it from the goodness of your heart and not because you want to do it." The woman spoke pleasantly, in English with a slight European accent. She looked to be about 35, and her face was glowing with friendliness. Suddenly I felt very honored to be standing in front of this total stranger, who apparently thought so highly of me.

I replied with a definite *gomboc* (this is Hungarian for "*knaidlach*," an expression that implies speaking with a lump in one's throat, a voice clogged by emotion). I said: "It is the happiest day of my life, as I am to become a grandmother. My daughter is having her first child."

Hardly did I finish this sentence when the whole crowd broke out in the loudest "*Mazal tov!*" I had ever heard, repeating it with great joy, for no other reason but the imminent birth of my grandchild.

I was overcome and could not hold my tears back as I heard my "friend" behind me say: "May Hashem bless you with many healthy grandchildren and may *naches* be your companion." Then she smiled broadly and added: "You must be a very good and loving mother. It is obvious you are not *datiyah* [religious]; it is also obvious that you are trying to get along with your daughter in her newfound joy in the religious life. May Hashem bless you and your family."

The queue had almost reached the door by now, but I could only concentrate on this total stranger who was so engrossed in my personal life.

Who is she? I wondered. What business of hers is it that I am to become a grandmother today, or better still that my daughter is a B.T. and that I am going out of my way to please her?

I was contemplating all this when the woman handed me a slip of paper that read: "This is my name. I am blessed with many children. I live in B'nei Brak, and we are here in Jerusalem only for *Shabbat*. I am sure it was *bashert* for me to stand behind you today. It gives me a good feeling to see a woman like you standing with me here, on a hot Friday morning..."

After I had read her lovely note, she said: "It would be my privilege to attend your grandson's brit," and again she wished me the heartiest *Mazal tov!* and *B'sha'ah tovah!* ("May it be in a good hour," a beautiful wish for pregnant women.)

I found myself inside the shop, the counter of which was laden with food of all kinds, mostly the kind that did not impress me. But I knew it had to be *glatt*. The chicken liver, the various salads, the herrings in every color and shape, the smell of it all, in that heat! It was overwhelming, and I thought: "I certainly could not eat even a mouthful of any of this." (How incorrect my assessment was!)

The people serving behind the counter looked even more alien than the food. There was a man with a long white beard, wearing a fringed, white-ish, sleeveless sort of tunic (which I later found out was his *tzitzit*, worn on top of his shirt instead of hidden beneath it); I had never seen such a strange garment before in my life. There were two men, both dressed in this "thing."

I looked at the people around me, all buying large quantities of this food; some also bought *shnitzels*, fried chicken breasts which were piled up high on platters.

Remember, this was my first-ever *glatt* shopping trip in Meah She'arim. The heat, the perspiration, the strangeness of the people, their garments — put all that together and you will understand that I felt closer then to fainting than to merrily shopping for our festive Friday night dinner.

I was also close to tears when I realized that my "friend" had disappeared. I was all alone in this "black," ugly world around me. I thought: I will *never* forget what my daughter made me do on the day of the birth of my first grandchild. Instead of being with my husband and celebrating it in our own fashion, with champagne and caviar, with our marvelous, secular Hungarian friends in Israel, I must stand in this horrible place and feel ill.

I was still holding the slip of paper my "friend" had given me and, in my desperation, while trying to make up my mind what to buy from all those awful things, I glanced at the note again, and read the following words: "May Hashem guard you and guide you in your new role as a grandmother, a *Savta* to your newborn religious grandson." I walked out of the *glatt* shop in Meah She'arim with my purchases and decided to confront this "black" world around me, with a new name and newly gained strength. From that moment on, I would be *Savta*, and proud of it.

The days following the birth of our first grandson, however, were considerably less glorious. The difficult times, it seemed, were not yet behind us.

Actually, we felt as though we were traveling through a tunnel, a tunnel with no end to it, a black tunnel which we tried to drive through blindfolded, and as far as we could tell, the end of it did not even exist. Every step we took was unknown to us, and every move we wanted to make on our own initiative was corrected or criticized. We adults, we parents, were suddenly ridiculed at every step of the way because of our ignorance.

Take the first day, that Friday afternoon, when we entered Natalie's hospital room and asked our first logical question: "Darling, tell us, what is the name of our grandson?" Both Natalie and Avi looked at us as if we had asked if the baby had two heads or something.

It was so good that I had my husband to share these days with. I don't think I could have endured them alone. At least we were able to glance at each other and exchange a look of disbelief over what was actually happening all around us.

Again it seemed that Natalie and Avi were out to see how far they could go, how much they could shock us. This was what we thought when we could not get a straight answer to our most logical question.

Natalie whispered to us: "You must never ever ask this question before the *bris*! Don't you know that?"*

Steven and I replied at once, together: "No, we don't!"

In spite of Natalie's remark, we still would have loved to

---

*We subsequently discovered that not telling the baby's name before the *brit* is a custom observed only in some Orthodox circles, not a Law as Natalie was so sure it was. Still it is preferable not to ask the name, just in case the parents do observe this custom.

know the name of our grandson. We felt it was really cruel to make us wait seven more days to find out, but there was no use arguing. We assumed they had their reasons.

Natalie looked very well and happy indeed. She was up the very first day, admiring her firstborn, whom she called her *bechor*. To us, not even the fact that he was nameless mattered, as he appeared to be the handsomest, most intelligent looking baby boy we had ever seen.

Just as I was looking at him, at his tiny, wrinkled face, I had a sudden vision before my eyes. I quickly tried to chase this horrible sight away, but it still remained.

It was a vision of this grandson of ours, grown up and already a boy of 12 or maybe 13, close to his Bar Mitzvah. I could see him clearly before me, standing there tall, dark and handsome, with long *payot* dangling on either side of his face. "Oh, what a horrid picture. How could I think of it at a moment like this?"I tormented myself. I looked again at our beautiful newborn grandson and wondered, "Could they have affected even our vision so much, and so soon, to make me imagine a sight as distressing as our grandson with long sidecurls??"

It must have been the sun, I told myself, and tuned back in to the chit-chat of our own secular friends, who had come all the way from Tel Aviv to join us in celebrating the arrival of our first Israeli grandson.

Later on I heard mention of many foreign-sounding things but I did not take much notice of it all. Not until Avi sat us down the next day and started to discuss the events which were to follow. With our full cooperation, he hoped.

First there was the arrival back home of Natalie and her son (unnamed). To us this namelessness was very strange and because of it, I could not associate myself with him as closely as I would have liked. But there was no time to waste with idle thoughts. Action was demanded of us.

My husband and I were numb, and we just did as we were

told, as nothing made sense to us, *nothing*. It was all foreign, unnecessary hocus-pocus, which they carried out in what seemed to us an almost hysterical frenzy. (Please see the next chapter for more details.) The big subject on the agenda was the circumcision ritual, the *Brit Milah*, which they called "the *bris*." Naturally they were to choose the most renowned *mohel* in Jerusalem to perform the ritual.

The confused but proud grandfather was to have the greatest honor: he was to be the one who holds the baby on the pillow at the actual *Brit Milah* ceremony, the *sandak*, as we later learned this is called. We knew nothing about an Orthodox circumcision ceremony, how it proceeded, what the participants were called. (Although I had attended a few such ceremonies for the sons of Natalie's friends, I never realized the magnitude of the preparations until our turn to make a *brit* arrived.)

All the expressions we heard were in Yiddish or Hebrew, neither of which we spoke. We, the new grandparents, were guilty of total ignorance of all the customs connected with this occasion.

Well, we thought, this little fellow was to have the *glattest*, "blackest" *brit* in Jerusalem. We were not too far off.

The site was chosen. It was to be in the Yeshiva where his Abba was learning, a most obvious choice. Just as it was at our big wedding, with hundreds of yeshiva *bachurim* attending, so it would be at our huge *Brit Milah*. All those healthy, previously secular, (mostly) sportsmen-cum-yeshiva *bachurim*, who always seemed happy to participate in a *simchah*, would attend.

We heard about the famous *mohel*, Yossele, the numerous *Ravs* who were to honor us with their presence, the food that was ordered from the *glattest* caterers for such occasions. But it was our first grandson's *Brit Milah*, certainly a worthy occasion. There was no further question about it; it was all arranged, and it was going to be *glatt*, big... and expensive.

Ever since the wedding, we were amazed that we, who had lived in Australia for over 30 years, could have a *simchah* in Jerusalem where we hardly knew anybody, and still have hundreds of "friends" attending. The feeling was strangely exciting for us, and a bit overwhelming. But where could we cut back? Should we not have the famous *mohel*?* Should we not have it in Avi's own Yeshiva? Should we not invite all those students that Avi had been learning with now for over a year, and would continue to learn with for who knew for how long to come? (This thought actually worried us: How long would our son-in-law continue to learn and when would he start to earn a livelihood?)

But there was no time to think on matters as trivial as these. The *brit* was all planned and everything was ready for the celebration. It was to be early, at 8:30 A.M., for me an unearthly hour to plan a *seudah*, a big meal. And naturally there would be this festive meal at the celebration of our grandson's *Brit Milah* to welcome him into the world of the B.T. *Their* world, not ours. Of this we were certain — at the time.

I tried to reason with Natalie, saying: "Why must we have such an elaborate and expensive meal so early in the morning, when all I think people would like to eat is a bowl of muesli?" Natalie hardly listened to my complaint. She just repeated her usual "Mummy, you really don't know anything about it. Just leave it to us."

And I did. With resentment and humiliation over how little we mattered. Not once did they ask our opinion or our advice. We were the silent bystanders. They would, without hesitation and in front of us, phone any young new friend of theirs and ask his advice before ever thinking of turning to us. To us, their parents, their elders, the ones who brought them up to become such clever people, to enable them to set their world

---

*The *mohel* usually does not charge a fee, but it is customary to give a respectable sum as an honorarium.

up against us.

Words cannot express the anger, the frustration, the animosity we felt.

No matter how sincerely my husband and I intended to accept our child in her "madness," it was very hard for us to do so, especially in these early years and particularly at a time when we were to celebrate a common joy with them. We felt outnumbered, outcast, as though we were only figureheads. We were to take part in their *simchah*, oh yes; after all, we were the grandparents. Saba and Savta were there to play their parts and to be *"mazal toved,"* but in all earnest, we felt that we were the very last ones on their list.

We were told what to wear, how to behave, what to say and, mostly, what not to say. We were to be, in a word, puppets. We were to act, move, talk, just as they pulled the strings. This was how we felt on the eve of our first grandson's *Brit Milah*: like two very tired puppets.

The day began at dawn. Who could sleep when at 8:30 we were to at last (we hoped) find out the name of our grandson? Not I, for sure. I was dressed: stockings, shoes, buttoned-up dress and even a *tichel*, a kerchief, on my head! Natalie this time had put her foot down, saying: "Mummy, you must cover your head at the *bris*." I looked in the mirror and saw that I looked like all the religious women, though not quite.

Saba was still under the impression that he was to hold the pillow with his first grandson on it; no one warned him that this role might be abruptly withdrawn from him at the very last moment. And this was the case. To our profound hurt, Saba was only to stand by while a very fine-looking *Rosh Yeshivah* received the honor of holding the baby, our grandson.

Such were the actions of B.T.s who wanted so much to do the right thing for the sake of their newfound religiousness, that they neglected to do the right thing for the sake of their parents. This was a matter that could only be understood and forgiven in the years to come, when I had gained a better understanding of the B.T.s and their life.

By relating this episode, I hope I can help you to accept these times of total upheaval a bit better, more easily. I mean the times still awaiting you, as there is no question about it: the new B.T. will always bow to *Halachah*, his new-found ruler. Although Jewish Law prescribes obeying even one's *secular* parents, whenever there is a conflict between the two, *Halachah* will govern the child's actions.

Just as at the wedding, I felt at the *brit* like a member of the audience in a theater, not an active participant. I did not feel that it was actually my celebration. I could not relate to the Yeshiva-style hall as the venue of our party. I could not relate to all the (as they called them) "big *Ravs*" as our friends. I could not relate to all the sidecurled, black-hatted, bearded young men, with hollow faces and sunken eyes (from the intense learning, as we later found out).

What really staggered me was that our few secular friends, who lived in Tel Aviv and even Haifa, all arrived on time, at 8:30 sharp to celebrate the *Brit Milah* of our religious grandson, still nameless but certainly not for long. I will never know what brought our friends to Jerusalem so early in the day to celebrate with us — curiosity, or true Israeli brotherhood. Whatever, they were delighted to be there with us, they said, and proud to be celebrating so important an event as the Orthodox *brit* of our B.T. daughter's firstborn son. They genuinely wished us all *Mazal tov* and told us how happy they were to join us in Jerusalem. We confessed to being tired but terribly pleased that they had come all this way so early in the morning to be with us for the occasion.

We were hushed down as the "big *Rav*" walked in. The *mohel* followed, and then the baby was brought in on a beautiful pillow that was covered with a pillow case from my trousseau. My pillow case, brought all the way first from Hungary, then from Australia, a pillow case which even had my initials embroidered on it.

A loud cry told us that our grandson had become a Jew in every sense of the word. Enthusiastic shouts of "*Mazal tov!*" followed. Did they actually say the name? I could not hear it.

I was naturally standing far away from where the action was, as the men all stood somewhere at one end of the hall, a much larger part of it, while we women were tucked away at the very opposite end of the huge room. I turned to someone a complete stranger, a lovely looking young woman, obviously a friend of my daughter's, and whispered: "Please, could you tell me what is the name of my grandson?"

And this lovely woman turned to me and exclaimed, "Oh it is you, but of course! Don't you remember me? I met you in Meah She'arim in the *glatt* take-away shop on the day your grandson was born. You must have given my name and phone number to your daughter, since she called to tell me about the *brit*. *Mazal tov!* May Hashem bless you with many healthy grandchildren!"

She kissed and hugged me with warmth and affection, and of course I remembered. I had told Natalie about our strange meeting and also made sure to ask her to invite this lovely person.

I felt as though I were in a dream. It was all so new and so strange, and people were all so happy at the *brit* of my grandson — *if only I could know his name!*

But Avi arrived at my side together with Saba, beaming with joy (not allowing his disappointment over not holding the baby on the pillow to show). And Avi said: "We will definitely choose Saba for the next *bris*, with God's help." (And let me tell you, they did, and what a wonderful *sandak* Steven made at the *brit* of our second grandson, the same time and the same place, a year and a bit later.)

"Well, do you like his name?" Avi asked. I smiled a sort of strange half-smile, not knowing if I should admit my ignorance or not.

As soon as he told us the name, we started shrieking with

joy. First, because we loved the name Yacov, and second, because although we were ready to accept even the hardest-to-pronounce name — no matter what, even *Pinchas* — we were ecstatic that they had chosen one we would have no trouble with.

I quickly mumbled a thanksgiving prayer, and asked for forgiveness for turning to Hashem on such a petty matter as a name for my first grandson. But I had asked that the name be easy for us to pronounce and also acceptable in our world, and even in Australia. A name something like Yacov.

I ran to the baby, who by now was in the arms of his mother, proudly and happily holding this little Jewish man, this little Orthodox boy, this sweet little boy called Yacov. My first grandson. May Hashem bless him now and always.

8 *The First Shema and Other Firsts*

I remember, it was at the first *Shema*...

I say this proudly and with such nonchalance, as though I have always known that every Orthodox Jewish male child who comes into the world has a "first *Shema*" on the eve of his *brit*, in the company of his new friends. It was only one of several parties for this sweet, Orthodox Jewish fellow, my grandson. And oh, what a lovely party it really was.

All my life, the *Shema* has represented for me "The Prayer for all Occasions." It is the prayer in which a Jew affirms his belief in the One and Only God, and I should have been reciting the *Shema* every single night of my life as this is how I was brought up.

As a child, I understood the *Shema* to be the ultimate prayer, the one we Jews should always have there — always at hand — for any special occasion, such as thanksgiving or begging God for His help in times of need. And if, to a "secular" Jew like myself, the *Shema* is so meaningful, can you imagine what it means to the Orthodox?

Because of my personal connection with this prayer, I was especially touched by the "first *Shema*" celebration for our first grandson. On the night before the circumcision, Avi's best friends and their little boys and girls all gathered around the crib to recite the *Shema* for the first time on behalf of the infant who was about to become a member of the Jewish people.

Speaking of the crib, it was the one that Saba Steven had gone to collect from the "*Sochnut*" (Jewish Agency), which provides a crib to the firstborn *Sabra* (a colloquial Israeli term for those born in the Holy Land) of a new immigrant couple. Although it was quite an ordinary bed, to us brand-new grandparents it looked anything but ordinary. And even if it *did* look ordinary, I, Savta, immediately ran to the most elegant nursery shop to buy all there was to make an ordinary Jewish Agency crib look like the most luxurious little prince's cradle.

In truth, the "first *Shema*" was not the first celebration in our grandson's honor. The very first, called the "*Shalom Zachar*," which means "Welcome, male child," is a party usually attended by men and boys only and held on the infant's very first Friday night, his first *Shabbat*. It is yet another celebration of thanksgiving for Hashem's present, in the company of the proud father and his close friends, and it takes place whether or not the tiny guest of honor is able to attend. (In this instance, Natalie and the baby were still in the hospital.) It is a lively, happy affair, with lots of eating and singing.

I had come to Israel six weeks before the birth, and thought I would fly back to Australia three weeks after Natalie had the baby. At that time I was still needed in various capacities at home. Two-and-a-half months seemed a long time to be away.

The entire week after the birth of a firstborn son, I discovered, is just one continuous thanksgiving celebration. Though exhausting for me, all in all I found it very interesting and enriching. But after the *brit*, when I told my daughter I had booked a flight back home for two weeks later, she looked at me with what I call her "What do *you* know!" expression and said: "Mummy, forget that flight. You would not want to miss out on the most beautiful of *simchahs*, the *Pidyon Haben*."

I smiled my ignorant-yet-self-assured smile and asked, "What, who?" And it was then, at the ripe old age of grandmotherhood, that I first learned about this truly impressive, once-in-a-lifetime event: the "Redemption of the Firstborn Son."

[This ceremony is connected to the Exodus and the liberation of the Children of Israel from Egyptian bondage. Immediately preceding the Exodus, Hashem subjected Egypt to ten plagues, the last and worst of which was the Plague of the Firstborn Sons, in which only the Egyptian children died. Because God chose to spare the Jewish firstborns, their lives "belong" to Him. Jews acknowledge this debt-for-all-time by "redeeming" their firstborn sons, that is, by paying a symbolic fee to God's earthly representative — a *Kohen*, who is descended from the Priestly family — in exchange for the life of their child.]

As in all such celebrations, food plays an important role and a *seudah* is served. But the star of the show is the thirty-day-old infant who is to be "redeemed." He is customarily carried into the hall on a silver tray, adorned with jewels and fine white clothing, and offered to the *Kohen*. The father of the "*ben*" offers five silver coins as a "*pidyon*" to redeem his son, and the *Kohen* graciously accepts the token sum.

My friend from Tel Aviv arrived with the biggest silver platter I had ever seen to carry our thirty-day-old *ben* on, and I searched high and low for all the family jewels that we possessed in Israel, with which to decorate our brand new firstborn grandson. I must say that when I took my most precious possession, the signet ring that my father had worn and I inherited and had never taken off my finger in thirty-seven years, and placed it on the chest of my precious little grandson, this little Orthodox grandson of ours, I felt something very close to perfect joy and satisfaction: *naches*.

And I was sure that my father was smiling Up There along with us.

9   *Names Can Be Tricky*

I am warning you, names can be tricky. Let us start at the very beginning, when you as a brand-new mother painstakingly search together with your husband, friends and parents for an appropriate name for your newborn child. You even buy books that consist of nothing else but names from which to choose the one you consider beautiful for your own flesh and blood, the name your child will bear for the rest of his or her natural life. Or so you think at the time.

Well, you can forget about that painstakingly selected and lovingly bestowed name. If this child becomes a B.T., suddenly this name by which you have called your child for let us say 27 years, a name you love and sort of got used to calling him, a name you think that your child loves too, since, after all, this was, is, his/her name... this name is suddenly *gone*. Let me explain.

Take our son-in-law's case, for example. His name was Andrew. I rather like the name Andrew. It is a good, short name, and his family liked it and they all called him Andrew. But Andrew became a B.T. and suddenly realized that "Andrew" was certainly the wrong name for him. How could he possibly exist as a religious Jew with such a non-Jewish name as Andrew? And so, without further ado, he changed his name, or more correctly, reverted to his Hebrew name, as he already had one (unused since his birth).

That he actually *knew* his Hebrew name was a blessing. If he hadn't known it, he would have had to choose one for himself, as many do. From that day on, Andrew became, religiously and irrevocably, Avi (short for Avraham).

His B.T. wife had no problem calling him Avi, as she had not known him as Andrew. His parents, brothers, aunts and old friends occasionally slip back into the nasty habit of thirty-odd years of calling him Andrew, thereby breaking an unbreakable rule. Well, this is not so good. The family must try very hard to stick with the name Avi, since after all this is his name *now*.

This phenomenon is more common among male B.T.s than females, naturally, as it is by his Hebrew name that the B.T.'s teachers in the yeshiva will call him, it is by his Hebrew name that he will be called up to the Torah in the synagogue, and it is the name he will use in the numerous other religious observances in which he participates. But female B.T.s very often adopt a new Hebrew name for themselves as well.

There are very few exceptions to the rule, but if you should see or hear of them, you must pretend not to have noticed as they would not like it if you were to make them conscious of it.

Rare are those who have learned to love the names their parents gave them so much that they simply cannot, at the age of 27, suddenly become a newly-named person. My daughter belongs to this select few, a B.T. who was so attached to the name Natalie that she stayed Natalie. I guess I'm just lucky, that's all.

So there was and is our daughter Natalie, and we and also everybody in the Circle call her Natalie, and I must say I am proud that we were so fortunate to have chosen a name which inexplicably suits both worlds.

But don't count on it happening to you. It's a pretty

isolated case as far as I can tell.

To give you another example, I'll tell you about my very lovely friend Eva who has a son, Anthony, called "Tony" at home. This is the name they all liked and got used to. Now, Anthony, a B.T., has become Moishie (Moshe). I really think Moishie is a good name, but it happened once that Eva and I were together at Moishie's house, and every time my friend called or referred to her son as Tony, she was politely but firmly interrupted. "Moishie," they reminded her repeatedly, and each time my charming friend, a very good sport indeed, apologetically smiled back and said, "Oh, yes, I mean Moishie...."

The name-change phenomenon is not exclusive to Orthodox Jews, or even to secular Jews. Immigrants have been changing their names possibly since the dawn of immigration. No doubt Guiseppe, the shoemaker's son from Sicily, quickly became Joe when he landed in Chicago, and most likely reminded his aging Mamma of his new name every time she lovingly called him Guiseppe. And didn't Bernie Schwartz from New York become Tony Curtis of Hollywood? Countless Israeli notables and less-notables obstinately cling to their newly Hebraized, Israeli names, regardless of religious orientation. It is the most natural thing in the world for newcomers to want to "fit in" in their new environment.

What I am referring to, though, is the Hebrew name change that comes about among B.T.s *whether or not* they immigrate to Israel, the Hebrew names they take on even if they remain in the land of their birth. It is part and parcel of their newfound religious beliefs and should not be taken lightly.*

But this name problem does not end with the B.T.; in fact this is where it begins. With each grandchild that comes into

---

*It is said that the Children of Israel merited redemption from Egyptian bondage because they retained their traditional dress, their Hebrew language, and their Hebrew names.

the world — with all the wonder of it — you must be prepared for the child to have a name that you might never have heard of before, or, worse still, that you can hardly pronounce. But nobody asks your opinion and they will only tell you what it is and what it means in their own good time.

I must say, today this all seems to me like an ancient history lesson. Today I would not dream of asking Orthodox new parents the name of their son — not a moment before the Rabbi announces it at the *brit*.

With my daughter's first pregnancy, there were very many "taboos." I was so totally ignorant that no matter what the subject was, I was kindly but firmly corrected. But I am a strong fighter and at the time, I was fighting for a name for my grandson that I could announce in every part of the world. After all, I reminded my daughter, there was a great-grandmother to consider, and she would love to be able to tell all her friends in faraway Sydney that she was to have a great-grandson.

"Please do give him an 'international' name," I begged. Yes, this was what I was fighting for: an "international" name.

I am stunned today to think what trivial things mattered to me a mere ten years ago.

When Is
My Grandchild's Birthday???

Imagine, if you will, the following scene: It is almost midnight in Sydney, and Saba and Savta are sitting up in their bedroom, ready and set to place a long-distance call when it will be 8:00 A.M. on the dot in Israel. Why? To be the first to congratulate their beloved Yacov on the morning of his second birthday.

At the stroke of midnight, Saba flies into the next room to pick up the extension. "Hello, darling!" we both yell from two different rooms on two different phones as we both want to hear our grandson's happy voice saying, "Hello Saba, hello Savta! You remembered my birthday!"

But it is Natalie's voice we hear. We do not know why but she sounds firm and commanding, as she says to us grandparents at midnight in Sydney: "Please don't say anything. I cannot explain it now in front of him but actually, you are wrong, as it is not his birthday today, not at all. It will only be nine days from today. So please just put down the phone and make a note of this date and call him then. At the same time. It is a very convenient time to call."

We both put the phones down and Steven and I look at each other in disbelief. "Are we so old and senile that we don't know anymore when our grandson's birthday is?" Saba asks.

"Or is this some new trick of our daughter's?"

"That's it. It must be a new *meshugas* of hers," I reply. "It must be something to do with *them*. It *cannot* be us. We know when our grandson's birthday is."

After all, any normal grandparents should be able to keep track of one, two, three or any number of grandchildren's birthdays, shouldn't they? All they have to do is write down the day the babies are born and they will always know when their grandchildren's birthdays are. Just as we had done. So of course we would know that our beloved first grandson's birthday was on the 20th of August. And just as every loving grandparent would have done in our place, we had wanted to catch him early in the day and say: "Happy birthday to you!" and maybe even sing to him.

But apparently, we had it all wrong. *They* in their wisdom had decided to observe the Hebrew date, that is, the date on the Jewish (lunar) calendar, which does not even remotely resemble the "normal" (Gregorian) date in any shape or form. And of course, the "normal" date is the only date which we, the grandparents, the uncle, the relatives and family friends, not to mention the proud great-grandmother, know.

So this poor B.T. mother receives all kinds of calls greeting cards, and presents which she must hide. She must use all kinds of tricks to protect an innocent child because of what those ignorant people all over the world *think* is the date of his birthday.

You might say, they *could* have let us know, perhaps sent us a note in advance saying: "Look, we are sending you a list. Please keep it in order. From now on, these are the dates of your grandchildren's birthdays. Do tell all the family and friends that this is the new date, the correct date." But it doesn't quite work that way.

You see, the "normal" Gregorian date that coincides with the Hebrew date *is different from year to year*!

In 1982, the 20th of August was the 1st of the Hebrew

month of *Elul*, so *Elul* 1 became Yacov's official Jewish birthday. In 1983, unknown to us, *Elul* 1 fell on the *10th* of August and our good wishes, which arrived belatedly (ten days later) were graciously accepted. Obviously no comment, explanations or trickery were required for the benefit of a mere one-year-old baby. But in 1984, *Elul* 1 fell on the *29th* of August.

Were I not so lucky, I would never have known about these new dates and we would have gone on forever in our muddled state. But thanks to a very kind friend who grasped my problem immediately, I now know the Hebrew dates of all my grandchildren's birthdays. She gave me this fabulous book called *The Comprehensive Hebrew Calendar* published by Feldheim. You can run to the nearest Jewish bookstore in your neighborhood and buy it or order it. You will be grateful to me forever, I know, as I will have given you the joy of knowing in advance when your grandchild's birthday is due.

11   *Our Summer Camp*

One of our greatest pleasures during our frequent visits to Israel is taking our grandchildren out for a treat. And what a treat it is! Their mother is treated to a day of freedom, the children are treated to a fun-filled time, and we are treated to the incomparable joy of being Saba and Savta.

In the summertime, our favorite treat is to take the children swimming. We recently became the happy owners of a hotel swimming pool membership card which, in exchange for a few hundred shekels, gives us unlimited entree to the luxury of the pool facilities and garden. And it is heavenly. One summer we regularly took Natalie's two boys, aged five and four at the time, all of us deliriously happy to make our own special "Summer Camp." They could have attended a real day camp organized by their *Cheder* (elementary school), but we had begged Natalie and Avi to allow us the joy of having the children with us for the four weeks' school holiday, and giving them what we called "normal family fun."

With a little reluctance, our daughter granted permission for swimming and fun, but she warned: "Please don't expect this to go on indefinitely, as you know it is already stretching the approval of the *Rav*."

We swallowed hard when she said that, but what was there for us to do about it? After all, who are we? Only the grandparents of these adorable children, who shlepp 12,000 miles each year just to have "family fun" with them. Who are we, we thought, compared to the *Rav*, who must know everything better, who must know it ALL. So we swallowed and gasped for air, and didn't say a word.

"Let's enjoy today," I said to Saba, "and not worry about tomorrow." With these wise words, we opened our Summer Camp, and got ready to enjoy our Family Fun.

The children loved it, and we loved it. They played and shrieked with joy and paddled in the children's pool and we didn't take our eyes off them for a second.

Between the two of us, it was a strenuous job but worth every moment. Then something happened, a small incident, actually, but I think it was significant in terms of my own personal development as the mother of a B.T. and the non-religious grandmother of religious grandchildren.

Whenever we picked up the children, they were always dressed very nicely in shorts (we had been explicitly requested not to buy them short-shorts as the *Rav* does not approve, but to search high and low for long shorts instead), T-shirts over their *tzitzit* (fringed garments), sandals and, of course, *kippot*.

On this particular occasion, while the boys were playing a fabulous game at the edge of the children's pool, their *kippot* fell off and I had to fish them out of the water. I put them out to dry in the sun while the boys played on. It was sheer joy watching them play with other children their own age in the pool and on the grass.

There was a *ganenet*, a kindergarten teacher who assembled all the four-to-six-year-olds and sat them down in the shade to play educational games. Saba and I were watching them from the distance, and we had one of those moments we dream about in far-away Australia. I thought to myself: This is what they call *naches* — watching your grandchildren from a distance, while you sit under a shady tree sipping a cool drink and they laugh and play with a responsible adult supervising.

Suddenly, as though I had been stung by a bee or by something much worse, I jumped up and started to run, struck by an incredible sight. I hardly had time to explain to Saba, who stared at me and asked in amazement: "What happened?" I grabbed the *kippot* and ran to the children shouting back at him: "Can't you see? They're sitting there bareheaded!" And it was *I*, with no help from anybody, no prodding or reminding from my daughter, I alone who found the sight of their bare heads strange and unacceptable — I, the "different Savta."

I was amazed at myself: I had actually missed seeing the *kippot* on my grandchildren's heads! It was obvious that I must love my grandsons with their *kippot*. For a fleeting moment I was happy, truly happy with the feeling of having progressed and gained understanding of the way of life which I am trying to fit into and find joy in — no matter what!

While I am praising myself so effusively, I must also mention our misgivings and the mistakes we still make, never intentionally, but accidentally. My relationship with Hashem is such that I feel pretty strongly that He knows me and lets me be myself, as long as He sees that I am trying my best. I doubt that He would be angry or, worse still, would want to punish me for making a mistake. After all, I am still learning.

On another one of our Summer Camp outings we made such a mistake. Usually I take along sandwiches from home, soft rolls with cheese or peanut butter, tomatoes and green peppers. (We grandparents of Hungarian origin are strong on the theory that green peppers are very good for you.) But on one exceptional day I brought meat sandwiches, a rarity for the children as meat is pretty pricey in Israel.

After lunch they saw some children with fantastic-looking ice cream cones in their hands. The boys looked at me and asked: "Savta, could we have one of those?" And I said: "Of course! Why not?"

We all walked to the kiosk where they sell all kinds of goodies. We bought our grandchildren and ourselves those marvelous ice creams, and then strolled back to the poolside. As the children sat around us licking their ice creams, suddenly Saba (this time it was his turn to be quick and smart) looked at me aghast and said in Hungarian so that they would not understand: "The boys are *fleishig* and we have just bought them *milchig* ice cream!" (It is prohibited by Jewish Law to eat meat and dairy products together, and even small children in many Orthodox homes wait up to six hours after a *fleishig,* or meat, meal before having something *milchig.*)

My ice cream nearly choked me on the spot. We just sat there, the two of us, and looked at our darlings with their half-licked ice cream cones in their sticky little hands and decided (still in Hungarian) that we simply could not take the half-eaten cones away from them.

We simply let it be and hoped to learn in the future not to fall into these traps. I, with what I think of as my special relationship with Hashem, think and hope and almost know that He was not angry with us. We just had not yet learned the Laws and traditions well enough. Even today, we are still a long way from being Ph.D. grandparents of our B.T. family. But we are careful to watch each step and hope to graduate in the not-too-distant future.

12   *Discipline or Self-Torture?*

I have often wondered: Is this very strict lifestyle of Natalie's and other B.T.s a form of discipline, or is it just self-torture? I suppose I will never know. I will tell you about an outing we had one night, and you can draw your own conclusions.

I am not really equipped to judge. All I know is that in a way it made me feel sorry for my daughter, though she tried to convince me otherwise by saying: "You must never feel sorry for me for something like this." I would have loved to ask her when I *should* feel sorry for her. But naturally I asked nothing of the kind.

What happened was really trivial, yet I, her mother, was sad to see that my daughter should add even more burden than I think necessary to an already difficult life. (Of course, only I think it is difficult; *she* has never ever said so.) But I must stress the point: I don't know enough to judge.

We were invited that evening to the *Brit Milah* party of my daughter's lawyer's son, which was to be held in a very high-class garden-restaurant. Unlike our affairs, which had taken place practically at the crack of dawn, this one was at a more civilized hour.

It was not going to be a religious *Brit Milah*, that much I knew from my daughter. But let me just say that Moshe, the lawyer, is a fine human being, even though he does not wear a black *kippah*, or any *kippah* at all, for that matter. And despite that, both Natalie and Avi like him a lot.

It was a rare opportunity: my daughter and I were to go out at last in the evening without children, without packs, bottles or diapers; just the two of us. Avi was babysitting. So off we went to have a marvelous time in an elegant garden-restaurant.

Or so I thought. With all the experience I had from the previous years, I should have known that with my daughter there is always some unforeseen, added complication.

As we parked the car in front of the restaurant, Natalie immediately went into her usual panic and started to look around feverishly, muttering to herself: "I wonder if it is *glatt*?"

I refused to start worrying. After all, this was supposed to be our evening out. I was not going to let it get spoiled before we even set foot in the place.

We got out of the car and Natalie started craning her neck, muttering, "Are there any men with black *kippot*?" I started to stretch my neck too (she has a certain hypnotic power over me) and I too started to mutter: "I hope there are some men with black *kippot* here." Only I was hoping for different reasons, as I knew if there were not then I could call the whole thing off, right then and there. Their presence would have reassured Natalie that the place was kosher enough.

As it was, Natalie was full of doubts; still, we went along and entered the truly luxurious setting of this lovely garden-restaurant, one I had never been to before.

The host came along, all smiles to see us both, and greeted us warmly. I started to look around, quickly scanning the crowd for black *kippot*. Suddenly I spotted one and I almost yelled out, "Natalie, look! There is a man in a black *kippah*, so this place is fine for us." (Had I said "for us"? I think I must have been losing my mind.)

But my daughter was not impressed. She said in that dangerous voice: "This place is not *glatt.*" And I started to feel dizzy as I had to agree that the majority of men were not wearing *kippot* at all, including the baby's father and his brother, and a judge, whom Natalie pointed out to me. All of them *b'li kippah.*

Natalie followed me as I started wandering casually towards the most splendid display of food I have yet seen in Jerusalem at a *Brit Milah.* (I am gradually becoming a *Brit Milah* expert.) But for my daughter, it was not good enough that it was in Jerusalem, in a kosher restaurant. It was not *glatt.*

I thought: If I were in her place I would figure "*Glatt* or not, I am here; I did not have to cook the food; I can sit down in this garden setting and have a waiter serve me delicious kosher food. Really, let's not kid ourselves, I'm being silly, when after all the food *is* kosher."

But it was not kosher enough for my daughter. She put on her most defiant face and said: "Mummy, why don't you just relax and enjoy yourself and I will bring you everything you want from the buffet. As for me, I won't have any of this food." And with these words she went to the buffet and started stacking my plate with all the wonderful delicacies available in Israel, and then returned... with one plate only. For me.

"How do you envision me enjoying myself while you sit opposite me, starving?!" I asked. She actually expected me to start eating with pleasure while she sat there, sipping her drink, without even a plate in front of her.

Now, you must understand, I was far from ignorant at this stage of the game. After all, this had been the week of *Tisha B'Av*; had I asked: "My darling, why are you fasting?" No, I had not. I knew better than to ask such silly questions. Fasting on *Tisha B'Av* is both self-discipline and self-torture.

But the evening of the *brit,* I had intended to have a ball, and here I was sitting with a plate full of goodies, and next to me sat my daughter, not eating a thing, yet somehow happy.

Suddenly I found myself remembering another very similar occasion, also a *Brit Milah*, but it was a family *simchah* that had taken place about a year ago...

Avi's uncle has lived in Israel for more than twenty years with his beautiful family — his wife Zsuzsi and their three children. What a marvelous, sporty family they are. They were the hosts at their grandson's *brit*.

For me it was a truly good eye-opener to see how it is to celebrate a family *simchah* with about a hundred guests in the well-established Israeli Jewish way of conducting a *Brit Milah*, with my family the only ones in the hall who were strictly observant Orthodox Jews, and B.T.s, to boot.

I remembered how Zsuzsa, the grandmother, looked stunning, wearing a sleeveless, low-cut, blue top, perfect for a hot Tel Aviv afternoon-secular-*Brit Milah*-celebration. Her three grandchildren were dressed in sandals — it was too hot to wear socks — and light-colored shirts and shorts. No *kippot*.

(Secular Israelis don't go in for outward symbols. They have their own philosophy about religion: Why should they be religious — is it not enough that they are Israelis?)

I looked around the elegant reception hall. The food was laid out in great abundance, people were dressed in light, cool clothing, and a nice friendly mood prevailed.

For a fleeting moment I was going to compare the terribly early morning, terribly darkly-clad, very buttoned-up *glatt brits* of my two grandsons. I was almost saying to myself: "You see how much closer it would have been to your lifestyle if you could have had such light-hearted *Brit Milahs*." But luckily I did not have time for any lamenting. A breathtakingly beautiful sight captured my eyes.

This sight drew everybody's complete attention: the entrance of a different, but oh what a beautiful, family. *My family*, with my four grandchildren (yes, *four*), had arrived.

Everyone stopped chatting. All eyes were on them. You could not fault them, no matter how different they looked. They looked magnificent.

My daughter wore a long-sleeved, black and white cotton suit that I had bought for her in Europe, with white stockings and black shoes. Her straight, long brown hair was naturally covered with a most unusual black and white studded *tichel*. You could hardly call this a *tichel*: it was more a crowning glory for her glowing face.

The *tichel* was made in my favorite way (yes, I even have favorite *tichel* styles), pleated all around her head. She only had a touch of eye makeup on, but then she had that special glow... She really has!

And the children! Blonde three-and-a-half-year-old Sarah with her English complexion and coloring, blue eyes, tiny turned-up nose, and cherry lips ready to sweet-talk everybody in the hall (and she did). Her tall, slim figure was clad in a white, puff-sleeved dress, knee length, black and white patent leather shoes with long white socks. She was dressed like a young lady. A religious young lady.

Yacov our *bechor* and Zevi were naturally in their *Shabbat* best. Baby Ruthi, one-and-a-half years old and a walking, talking doll, a replica of her Ima, also wore long socks (already) but with little white sandals, her very first shoes, bought for this occasion. She was so cutely dressed in a purple cotton dress with a white lacy apron that she could have fooled everybody — no one would have known that she was a religious little toddler. But what did I care? I had nothing to be ashamed of, nothing at all.

Abba was wearing a dark suit, as always. His black *kippah* was hidden under his black hat. (When a religious man goes out, he makes a point of demonstrating which religious circle he belongs to. Consequently Avi wears a black hat.)

I must admit that I find it overwhelming to see my beautiful family arriving like this. Don't forget, I spend nine or ten months without them, and only two or three months with them. That day I had tears in my eyes from the sheer joy of seeing them looking so lovely, so elegant.

And then the party started. Children ran around (children will be children), grown-ups talked loudly (grown-ups will be grown-ups). It was a very jolly affair. Slowly we arrived at the reason for our being there: the grandfather held the tiny baby, the *mohel* did his duty. Avi, being the only obviously religious man there, was asked to chant the prayers and people took notice. Then everybody rushed to the laden tables. *L'chayim*, drinks for everybody! Let us be merry! *Mazal tov!*

I took a lot of photos, as after all, when else could I photograph my family all so nicely dressed in their *Shabbat* clothes? Then I stacked a large plate from the feast-like buffet, made my way to our table and started to eat.

My family sat around me, drinking their colas from paper cups. But besides my plate, which by now was empty, there was not another plate, not another bite of food, on the table. Just the smiling, happy faces of my family.

It was just then that I realized that my family, my three grandchildren (the baby did not count yet), would not touch anything. It must have been predetermined, pre-discussed and pre-decided upon, that if the *kashrut* in this place did not meet their standard, they would drink, they would enjoy themselves very much, but eat they would not, not one solitary bite.

The boys understood, as they had been carefully taught in their *Cheder*; they didn't even have to be told. Yacov and Zevi asked: "Ima, is it our *hechsher*?"* Ima, with a knowing, classic smile, shook her head. The boys looked at each other and nodded, and with this the subject of eating was closed.

Please try to visualize two ordinary six- and four-and-a-half-year-old boys in a similar situation. They would start crying for food, maybe perform quite badly, simply demanding to eat, like all the other children around them. But not my two grandsons.

* Rabbinic approval of the *kashrut* of the food.

They were dignified about it. It would not have occurred to them to go near the food, although they did have several drinks. But they knew what was expected of them and they acted accordingly. It was really as simple as that....

So here we were this evening, at the *Brit Milah* party of Natalie's lawyer's son, and once again I witnessed that special form of self-torture/discipline. Everyone gorging themselves, and my daughter not eating a thing, yet somehow happy.

That's the funny thing. She really did not mind it at all. I mean it! My daughter, who cooks dinner after dinner (when I am not in the country), who hardly ever goes out. She sat with me and all the others at the table, all *fressing*, and she nursing a cola and nothing else. And she looked as if she were having a great time. Not like someone who was torturing herself, but like someone who is disciplined and pleased with herself for it. As if she were on a special diet or something.

I was not going to let it spoil my outing. Oh, no. I had really been looking forward to this evening. There was a group of very nice and interesting people there, and Natalie pointed out some famous people from the elite of Jerusalem — she has not lost touch with the "real world." And why should she, just because she only eats *glatt*???

I really was asking for more trouble when I decided to get up and bring Natalie a large plate of fruit from the delicious-looking display. At least she could eat *fruit*.

It was at this point that I lost my sense of humor, or whatever it was that had kept me in relatively good spirits the whole of the evening. Natalie looked at the plate, piled high with luscious fruits, then she looked at me and asked: "But Mummy, have you forgotten about *Shemittah*?"*

I must admit that for one fleeting moment I had.

---

*Meaning the special regulations regarding the fruit of the Holy Land that are in effect every seventh year, but which were unlikely to have been stringently observed at a non-*glatt* restaurant.

13   *Shabbat*

I think that there is nothing harder to define than one's degree of *Shabbat* observance. What in our (secular) opinion would be a Sabbath observer (*Shomer Shabbat*) would certainly not be considered as such by the B.T. *Shabbat,* in some ways, is the most important holiday of the year — only it comes in weekly installments.

Shabbat is the span of a twenty-five-hour day, starting from dusk on Friday and ending on Saturday night when the stars appear. At least that was the considered and educated opinion of my parents and their parents before them. My children, however, have a far different understanding of the meaning of *Shabbat* observance.

In all the Israeli newspapers, including *The Jerusalem Post*, the exact time of the beginning and the end of *Shabbat* is printed each week, as it varies according to the time of sunset in different localities. (Candlelighting time is usually eighteen minutes before sunset, but in the Holy City of Jerusalem it is customary to usher in the Sabbath an additional twenty minutes earlier. But even in Jerusalem, the Sabbath ends when the stars come out.) This is the time ordained by the Israeli Rabbinate; nothing less would be published in the local papers. But my children, my wonderful B.T. children, do not adhere to this. They will, in their own words, "stretch the *Shabbat*" to any length they feel inclined to. As my daughter says, "Mummy, there is nothing more marvelous than to stretch the *Shabbat* late into Saturday night."

I have my reservations about this, as by that hour their kitchen is overflowing with dirty dishes piled up in disarray, because they don't wash dishes on *Shabbat*. Their bathroom is full of the children's soiled clothing. But who cares? It is *Shabbat* and all we do is throw things in a pile and leave them.

The beauty of *Shabbat* is that you don't do a thing except pray, eat, sleep and dress nicely. Especially the male children, who wear a sort of uniform: navy long pants, white shirt, dress shoes and socks, and a special reserved-for-*Shabbat* velvet *kippah*. Comes *Shabbat* and all the religious children all over the country become little princes and princesses. In fact, they look like one huge family, all dressed in the same uniform.

Truly, there is nothing more beautiful and festive than *Shabbat* in Israel. It is there, and only there, that the sirens go off on Friday at candlelighting time, to let everyone know that *Shabbat* is coming, and they had better get a move on. And they do!

Here I must add something very personal and private, but I think I must share this with you, since everything I say to you in this book must be honest. You must be able to follow every detail clearly, so that you can identify with me, and the personal conflicts that rage inside me, as a result of my B.T. family.

Back in Australia we are still not *Shomer Shabbat*. We are thinking about it, weighing the pros and cons, talking about it occasionally with our Rabbis, but we've taken no final decision — yet.

But let me spend my *Shabbat* in Givat Dat with Natalie and her family, and from Friday afternoon till late Saturday night (remember, they love stretching it), we become just like them: strict Sabbath-observers.

So take a normal *Shabbat* afternoon, when all the kids play on the roads, carefree, happy, unconcerned about traffic, as in theory there should be no cars at all going through this religious neighborhood on *Shabbat*. Unfortunately there are still a few, and when suddenly a car appears, I — yes, *I* — get so furious that I lead the chorus of shouting children, "Booo! Booooo!" as I find it most disturbing and disrespectful to disrupt "our" *Shabbat*.

This really does infuriate me. And then, deep inside me a little voice laughs a very sarcastic laugh, saying: "Who are you to criticize somebody for driving on *Shabbat*!" And I get very indignant and talk back to this little smart voice, saying: "Do you want to know who I am? Well, listen: I am the mother of a B.T. and the Savta of those children on the road, and I say to those *Shabbat*-desecrators and grandchild-endangerers: BEWARE!"

Another incident comes to mind about *Shabbat* vis-à-vis me and some of the mistakes I was capable of making in the old days, in my total ignorance. I have learned a great deal since then.

The most important advice I can give (which I wish somebody had given me back in "My Ignorant Days") is: "Don't overdo it. Don't volunteer. And furthermore, do not try to do things that you don't know about, or have never heard about, as this will only get you into a great deal of trouble."

This is what happened to me one Friday night. I was feeling so dreadfully sorry for my daughter, what with the tension of a hectic Friday, the panic before the onset of *Shabbat*, the rushing, the final scream: "Is the *blech* on? Is it hot?" (referring to the electric warming tray which keeps the Sabbath meals hot, as there is no cooking done on *Shabbat*). I saw my daughter collapsing from tiredness. She was feeding her second or third, or maybe fourth child (sometimes these events run into one another), and so I said to her: "Natalie, you stay put. I will serve the dinner." She smiled a tired smile and nodded. I was happy.

As is customary in religious homes, Abba sits at the head of the table with the *siddur* open in front of him, ready to do all the necessary, important things such as reciting the blessing over the wine and pouring grape juice into each one of the boy's little silver "*bechers*," making the *berachah* for the challah and distributing pieces to everyone, and so on.

After that's done, he questions each child about the weekly *parashah* (the specific portion of Torah read on that *Shabbat*) — even two-and-a-half-year-old Ruthi, who offers something she learned in nursery school — and he tests the children's knowledge. (To me it is mind-boggling that even at the tender age of Ruthi they know so much.) This is Abba's most important obligation, and he certainly is not to be disturbed with so mundane a thing as moving a pot or serving a dish. *Chas v'shalom!* (Heaven forfend!)

So I was to perform this highly qualified task (little did I know how highly qualified one has to be for it!) of serving soup in the red plastic *fleishig* bowls for the children, and the brown glass ones for the adults. And then, just as I finished serving all the soup, I heard my daughter cry out as though I had committed some horrific act of violence.

"What is wrong?" I asked, frightened.

Baby in arms, pale yet composed, she announced: "Well Mummy, there goes our whole *Shabbat* meal."

I was spellbound. "Why?" I asked, and she looked at me and answered with that air of superiority, but still with a kind face, as one talks to a very hopeless, dumb kid: "Mummy, it just is! Once you removed the pot from the *blech* and put it down, you BLEW IT! Now we won't be able to have any soup with tomorrow's lunch."

I stood there, really and truly dumbfounded. But I knew (and this is another good piece of advice) that one must never be surprised, whatever they say or do, as the B.T.s are almost always right! It has taken me years of blood, sweat and tears to reach this wise conclusion. In all religious matters the B.T. is superior in religious knowledge to you. The sooner you accept this, the happier you will be.

I also have a very sweet incident to tell you about "never being surprised," one that shows that it sometimes works in reverse too. If this should happen, it causes great joy to your B.T. children, when they see that after all you are learning from them and doing things *their* way.

One hot, sweltering July *Shabbat*, Natalie and her whole family, including me (I was visiting at the time), were invited out for the *seudah shelishit* (the third Sabbath meal). I love being invited out for this last meal on *Shabbat* as by that hour Natalie's home is usually in a state of total chaos, what is known as a "*balagan*." By then, for me to leave the house is sheer joy, so off we went.

The streets were filled with families going to and fro. Everybody was a little bit wilted from the heat, but still we marched: baby carriage, baby, kids, bottles, diapers, Ima, Savta, the whole lot. But at least we were out of the house!

We were invited to a very nice South African family who, through no fault of their own, live on the top floor of a beautiful building in Givat Dat. Now I don't want to admit to being so old as to be unable to walk up three or four flights of stairs easily, but with the second youngest in my arms, the baby in my daughter's arms, the boys pulling the stroller and all the things we brought with us, by the time we made it to the top floor, I must confess I was breathless for a few minutes. Avi was out at afternoon services, and would join us later on.

As usual, I was given a few last-minute instructions and an oral list of do's and don'ts. By this time, I was no longer fooling myself, thinking that, after all, we parents are the elders, the educators, the wise, experienced ones who don't need to be kindly but firmly instructed by our B.T. children. Instead, I take notice and try to comply.

When we arrived at the top-floor apartment, from where the view was stunning, all I wanted to do was collapse into the nearest chair, but my daughter gently prodded me on, saying: "Watch the children, please, Mummy. Don't let them lean over the edge of the balcony."

The third Sabbath meal was enjoyed by all except the women. The hospitality was great and the children were very well-behaved, but still they are children, and had to be watched. While the men (who returned from services in good time) and the older boys sang those beautiful *Shabbat* songs in full voice, we mothers and Savta hardly sat down for a moment. Nor did we have a decent bite of the delicious-looking food. But, really, who cared? The family atmosphere all around us was delightful.

We could hear singing from other families' third meals. It was as if the whole of Givat Dat were one happy, exhausted, singing family, singing in harmony and in the joy that yet another *Shabbat* had passed blissfully and we could start looking forward to rejoicing on the next one. *B'ezrat Hashem!*

After the meal, we slowly descended from the top floor. Abba was now attending evening prayers. My daughter, my four grandchildren, and I strolled towards Natalie's home in the dusk. I hardly realized that it had turned dark already, when I saw a car pass us by, obviously one of "ours."

It was at this moment that I surprised my daughter by exclaiming: "Don't tell me *Shabbat* is over already?" And my daughter looked at me with those laughing gray eyes, and with a real loving voice replied: "I never dreamed I'd hear you say that."

Neither had I, but I did say it, and furthermore, I meant it!

Over the years, I really have come to love the sublime observance of *Shabbat* and its special place in the weekly cycle. One *Shabbat* ends and then you start the week anew till the next festive *Shabbat* begins. It is quite rhythmic. One can easily become addicted to the long, idyllic state of compulsory idleness which characterizes real *Shabbat* observance.

The days that we spend in Givat Dat with our children are unforgettable for me, but they are still not entirely problem-free. One of the problems has to do with our accommodations. When we helped our children to buy their beautiful apartment in Givat Dat, a brand-new Jerusalem suburb occupied mainly by Orthodox Jews and hundreds and hundreds of young B.T. families, we realized that it was quite far from our Jerusalem apartment in Rehavia. We certainly could not walk from Rehavia to Givat Dat and back on Friday night, and then again the next day. It was not a question of our observance of the Sabbath; it would simply be offensive to our religious family and all their religious neighbors were we to drive to and from their neighborhood. And we weren't about to forego the pleasure of spending the weekends with our children and grandchildren during our always-too-brief visits to Israel.

So in our wisdom we decided to purchase what is called a "*machsan*," a sort of glorified cellar-*cum*-utility room, in the basement of their Givat Dat apartment building. In our vivid imagination (the parents of a B.T. must have a vivid imagination at all times), we saw this room becoming the comfortable old-age refuge we had waited for all our lives: a beautiful bed-sitting room, with its own little bathroom and kitchenette. All tastefully furnished, and all for the purpose of making our *Shabbats* with our children sweet, pleasant and comfortable.

Without further ado, and for an additional large sum, we bought this permanent weekend retreat. At least, this was our plan and our dream. But with B.T. children, somehow plans can become a bit confused and dreams a bit blurry. The parents always have to come up with some useful ideas as to how to solve the suddenly unexpected problems that crop up.

This is what happened to us, when one day the phone rang in Sydney, Australia, and it was our daughter with her bubbly, ever-cheerful voice, calling us from Jerusalem. After the first five minutes of preliminaries, she came to the point and said: "Dad..." (Somehow she always says "Dad" when she wants something serious. "Mum" is only for unimportant things, such as buying clothes, cooking meals and doing a million-and-one chores. But "Dad" is the master of the house.)

So: "Dad, we have a great idea. Listen. Avi wants to leave his job and finally open his own office. We thought how marvelous it would be if he could have an office right in our hardly-used, empty room."

A long pause. I was listening on the extension, and I started to signal and whisper frantically: "*Theirs?*" I was waving madly to "Dad," and pointing to us, meaning "*Our* empty room, not *theirs!*" And as "Dad" looked on helplessly, hopelessly disturbed, I covered the phone and said to him, "What next?"

"Dad" composed himself and calmly continued: "Well, let us think this over, as we really hoped to have this room for ourselves for all the family *Shabbats* we will have with you in Jerusalem." Now there was a long pause on the other end of the line. Neither side broke the silence. We were each waiting for the other to say something.

But what was there to say? We knew already that we had lost, and that they would have our beloved room for their own use. But one has to at least *pretend* to have some decision-making authority. One cannot simply submit immediately and just say: "Yes, darling, go ahead, move into the room that we bought for ourselves, for our old age, to spend our *Shabbats* with our grandchildren. Just use it in health and wealth. *Mazal tov.*"

But that was exactly what we wrote to them in a letter we posted after the internationally accepted time span between so-called decision-making and resigned submission. Besides, who was I to complain if my son-in-law not only was *working* but was about to open his own office!

In retrospect, I realize that their annexation of "our" *machsan* (and many other things they do that I find fault with) had nothing whatsoever to do with their being B.T.s, but at the time it really did seem like another one of their crazinesses. Whatever the cause of it, however, the outcome was the same: we did not possess one square meter of space in which to rest our weary bodies at the very late end of a Friday night in Givat Dat, spent in joy with our children and grandchildren.

But I am exaggerating. We can and do use "our" room, which Natalie cleans from top to bottom on the Friday before we come.

Friday night dinner ends in my daughter's house (although not necessarily in all Orthodox households) at almost midnight. Let me digress to explain to you why that is so.

In summer it only gets dark at about nine o'clock. The children all wait for Abba to return from the synagogue, and then the festivities, the singing and the dancing, start. One would have thought that eating would be the highlight of Friday night, as so much work has been put into the cooking and baking of the *Shabbat* meal (so much that meals during the rest of the week mostly consist of the leftovers from *Shabbat*). But who am I — certainly not an authority on *Shabbat* — to wonder why the singing, the dancing, and the merrymaking should take up the major part of Friday night?

By the time the meal is served, the children are worn out and the younger ones are too weary to sit at the table and eat their festive meal. Instead they nap on the carpet or sofa. They usually manage to hold out for the *kiddush*, the hand-washing, and the *berachot*, which they adore (and so do I), and even the baby, whoever is the baby at the time, says "Amen" at the right time, and is taken out of the high chair by the smiling mother of the house.

Abba, as I mentioned earlier, sits at the head of the table; he asks his children about the *parashah* of the week; he wakes them to sing those wonderful *Shabbat* songs, while the dinner on the hotplate gets more and more dried out by the minute. And I, the poor grandmother (who, by the way, cooked all the dinner which is getting ruined out there) practically dies of hunger, as I have not quite gotten used to these eleven o'clock Friday night dinners. I am so old-fashioned and unimaginative that I always thought Friday dinner was really on Friday evening, and not late at night.

When the time comes round for the *bentching* (Grace after the meal), a truly magnificent part of the Friday night dinner, our grandsons, who have rested during the meal, are back at their places, sitting upright and singing the whole of the rather lengthy blessing by heart. But by then my eyes are hardly open.

When Saba is with us, during those few wonderful weeks when he is able to join me in Israel (as he is still a hard-working grandfather back in Australia), he is more than ready for a good night's rest. So down we go to the room that was to be our beautiful bed-sitting room for our *Shabbats* in Givat Dat. Then reality hits us. The room is full of the right things for a lawyer: a medium-sized desk, two small arm chairs, two tall filing cabinets. And there in the corner, under the bookshelf, are two "Sochnut" beds with two thin mattresses, made up with clean sheets and one pillow.

Our night lodging is unique, but luckily, as it is Friday night, we can hardly see it, as only in the small bathroom is there a 25-watt bulb lighting up the whole area. So we can only guess where the beds begin or end. But who cares.

It is far past midnight. Let us just drop down and have a few hours' rest in a horizontal position, and let us not think about the room as we envisaged it, before our wise decision that it really would serve a much better purpose as a law office than as a bed-sitting room for elderly grandparents who occasionally travel 12,000 miles to share beautiful *Shabbats* with their family.

As we wake up on *Shabbat* morning, we hear faint tapping on our window at ground level, and whispering voices calling: "Saba, Savta, are you awake?" And we whisper back: "Yes, we are!" Then the door bursts open and there stand four little people, our grandchildren. Yacov, Zevi, Sarah and Ruthi, all dressed already in their best *Shabbat* clothes, eyes shining with joy at seeing us. They stand and look at us, their grandparents. We all rejoice in one another: they in us, their grandparents, there to greet them on a *Shabbat* morning; and we in them, our adorable grandchildren.

This sight is something so heartwarming, so uniquely marvelous, so incomparable to anything else, that words fail me.

We have had better accommodation in our lives: *en suite* bathrooms, all the luxury of our Sydney bedroom, with its king-size beds and push-button blinds....

But! ONLY here in "*glatt*" "black" Givat Dat do we have this joy in our grandchildren and their joy in us. What else matters, really?

AUTHOR'S NOTE: In recent years, with Avi's acquisition of his own proper office, our little *machsan* has been transformed into the lovely retreat we had envisioned from the start, adding an element of comfort to our already joyous *Shabbats*.

14   *A Glatt Concert*

During a recent summer vacation in Jerusalem, I was invited to the President's House, where an Australian reception was being held. I am very involved in Sydney with the local Jewish newspaper, *The Australian Jewish Times,* with the United Israel Appeal, and with all kinds of Israel-oriented activities, and was therefore not surprised to be included in the guest-list, but it pleased me all the same.

I must confess that I love being invited to the President's House and, in the past, nothing in the world would have made me refuse such an invitation. This time, however, I surprised myself when instead of replying immediately and enthusiastically, "Oh, yes, I am coming, thank you!" I answered with a polite: "Maybe."

The reason for my hesitation was a phone call I had received that same day. It was Natalie, with her usual bubbling voice. (Here I must say something about my Natalie's voice, which unfortunately I hear more often over the telephone than I hear live. We have never yet rung her — long-distance or locally — without her answering us in a voice full of anticipation. In fact, when we call her from Australia, we are always under the impression that all our daughter does is sit at home, peacefully awaiting our call. This is how her voice sounds to us.

Of course this is not the case, as Natalie hardly ever sits at home peacefully. She works from dawn to dusk and still her voice always sounds as though she might have just thought: "If only my parents would ring this minute!"

Not once has she said: "Please call me back — I have the baby in my arms," or "I am just in the middle of changing a diaper," although in the mornings my daughter not only has her own four little ones to attend to, but she sometimes minds another three to five children as well.)

On this occasion, her bubbling voice had asked me, "Mummy, how would you like to come to a concert with me?" (Another important rule to note: Always try to accept your child's invitations. It will make her, and ultimately you very happy.)

Noticing my hesitation, Natalie chuckled and said: "Mummy, it is a Givat Dat Women's Club benefit concert with a famous pianist, in a beautiful concert hall. All of the neighborhood women will be there — it's for women only." And it was on the same day as the President's party.

I considered this for a moment. The Herzogs' party would surely be elegant and nice, but not as unique as a concert for-women-only, and only for Givat Dat women, at that. Soon my mind was made up. "It will be my pleasure to come to the concert with you, darling," I said, and I could tell she was really happy.

We made a date. Before hanging up, she added: "Wear something nice, not too elegant, not too casual, something in-between." I knew behind this coded message was the following: "Mummy, wear something nice, with long sleeves if possible, high-collared, and if you really want to please me, stockings."

I filled the silent request, more or less, and my mirror told me I looked decently covered and proper. And I was sure I would have no trouble blending in with the crowd. I gave no thought at all to the one aspect of my appearance that would be a total giveaway and make me stand out as "different." But I'll come to that later.

Natalie picked me up looking beautiful, with all matching accessories. My daughter loves matching things and is far more meticulous about colors and jewelry than I am. She was wearing the very latest, gold-beaded, French-influenced Meah She'arim head covering. (You, my ignorant reader, might shudder at the mere mention of this historic neighborhood that appears in photographs to be a benighted *shtetl* transplanted to modern Israel, but beware not to judge by appearances and your own prejudice, as you would be in for a surprise. There are a lot of chic and beautiful things to be bought in Meah She'arim. Trust me; I have years of experience and I too would once have laughed out loud if anybody had suggested that I go and buy *anything* there, let alone a chic French scarf.)

We kissed and I saw her approving look. She said: "You look nice, Mummy." I returned the compliment and we were off to our concert.

I had never been to this concert hall. It was in the center of town and, as I discovered in the interval, it was one of the hundred-and-one places in Jerusalem which are dedicated to someone very precious, very young, and very brave. These places are usually endowed by the parents in the memory of a deceased child, or, as in this case, to a young man killed in an accident. The hall was called Gerard Behar.

Upon arrival I immediately noticed that all those same women whom I usually see in Givat Dat rushing with four, five, six, seven, nine children surrounding them, shlepping on them, pushing them, women who were often pregnant on top of all the load they were carrying, were tonight looking relaxed and radiant, elegant and happy. Happy to have a night out without the children, happy to be seen looking their very best — by other women.

The strangest sensation for me was the feeling that I was just like them, happy and pleased to be seen among them. These women of Givat Dat are a rather special lot. Probably half of them are B.T.s; they are all young and very attractive, and they all know one another. And now comes the most interesting observation: in stark contrast to any women's gathering I've ever attended in Australia, where the women love nothing better than to talk behind one another's back, here they all seem affectionate and sincerely concerned with each other. Gossip-mongering — *lashon hara* — is very much frowned upon among Givat Dat women.

Natalie linked her arm in mine and gently urged me around the foyer, introducing me here and there to women I did not know, saying in her special, loving voice: "This is my mother." They each smiled in turn and several remarked: "She looks young to be your mother," which in my one-track mind sounded like: "She looks different, your mother." But this was only my interpretation.

Then we met some good friends, like Pearl, who could easily be mistaken for a Miss America contestant, but in reality is the mother of quite a few, *baruch Hashem*! Actually, I have a memorable story about her which could again be a good example of never underestimating the mother of quite a few children.

A while back, the Givat Dat women were having a charity swimming gala, and Natalie asked me to sponsor a few of the contestants. When it came to sponsoring Pearl, I offered a rather high figure for each lap she would complete, thinking, With so many children, how well could she still swim anyway?? Let me tell you, my wrong assumption cost me quite a lot of money. She swam ten times more than I believed she would. She had been an All-American swimming champion in her teens!

Back to the night of the concert. We eventually went into a beautiful, spacious theater, where the stage was most tastefully decorated with, among other things, a large banner that read P'TACH [an acronym for Parents for Torah for All Children]. I whispered to Natalie: "Does that mean 'open'?" and she, with that expression of genuine joy reserved for when I say something correct, exclaimed: "Good girl, Mummy!" (my favorite praise from my daughter; the irony of it did not strike me at the time).

The praise was doublefold, as it meant that she was happy that I not only could readily translate the Hebrew but also understood the implications of the term. It represented the open-hearted women who, with their Torah understanding and human kindness, help children with learning dificulties to reach their maximum potential.

This was what the concert was really all about. Getting dressed up and getting out of the house for the evening were secondary; the main issue was to help these children. They were all dedicated women, this was obvious to me.

Sitting there in the concert hall surrounded by women, all women, I had a little, quiet laugh. Not for a second did I feel that I was missing anything; in fact, I found it very relaxing.

At the interval, we retired to the hall for another round of socializing, and there we saw a very pretty woman with a fabulous hairdo, fashionably untidy and terribly natural. I could not resist the urge to touch her hair and, in the most polite yet curious and stupid way ask: "This is a *sheitel*, is it not?" knowing full well that it had to be, but I had never seen one that looked so much like real hair. And Natalie and her friend burst out laughing and replied together: "But of course it is."

It was then that this sweet young American B.T. touched *my* hair and asked the same question, whereupon the realization struck me like lightning. I looked around and up to my own hair. I even touched it, as if I were not sure if it was my own hair or not. One gets quite confused sometimes.

I think I was the only married woman in the concert hall without a hair-covering of some sort.

I could have mingled with the best, with the high society of Jerusalem in the magnificent home of the President of Israel, but instead I had gone out with my daughter, and had had a uniquely interesting and rewarding night. It had been another first: my first *"glatt"* concert — with the marvelous women of Givat Dat.

15   *Voodoo Magic or Berachah?*

I cannot help but hear some incredible stories in my daughter's house. "Overhear" might be the more appropriate word as the kind of stories I am talking about are usually not told to me directly, but are reported to Natalie by her visitors or discussed among her friends. I often have the feeling that her friends still do not quite accept me in their close Circle.

By the way, I must comment here on what an odd feeling it is to be the "outsider," the one who is "different" and yet always painstakingly trying to fit in, regardless of the re-quirements this entails. It is a very peculiar sensation for someone like myself who has never had a problem with fitting in wherever I've been, and it makes me wonder why my daughter, who after all is the one who has changed her lifestyle so dramatically, should be the "insider" and I, her mother, the "outsider."

But back to the story that I overhead at Natalie's house one evening. It had to do with the *mezuzah*, a most important religious symbol, the sign of a Jewish home. On this subject, at least, I can safely say that in our home back in Hungary, in Australia, and at all times and everywhere we have dwelt, we proudly placed a *mezuzah* on our front door on the right-hand doorpost as prescribed by Jewish Law.

As our daughter's religiousness increased, so did our knowledge concerning *mezuzot* and other Jewish signs and symbols in the house. Not only do we now place a *mezuzah* on our front doorpost, but upon moving into our new home three years ago in Sydney, we invited our Rabbi to make a festive occasion of it and to give his blessing over our *mezuzah,* that it should safeguard our home for years to come. Nowadays we are no longer satisfied to have a *mezuzah* only on our front doorpost, but are placing more and more beautiful Israeli "kosher" *mezuzot** on the right-hand doorposts of practically all the rooms in our home. And we're doing so with great joy and pride.

You see, we *do* learn and we *do* progress, and we rejoice in our new-found higher learning and understanding of Judaism.

But what I overheard the other day was a completely new concept for me as far as *mezuzot* go, and I stress the point that I do not doubt the validity of what I heard; in fact ever since that afternoon I have been seriously considering taking down and examining all the *mezuzot* in my home in Jerusalem and in Sydney as well. Here's why:

Little Naomi, the third child of my daughter's good friend Susan, had been unwell lately. The parents had become more and more concerned and watchful as little Naomi had not been eating well at all, and the little she ate, she could not keep down. Terribly worried, the parents made appointments with various physicians.

Before anything else, a very wise and learned Rebbe of the community advised the concerned parents to examine all the

---

*A *mezuzah* is the small scroll of parchment on which is inscribed in Hebrew the words of the *Shema*: "Hear, O Israel..." Most often it is housed in a protective case, either simple or ornate, which has no particular sanctity attached to it *per se.* A kosher *mezuzah* is one that is accurately and professionally handwritten on genuine parchment by a religious scribe.

mezuzot in the house, because, he said, often it is the presence of damaged or faulty *mezuzot* that causes unexpected upheavals in a family's life.

When I heard this, I smiled a sort of doubting and "What next?" smile, reserved for strange and unexplainable weirdnesses of the Circle. But as the story unfolded, I stopped smiling and started to listen.

The parents followed the Rebbe's suggestion and checked all the *mezuzot* in their home, and to their utter surprise found in none other than Naomi's room that the parchment had a letter missing. And which letter was it? The first letter of their daughter's name! (Apparently, with handwritten parchments, mistakes can be made in the writing; sometimes, the ink gets dried out and the letters crack.)

The story stopped at this point and the parents were going to take Naomi to the physician to have her checked out thoroughly, but since they had immediately replaced the faulty *mezuzah*, there were great expectations for the child's fast and complete recovery.

Some of you will smile your own doubtful smile, saying "What voodoo magic is she writing about???" and quite honestly this is just what it resembled to me at the time. But today I can truthfully say from my very own life experience (which, to protect the privacy of someone very dear to me, cannot be retold here), that it is not voodoo or witchcraft or the like. It is a *Berachah*, a blessing from Hashem. It's really quite simple: if one's belief is strong enough one may be worthy of Hashem's blessing.

Have you ever stopped to think what the significance of a *mezuzah* might be? Because it contains the text of the *Shema* — that very central prayer to Judaism which declares one's belief in Hashem — by placing it on our doorposts we state clearly that the people who live in that house are Jews who believe in One God. But if the *mezuzah* case is empty, then affixing it to the doorpost is an empty gesture, and if the parchment scroll is faulty in some way, then the declaration of faith is also faulty. Now, how can one be worthy of Hashem's *Berachah* with empty gestures and faulty declarations?

A friend of mine who is an Orthodox Rabbi explained that the three letters on the outside of the parchment form one of the names of Hashem, one that is the acronym for the Hebrew expression meaning "God is the Watchman of our doorways." But only if the declaration on the inside of the parchment and inside our hearts is intact will the Watchman guard and keep us safe from harm.

There are other means of invoking God's blessing for someone who is sick. Sometimes, people will turn to a known *tzaddik* — a very righteous, pious Jew, and ask him for a *Berachah*. What this means is that they feel they themselves may not be worthy of Hashem's blessing, but they are sure the *tzaddik* is, so if he petitions Hashem on their behalf, *his* prayers are more likely to be answered. They too will pray and ask others to join them, as no one knows for certain whose prayers will be answered. From personal experience I would say one should never doubt the "magic" of religious belief and the *Berachah*, or the value of prayer by people who believe.

Let me tell you what I have learned and how I pass on my belief in the *Berachah*. I have a friend who has a very sick little granddaughter back in Australia. When I heard about it, I told my daughter. She immediately instructed me to find out the little girl's Hebrew name and her mother's Hebrew name. I did all that, and from then on my daughter in Jerusalem, in Givat Dat, together with all the friends she has asked to join her, have been praying for this unknown little girl in far-off Australia. I told the parents that there was a *Berachah* and that back in Jerusalem a lot of people were praying for their child, and this gave them hope and comfort. Every time we speak on the phone or by FAX, Natalie asks how the sick little girl is doing. This has been going on now for over seven months, during which the little girl has gone through incredible ordeals.

The doctors were amazed that she still had the strength to hold on.

Today, against all medical beliefs, but certainly not against the believers in the *Berachah*, the child is getting better.

I will seriously say that, with my present knowledge of the power of *Berachah*, I would not accept any medical verdict as the final one, but would place great hope in the Upper Hand, in Hashem and His *Berachah*.

16   *A Simchah in Sydney*

It was a rare occasion when I could show off with my new-found circle of Orthodox friends to my own elderly mother, who simply could not comprehend the great joy I have gained from their acceptance. I would tell her about my experiences in Jerusalem after each visit, and she would say: "I cannot imagine how you can move comfortably in a world as different from ours as that of the 'black' ultra-Orthodox."

I said to her one day: "Let me take you along and show you how well I do fit in with them." And off we went, to the Bar Mitzvah party of the son of our local *Rosh Yeshivah, Rav* Pinchas Feldman.

Unfortunately my mother had not been well enough to fly to her dearest granddaughter's wedding in Jerusalem, or to any of the *simchahs* that followed. No matter how many photos, video cassettes or high-quality tapes I brought back for her, it was nothing like being there. I thought taking her to a Sunday afternoon Orthodox *simchah*, the kind I have grown to love so much, would be an eye-opener for her.

And it was.

Rav Feldman had been instrumental in our daughter's be-coming a serious B.T., and despite the many learned friends and acquaintances Natalie has acquired during her many years in Jerusalem, there remains a strong, personal bond between her and *Rav* Feldman.

Over the years, I too have become a great admirer and friend of this young, Orthodox Rabbi and his family, and I never hesitate to go to them for advice or just for a friendly chat. (At an earlier stage of our friendship, I thought nothing of dropping in to his office or home dressed any way I happened to be dressed when I left my house, but today I can no longer claim ignorance and therefore take care to be decently clad and covered up.) Their children have gotten to know and like me as I am, and I have come to love all of that clever, beautiful bunch, all (blank) of them.

[It is customary not to mention the number of children in an Orthodox family. No Orthodox grandmother will ever say: "I have 40 grandchildren." The most she will say is: "*Baruch Hashem*, I stopped counting after the first few," or something to that effect. Although I know of this custom, when somebody asks me how many grandchildren I have, I still tell them, unhesitatingly. Perhaps I should start thinking more seriously about the custom of not telling the exact number, as there may be something deeper to it than we realize.]

I had explained to my mother upon arrival at the elegant hall which had been made *glatt*-kosher just prior to the *simchah*, that for me to enter the world of the ultra-Orthodox was, by now, very easy. It was a world that I had learned to love and respect and even to be proud of. Still she looked on with real amazement as I was greeted by a number of Orthodox men and women, all of whom I had become acquainted with in one way or another throughout the years of my daughter's and my own religious development.

When we entered the hall it was truly as if we had entered a different world, for this hall was situated in the middle of the most elegant "WASPish" part of Sydney. It was astonishing to suddenly find it occupied by masses of black-coated ultra-

Orthodox with their multitude of children. The contrast between the sedate streets of the area occupied by typically small, wealthy Australian families, and this world of pregnant mothers with happy faces and *sheitels* (that often look better than any natural hair does, something that will never cease to amuse me), was striking.

When the speeches ended and the merrymaking began, I seated my mother at a good vantage point and went to greet all the members of the family tribe, including the beautiful *Rebbetzin*.

It was a great honor to meet *Rav* Feldman's parents at the Bar Mitzvah, which they had come all the way from Baltimore, Maryland to celebrate. *Rav* Feldman, you see, is their one and only son, their one and only child.

His mother is a remarkable lady, very young, very modern, very elegant. I wanted her to meet my mother, who probably thought the mother of *Rav* Feldman would be a little old lady with a gray *sheitel* or a dark *tichel* and not anything like the lady she was introduced to.

The two struck up a conversation and as I sat and listened, I became aware of an amazing phenomenon. Most of the words and expressions so common in the world of the Orthodox were totally alien to my mother, words such as *kallah, bashert, im yirtzeh Hashem*, not to mention *baruch Hashem*!

How simple and self-explanatory, then, was my mother's reaction to me. Those words had been alien to me too only a short ten years ago. Had I already come such a long way? This discovery really made my day.

I felt very "in" at *Rav* Feldman's Bar Mitzvah celebration, this very ultra-Orthodox *simchah* in Sydney. I certainly did not try to fit in by indulging in hypocritical falsities such as wearing a hat or behaving differently from the way I would with my friends from the "other" world. But I did take the trouble to wear a long-sleeved dress and look neat and tidy. It was the very least I could do.

Oh yes, the world is a big place and there are many shades of black and white. But while the "black" ultra-Orthodox world may have looked and felt alien to me a decade ago, I have slowly learned to accept and even love it, thanks to my own B.T. daughter. It is to her that I owe this new and exciting chapter of my life, and it is through her that I have been able to broaden my scope of understanding of a world which had previously been closed to me.

17   *The "Non-Event," Purim*

Way back in "My Ignorant Years," I had decided that *Purim* was a non-event. We had never celebrated it at all in my childhood, nor in my early Australian days. I don't remember ever buying special cakes at *Purim*, or keeping the children home from their secular schools to celebrate this minor (in my opinion) Festival. And I certainly never thought of giving *Mishloach Manot*, or as it is known colloquially, "*Shalach Manos*." Nor did the children ever dress up for *Purim*. In other words, I had never consciously enjoyed this thoroughly joyous Festival.

I think it must be this previous total lack of awareness of *Purim* that brings me to my present elation and conscious enjoyment of the (for me) newly-discovered, exciting fun of *Chag Purim*! And what could be more fun than celebrating it in Jerusalem, which, for Talmudic reasons, observes *Purim* on the day after it is observed almost everywhere else, and people come from all over the country to enjoy an extra day of fun with the Jerusalemites.

It seems to me that no Jewish families anywhere could possibly get into the frenzy of *Purim* as excitedly as the B.T. families, as whatever they do, they do it more so. But with a family consisting of four children under the age of seven, *Purim* is absolutely incredible.

It is pure, delicious fun dressing up either as Queen Esther the *Purim* heroine, or Haman the villain, or some other famous figure from the Bible. The whole country becomes one big, colorful carnival. There is the nighttime reading of the *Megillah* on the eve of *Purim*, the reading again the following morning, the huge festive *seudah* in the early afternoon of *Purim* day, and the special *mitzvah* that all members of the family must fulfill: delivering *Shalach Manos* — gift packages of at least two food items, usually cakes and fruits — to at least one other celebrant of *Purim*. And the constant stream of friends and neighbors bringing *you* such packages. Just imagine it! It all adds up to a most colorful celebration.

I am sure *Purim* is a pretty merry festival in every religious neighborhood everywhere in the world, but I still think that it must be the best in Israel, where the whole of the country is taking part in the religious as well as the traditional festivities of the holiday.

Natalie asked me if I would mind making the *Purim seudah* for the entire Israeli contingent of the family (at present, *baruch Hashem*, consisting of almost 20 members). I am easily drawn into things like that, especially when I know that the holiday is not like *Shabbat* and I don't have to deal with *Shabbat*-related restrictions. Everyone can drive to my house and I can use all my appliances. Who could ask for more? I eagerly agreed.

It was *erev Purim* and the day was fabulous, with my four grandchildren fooling around, dressing up in various costumes. Yacov's favorite home-made costume was a *chassid*. Naturally Sarah, the blonde beauty, would be Queen Esther — what else? Zevi thought he should be the king, and little Ruthi was not sure yet if she wanted to be a clown or not. All day long we packed *Shalach Manos*. Why "all day," you ask? Well, it is a *mitzvah* to give a *minimum* of one package, but there's no *maximum*, and you certainly want to be able to give one to everyone who gives to *you*.

There was such a good mood among us with the approach of the Festival that I was not at all worried about managing with the hectic schedule: preparing the packages, staying up late at Natalie's house for the *Megillah* reading, going home to Rehavia to sleep, returning to Givat Dat in the morning for the second *Megillah* reading, sending *Shalach Manos* (Natalie had decided that I should have a really kosher *Purim* and participate in everything. I agreed with her as, after all, if not now, when?), and finally hurrying back to cook and serve the huge *seudah* at my place. Still, I was relaxed and content.

Until this occasion, I had thought that the *Megillah* reading was something very long and drawn out, something that would be of no interest to me, so I never bothered to find out about it. But that night, in my marvelous mood, I went with the family to the synagogue and found myself sitting quite happily in the very crowded room, even though I was separated from my daughter who had had to take little Ruthi out as she was fussing and disturbing the women around us.

The reading had begun, in Hebrew of course, and I was sitting and quietly meditating when suddenly the most incredible noise shook me, such a noise that for a moment I thought there might have been an earthquake!

I quickly realized that this was part of the *Megillah* reading: the congregants are all *supposed* to make the wildest noise, to blot out the name of the villain Haman every time it is read. All sorts of noisemakers are used for this purpose — horns and rattles and cap pistols — and the tumult is deafening and joyous at the same time.

As the *Megillah* is a rather long recitation, I had time to look around and acquaint myself with the whole scene. Close to me sat a young, fascinating, calm, and intelligent looking mother of four identically dressed, beautiful girls, from the age of seven to a baby just starting to stand. This baby was not at all disturbed by the great noise; in fact she had not even gotten a fright as I had. She just stood there and tugged on her mother's skirt. The mother patted her and followed along with every single word of the *Megillah* undisturbed.

I gathered my best Hebrew and asked the tallest girl if they were all sisters, and she smiled and said, "Yes." As they had fabulous costumes on, I asked if Ima had made all of them, and the girl answered again, "Yes." Then I asked if there were some boys in the men's section belonging to them, and the seven-year-old answered calmly, "Oh, yes, five of them."

I must say it never ceases to amaze me how these young religious mothers can look so smart, so slim, so calm and so happy, with, as in this case, nine children. I was impressed.

When I am impressed, I like to tell the person who impressed me that I am impressed. I decided on the spot that after the reading of the *Megillah*, I would go over to this young beautiful mother of nine and tell her how impressed I was. I was just getting up to walk towards her when suddenly that all-important rule flashed in my brain: The religious do not like to count out loud the number of children they have. They just like to say *baruch Hashem*.

So with my mind working overtime, I walked up to the woman and said: "*B'li ayin hara* ("May they be protected from the evil eye"), your daughters are lovely — one sweeter than the other, and I believe you have some fine boys too."

The beautiful young woman smiled back at me and said simply: "*Baruch Hashem*."

When I told my daughter this story later in the evening, she exclaimed happily: "Congratulations! You should really write this down in your book, to show how much you have improved from earlier, when you still thought that most of the things we do are just plain nonsense."

To get that sort of praise for my new-found knowledge really makes it all worthwhile!

18   The Dark Clouds of Tisha B'Av

Tisha B'Av deserves a separate chapter. I don't think I knew about *Tisha B'Av* before....

I have come to realize that non-observant Jews, and I mean good Jews like us, are missing out on a lot, in terms of both experiencing the beauty of what it really means to be a Jew, and knowing about our incredible history. Our history is our religion. Being a Jew involves KNOWING about our history.

Tisha B'Av, the ninth of the month of *Av*, is a symbol for many of the misfortunes that have befallen the Jewish people through the ages. It is the blackest date on the Hebrew calendar, marking the destruction of the First and Second Temples in Jerusalem, as well as several other calamities.

But all this happened so long ago — why must we, today, here in our own Land, in Jerusalem, still weep about it? Or is it only by keeping alive these bitter memories and teaching them to our children (or vice versa) that we can hope to prevent their recurrence?

I have been coming face to face with the dark three weeks preceding *Tisha B'Av* and the even darker, blacker nine final days, for years now, but somehow I never went into it, except to let it either irritate me or pass me by. But this year I had an insight into it that was an experience on its own.

In the Circle, not only did everyone go into semi-mourning for three weeks, not only did the dark mood descend on the whole of Givat Dat, not only did this darkness influence every suggestion I made connected with either serving meat (which is forbidden during the final nine days), or doing something lighthearted (which is prohibited for the whole period of mourning), but it also changed people's faces. I mean this!

For instance, some young men became old men. How? you ask, Why? Because men do not shave for the whole period of mourning, and consequently some of the normally clean-shaven 35- to 38-year-old friends of my son-in-law produced beards which were turning gray. And these happy, boyish-looking fellows suddenly became old men with gray beards, looking twenty years older than they had looked three weeks earlier.

Once, on the day before *Tisha B'Av*, I went into town to a book shop. I saw a somewhat familiar face and it smiled at me. Naturally, I was recognized, as I had not changed, nor aged very much in the previous three weeks. Though I certainly could have, with all the aggravation I had had. But I also had learned a lot of new and interesting things about the Circle.

So this face smiled at me and I wondered, "Who is this old man?" Well, it happened to be one of our best friends, one of our handsomest friends, who actually, though he is a *Rosh Yeshivah*, for some reason (unknown to me) does not normally have a beard. But on this day he turned to me with a white — snow-white — beard, and it really took me a long time to realize that this face belonged to our very close friend!

With two totally different behavior patterns within one family, any time of religious observance is complicated, but when the religious observance lasts for an entire three weeks, the problems multiply. To sail through those rough waters is not easy, believe me.

For instance, I had been invited by good friends of mine to

see a play at the Jerusalem Theater, a superb production with outstanding performers. Theater at its best. I told my daughter about it after a heavy day in Givat Dat, helping her with Sarah, who was sick with high fever from a virus that was going around, and minding baby Ruthi.

I excused myself around six to leave for home, to get ready to go to the theater. My daughter turned to me and with obvious shock asked, "You are going to the theater tonight?" She looked at me as though I had said I was going on an African safari; she could not have been more surprised.

"Yes," I answered politely. "I was invited weeks before I even knew about the dark clouds of *Tisha B'Av.*"

Natalie continued most indignantly: "Well, *we* will be washing all the laundry we have, then we will put on all the clothes we washed [I was totally lost at this stage],* and altogether we are going to start observing the very last important nine days before *Tisha B'Av.*" She also added that she thought it was in very poor taste for me to go to the theater that night.

"But this play is on for only three nights," I said most apologetically, and Natalie's sharp voice cut in: "You could at least have gone last night [equally bad, I thought], if you so desperately needed to go out."

I was at a loss. I knew it was one of those times when whatever I said would be turned against me, so I said nothing. I thought my daughter was being quite unreasonable. Since we had never made any sort of "deal" that I was to be as religious as she was, especially outside of her home, I didn't understand why it should bother her that I was going to the theater that night.

---

*Since it is customary not to launder or wear fresh clothing during this semi-mourning period, all the laundry is routinely washed before the nine days. Some people select the items of clothing they intend to wear during the nine days, put them on and wear them for a little while so that they will no longer be entirely "fresh," and therefore will be permissible to wear.

I've given this a lot of thought and have come to the conclusion that Natalie tolerates my being "different" because she assumes I am ignorant of the importance of certain religious observances. If only I knew how important some practice was, she tells herself, I would observe it, and in truth that is the way it is in many instances. But some things are totally beyond me. It is not that I don't want to know, don't want to respect Natalie's and Avi's ways — but they don't explain things! They just take it for granted that I should know. Well, I don't know everything YET!

So how could I have known that the mere mention of this "distasteful" thing I was doing on the eve of the nine days would distress her so?

Or take this incident, typical of these "dark, cloudy days." It was terribly hot and I begged Natalie and Avi to let me take the boys swimming with me. This was just before the final nine days, but still they were reluctant as they felt the boys were getting older and it would soon not be right for them to go mixed swimming (that is, boys and girls together, as was the case at our pool). I begged them some more, and they told me that I really should not act "worse than a child," that they find it hard enough bringing up their children the correct way without having to deal with my undisciplined nature besides.

In the end they succumbed, and graciously allowed me to take the boys. "But only for two hours and then straight back home!" This was the order. I left feeling quite exhausted from the dilly-dallying, and feeling guilty, as I knew that actually I should not have taken them; Natalie and Avi had agreed only as a favor to me.

At the pool, it was so lovely that I almost forgot the initial conflict. Yacov, my eldest grandchild, is terribly sociable and loves making friends. On that day he first made an "enemy" but I helped him make peace. How? He told me that the boy he was playing with was collecting bottle tops and had asked him to help. Yacov had found quite a lot of bottle tops, but the bigger boy had taken them all away from him. I said to my grandson: "When you know that you are in the right, you must never give in, you must fight for it." (I thought this was in the fine spirit of real Israeli soldiers.)

I was pleased to see that after my rousing advice, the two boys became very friendly, so friendly that I had to spend the rest of the time sitting in the wading pool with Zevi, our four-year-old, because he was not accepted by the big boys, who were over five. When I asked Yacov the name of his new friend, he said: "It's Yanke'le." The old me would have said: "Yanke'le! How horribly *Jewish*, how terribly Yiddish, absolutely uncivilized to be called Yanke'le nowadays." But the new me said, almost with tears in my eyes: "Oh, Yanke'le. How terribly sweet! It really does sound so much nicer than Johnny, not to mention Janos, or worse still, Johann." And I meant it.

This Yanke'le had his parents with him, not religious, but nice young Israelis, who obviously enjoyed our Yacov's company. (He really is a riot, a born entertainer. He can make the most boring *sippur* sound like a detective story.) Yacov was a success with the parents as well as with Yanke'le, I could tell just by watching them from a distance.

Later on the father came over to me and said: "Can what your grandson has been telling us be true — that he has been to America and Australia twice? He also tells such wonderful yeshiva stories about his *Rebbe*, the teacher he loves so much." And then, between laughing and praising my grandson, he said: "I would not be surprised if our Yanke'le would want to become a *Baal Teshuvah* after this."

Now I thought this was a cute story, and while waiting for my son-in-law — who was kind enough to pick us up instead of letting us take the bus, tired, hot and all — I decided I would share it with him.

Well, it's never a good idea to share what I think is a good story with them, as it is unlikely to be funny for them. I should have known by this time.

It was not funny to my son-in-law. In fact his face became quite stern and he said to me, while driving: "It would not be wise to get too excited about taking the boys to the swimming pool, as they certainly will not go during the next nine days, and possibly even after that. I don't think I want our sons to mix with that kind of company."

I was shocked and furious, but I did not say anything. It was one of those curiosities I did not know enough about, so why get myself into a real mess, something I would not be able to get myself out of? Clearly Avi did not wish the boys to associate with non-religious people, as who knew what they might pick up? I had thought it was all quite harmless, but obviously my son-in-law did not agree.

When he stopped in front of my own house, I kissed the boys and got out of the car. We waved good-bye and I thanked Avi very much for the lift.

I did not slam the door of the car, although the temptation was great. Instead I blamed the whole thing on the "dark clouds of *Tisha B'Av*" which seem to make everyone a bit irritable.

On the day after *Tisha B'Av*, I felt a kind of elation all around me. In the Circle, my family and their friends were all smiling again. They did not object violently, as they had done during those dark days, when I suggested that as the temperature was well over 100°F, I would take the boys to the swimming pool. At last I could make full use of my membership card to the most beautiful swimming pool in all of Jerusalem.

Even at the pool there was a happier mood. The surrounding garden was packed with religious people on holiday, merrymaking men with black *kippot*, their wives in long-sleeved dresses with buttoned-up collars, wearing stockings and "*tichelach.*" They were happily allowing their small children into the water while they sat vigil at the edge of the pool. But I did not feel sorry for them. After all, as my Danny always reminds me when I feel sorry for Natalie over something she does which only seems terrible to *me* (never to *her*): "Mum, don't ever forget, it is clearly what she freely chooses to do."

19   *Hair vs. Sheitel*

In my opinion the subject of "hair vs. *sheitel*" could indeed be one of the hardest to face among all the others connected with your daughter's total change. It was certainly so with me.

To cover or not to cover one's hair is obviously a matter that comes up a lot between me and my daughter, as you might have guessed by now from the way it crops up in chapter after chapter. There was never any question in Natalie's mind about what she would do: as a married woman she has always covered her hair, just as all the other women in her circle do. But as for me, regardless of all the religious observances I now follow in order to please her (and often to please myself), on this subject I have remained adamant. As a result, there has always been an element of non-acceptance between my daughter and me, between her covered head *vs.* my uncovered, old, unchanging head and hair, just as it has been all my life.

The truth is, I wasn't particularly happy about Natalie covering her *own* lovely hair, but was somewhat relieved that she had chosen to do so with, first, a *tichel* or headscarf, and later on, more chic and stylish headgear, rather than a *sheitel*. I had always had a terrible aversion to *sheitels* and all that they symbolized for me. The thought of Natalie wearing one was just too much to bear. I was afraid that this would be the one thing I would not be able to accept. Ever.

It was in 1989 when the "breakthrough" occurred, seven years after my daughter's wedding.

Now you mustn't think that my daughter's changing from wearing a *tichel* (which I had become accustomed to) to wearing a *sheitel* had anything to do with my feelings in any way. It was not a step she took out of spite, although she was well enough aware of my preference for and acceptance of the headscarf and my negative attitude towards *sheitels*. Today most Orthodox married women, B.T.s included, will cover their hair in one way or another, especially outside their own homes and in the presence of men other than their husbands. The choice of *sheitel*, *tichel*, or other form of headgear is determined by factors such as: fashion, occasion, local custom, and the ruling of their *Rav*.

Mothers and their opinions, for or against, are not deciding factors.

Sometimes, it is merely a question of comfort: a woman might feel physically uncomfortable wearing a wig, or emotionally uncomfortable because none of her friends wear one (her circle might all be *tichel*-wearers). Whatever the reason, I was glad Natalie had from the start not chosen to wear a *sheitel*.

Recently, Natalie reminded me of something I had forgotten completely, something that had occurred over ten years ago, when she was already religious but still single and had come on her first visit back to Sydney.

We had been walking along the streets of Sydney when we met a young woman, very obviously wearing a *sheitel*. Natalie remembered what I had said at the time, word for word, remembering even that while I had said it I had been stroking her beautiful, shiny, dark brown hair: "This I could never bear, touching a horrible *sheitel* instead of your beautiful hair.

Darling, please remember this." And she did.

I guess I was just born lucky, *baruch Hashem*, as the circumstances in which I ultimately came face to face with my daughter wearing a *sheitel* were ideal. I was looking at a photo she had sent to us with a friend, holding the picture and turning it this way and that. I called my husband to look at it with me, as I did not know why or what, but somehow Natalie looked different. She looked particularly gorgeous in the photo. As we were looking at it together, I suddenly realized what it was. "Where is her *tichel*?" I shouted. "And if she does not have a *tichel* on, then what is this on her head?"

We knew that her head had to be covered, as our daughter simply does not show herself, even to us, without some headcovering or other, even at home. This is something she's always been very conscientious about.

A stored-away memory suddenly popped into my mind. It was a very small part of a much larger event: the birth of Natalie's third child, her first daughter. I was privileged to have witnessed this event, an event so unforgettable that words cannot describe it. It just happened that I had been sleeping over in the apartment with them, and in the middle of the night Natalie appeared at my bedside. "I think it's starting," she said.

There was simply no time to do or say anything. I jumped out of bed, and within minutes we were on our way to Bikur Holim Hospital. Avi would stay with the boys, who were sleeping peacefully.

Before I realized what was happening, I found myself in the delivery room with Natalie. We hadn't discussed it at all, but I suppose she must have thought: "She is really such a good mother, let her stay — after all she LOVES every happening."

Well, let me tell you, to have had the privilege of seeing my own daughter give life to her own daughter is something for which I will always be grateful to Natalie. It happened so fast, and it happened miraculously, as in my opinion each time a newborn arrives into the world it is a miracle. When I saw with my own eyes that it was a girl, I clapped my hands with joy. The midwife, a marvelous woman, signaled angrily to me that this was no time to make noise; it was time only for the newborn baby to cry out for the first time.

And my daughter, this B.T. daughter of mine, this real *mensch*, opened her mouth to speak and the first words that came out were: "Don't be angry with my mother. She so wanted to have a granddaughter this time."

And it was then, straight after the birth, mere seconds after, that she pulled her *tichel* over her hair (it must have fallen off during the delivery), and tidied it with the same motions she always uses to tuck her beautiful hair under her scarf. Then she turned to me and said so sweetly: "Okay, Mummy, the camera is in my bag. Now you can take a photo." And though I was in a rather dazed and delirious state, Natalie's utter normality helped me to come back to this world and remember that I should be rushing back to her house to take over for Avi so that he might come quickly to see his wife and newborn daughter.

After this beautiful interlude, we must come back to the original story of how we, my daughter and I, crossed the uncrossable barrier between hair and *sheitel*.

Looking again at the photo she had sent us, I exclaimed: "If it is not a *tichel*, it must be a SHEITEL!"

Now, did I say that she looked unusually gorgeous in the photo? Yes, I did. And if I did say so, what does this mean in practical terms? You guessed it: acceptance.

It was at Ben Gurion Airport, a few months later, that I saw this new reality in the flesh, not in a photograph, as my daughter came towards me to welcome me. Now, clearly there was no point in saying anything to her other than: "Natalie, you look marvelous, and it is really almost the same as your own lovely hair that I adore so much." If I had said anything against the *sheitel*, there would have been nothing gained and a great deal lost. So why not be a winner?

It was some time after that that my daughter reminded me of the remark I had made years ago, practically begging her never to wear a *sheitel*. The occasion was really such an incredible one, that I could hardly believe it myself, but as I have already told you, nothing is impossible in the world of the B.T., absolutely nothing.

Natalie was never a sportswoman by any means, even in her youth, but she was an excellent equestrienne. In Australia, as a young teenager, she loved going to holiday camps where horseback riding was a great feature. She loved horses.

We have many old home movies back in Australia, which we sometimes, in our loneliness, put on our video screen, and we sit and wonder how a girl as outgoing as Natalie could have turned into a B.T. who locks herself away from most earthly pleasures such as sports and other similar types of amusement. She who used to ride horses, and so well, at that.

But not long ago, Natalie called us and said: "Don't ask questions. Just come this afternoon and bring your video camera." Naturally we wondered why, although making video tapes of our grandchildren is one of our favorite pastimes. (Watching those tapes back home in Sydney helps pass the lonely times, the in-between times.) But we asked no questions; we simply jumped into the car and took off for Givat Dat, armed with our camera.

When we arrived at their house, the whole family was waiting for us with great anticipation. The children were dressed very casually — the boys in old, long pants and shirts, the girls in jeans skirts, little blouses and very tatty shoes.

"Where are we going?" we asked eagerly. "Where are you taking us?" But the children only giggled. There was a marvelous, exciting mood.

"Where else, but right here in good old, 'black, *glatt*,' Givat

BLACK BECOMES A RAINBOW

Dat?" Natalie answered with the most mischievous smile.

We thought that whatever the surprise was, it could not be much fun, if we were not going to move out of Givat Dat. What new, exciting pleasure could possible await us *there*??

We drove to the outskirts of the neighborhood, and Natalie ordered Saba to stop and start videoing IMMEDIATELY. We looked around and sure enough, we saw a sight that took our breath away. It was so unexpected, and so very exciting.

There in the valley below Givat Dat, were horses, handsome horses, and it was precisely in this direction that Natalie instructed us to follow her and all our four beautiful grandchildren.

I was speechless. You could have knocked me over with a feather.

Natalie greeted an interesting-looking man, not religious, and I wondered if he were even Jewish. "Is he Israeli?" I whispered to Natalie, and the man, who had overheard me, replied, "Only eighteenth generation." He and Natalie exchanged a grin. They seemed to be already acquainted from previous visits.

Well, let me tell you, after this surprise, nothing will ever surprise me anymore. It showed us that we really should not think that our child has changed into another person altogether, while becoming an observant, Orthodox, disciplined woman. She has remained the same fun-loving, wonderful human being, with some additional wonderful human characteristics, some added marvel to her life, that is all.

And our daughter, naturally wearing a skirt (strictly religious women and girls would never wear slacks), and naturally wearing her *sheitel*, mounted a horse, and proceeded to give each one of her four children a good ride around the spacious grounds.

I was so excited, I was laughing and almost crying from the unexpected joy. For the first time in all these long years I felt that Natalie wasn't a stranger at all. It was like having my old

Natalie back — no, it was the realization that I hadn't lost my daughter at all.

Later on, back in her apartment, Natalie said: "Mummy, do you know what you did today at the riding place?"

"Of course I know!" I answered laughingly. "I loved every minute of it. I ran around like crazy taking photos, and I kissed and hugged the children, and I think I kissed and hugged you too."

And Natalie, with happy tears shining in her eyes, said: "Yes, you did. And do you know what else? Mummy, you stroked my 'hair'!"

20   *What You Could Miss Out On*

I don't think that I am exaggerating when I say that one has the potential for achieving perfect joy by just being a Savta. Of course, enthusiastic and happiness-oriented Savtas can always find joy in their grandchildren, whether they are religious or secular. But I am talking to YOU — the thousands of Savtas who have denied themselves the possibility of attaining this joy, because you have cut yourselves off from your own children.

Let me tell you about my day — just one of many — and I will leave you to be the judge. I challenge you to sit for a moment after reading this chapter and honestly ask yourself why you are missing out on all this joy.

Because only if you bend over backwards to join your B.T. children and let yourself be drawn into THEIR world, willingly and lovingly (as I have finally learned to do), only then will you be able to have a day like mine.

My day started early. Luckily I am an early riser — a very important asset in Israel, where people go to bed very late and get up very early. After the few exercises I do every morning, to the amusement and amazement of my grandchildren (who love to do them with me when they sleep over), I decided to make the day a real "writing day." Since I was on the last leg of a five-week pre-*Pesach* visit (I had to be back in Australia before *Seder* night to prepare the food and be with my own mother, husband and son), and since I can only write here in Jerusalem, I wanted to make all my remaining time available for jotting down the inspiring events of the past weeks. I know that when I leave the "source," I simply dry up until the next visit.

I had already cooked for my daughter for the whole week, so as to give her the time to spring-clean her house extra-thoroughly before *Pesach* (an incredibly rigorous and demanding job for the Orthodox), and I thought I still had some spare time for writing.

With four little ones of her own, Natalie at this time no longer went out to work, but she minded three or four small children every morning in her house to earn a bit of money while having her own youngest child home with her. But this morning the phone rang bright and early and her happy voice informed me that her "children" were not coming. She asked if I could be ready in an hour to go to town with her to do some shopping.

My idea of having a peaceful and fruitful day writing vanished the moment she said that. I was immediately all set to go shopping with my daughter. We were to meet in town to buy *Shabbat* shoes for Ruthi as she had outgrown her old ones. *Baruch Hashem!*

As always, waiting for my daughter and her baby fills me with tremendous joyous anticipation. Just knowing that they will suddenly appear excites and elates me. And soon they did appear, Natalie waving cheerfully and tiny Ruthi calling out, "Savta, Savta." This was sufficient to make my day!

We bought not only *Shabbat* shoes but, as I love buying shoes for my grandchildren, also a pair of adorable sandals for the coming summer. We strolled on the busy streets where the hustle and bustle of the coming *Pesach* festivities was evident and was for me an extra bonus, as there is nothing even faintly similar to it in Sydney.

It is my good fortune that I have such tremendous love for this Land, and that I can combine the joy of celebrating a holiday in the Jewish state with the joy of being the grandmother of an Orthodox family for whom the glorious Festival of *Pesach* is even more festive than for secular Jews. I pity the many Jews who have never experienced the exhilarating feeling of being part of the Land and its Festivals.

Close to one o'clock we parted company, Natalie naturally taking the "family car" to rush home to her own children who were due to return from school, and I, who loves traveling by bus, to go home, and despite my fatigue, possibly to pursue my writing for the rest of the day.

Just as I finished my lunch, the phone rang again and there once again was the bubbling voice of my daughter. She seems to call me all the time with the most marvelous, irresistible propositions. This time she suggested that as I had only one week left, and as I had not given the three older children a "special treat," I might like to take them to the Israel Museum for Children's Story Hour. "You could also do a little shopping in the museum store which you like so much," she added, while she would send Ruthi to a neighbor and clean the house for three hours solid.

But she had already convinced me. It was not easy to get ready to go out for the second time on the day I was going to spend at home, alone, peacefully writing... but just think what I would have missed if I hadn't gone!

I had hardly finished my coffee when I heard the car horn outside, hooting for me to come and take the children for their special treat. How wrong my daughter was — the "special treat" was for *me*. From the first moment to the last. It is not possible for my daughter to take her children on an outing like this. This is what Savtas are for.

As I sat with the other grandparents in the youth section of the museum, where the storytelling session for four- to seven-year-olds took place, and watched my three beautiful (*b'li ayin hara*) blue-eyed grandchildren with their varying shades of blonde hair, sitting, absorbed, in a circle with other children (whose own grandparents were probably convinced that *theirs* were the most beautiful, while I KNEW that mine were really so), I simply *enjoyed*.

I missed Saba this afternoon as I knew how much he would have enjoyed a day like today too. But I was already dreaming of the time when we would come back to Israel together and be able to give our grandchildren these special treats. For what can fill a grandparent's heart more than to be able to provide special times for special grandchildren?

I asked my little ones if they would like to look around the "adult" part of the museum. They said: "Savta, *bevadai!*" ("Of course.") and we were off, up the staircase to the beautiful museum.

The moment we walked in I knew this was going to be one of those emotional museum visits (though for me *everything* in Israel has an element of emotion to it). In one of the wings of the museum, we came across a door, a door that was made to look like one huge piece of MATZAH. Have you ever been to a museum, anywhere in the world, where you walked through a matzah door? We entered a room filled with *simanim*, symbols of various *Pesach* celebrations in different countries all over the world. I was spellbound. The children looked at me and smiled, as they enjoyed seeing how much their Savta was enjoying herself.

Afterwards the children waited patiently while I purchased some of those wonderful gifts that I always buy in the museum shop, and they even suggested what to buy for Saba, and Uncle Danny, and offered to give me their pocket money to buy *Pesach* gifts to take back to Australia.

That religious children are unusually well-behaved is a well-known phenomenon. The fact that they have new brothers and sisters on a regular annual basis, and grow up together without any wide age gaps between them, as is the case in secular Jewish families, is possibly a contributing factor.

I don't want to generalize, but it seems to me that in the Circle the children do not fight, scream and demand so much, but grow up devoted to and adoring their siblings. I am convinced that the very thing that we mothers of B.T.s are most against — that is, our children having these large, closely-spaced families — is the very making of a unique closeness among the children of the Orthodox.

The older children are brought up to help with the younger ones, and instead of this being a burden, it somehow becomes a joy for them. Instead of being jealous of their little brothers or sisters, they seem to love them and take care of them. At least that is how it is in our family.

When we walked down the steps from the Israel Museum in the dusk, holding hands and very tired and happy, we almost danced. And we did not talk — we *sang*. We were very "together" somehow, I, the "different Savta" and my ultra-Orthodox grandchildren.

But the day was not yet over, as I took the children home with me for supper. We were stretching the day as much as we could, just as my daughter stretches the *Shabbat*. Upon arriving at my place they asked if they could ring Ima. Then they asked to speak to Ruthi, the two-year-old, and you should have seen the excitement on their faces as they talked to their little sister, who had not shared this day of special treats with them. They passed the phone from one to the other, each child wanting to say something sweet to their little sister.

I could not but be amazed at the degree of love and unity there was in my daughter's home, and I could not help but be grateful that I was part of it and privileged to share the very special gift that religious families seem to have.

And so my day came to an end, after 8:00 P.M. when the children were taken home and I was left with a house turned upside-down, a kitchen full of dirty dishes and crumbs. A very tired, but very happy Savta collapsed on a chair with a contented smile.

And as I sat there I had a vision of those many angry, hostile grandmothers who still do not want to share the lives of their B.T. children. And I decided that no matter how tired I might be, I must sit down (hopefully without any more interruptions) and tell you what you are missing out on if you don't come to your senses and TRY.

You could be missing out on the best times of your lives. You could be missing out on a "special treats" day, like the one I had today with my religious B.T. daughter's children. You could be missing out on story hours, and matzah doors, and pocket money for *Pesach* presents, and the profound love of sisters and brothers for one another. You could be missing out on a little piece of Heaven on earth.

21   *The Visit*

Unlike the other chapters in this book, this one does not apply
to all mothers of B.T.s, but only to those whose children have
moved away from their original place of birth. With this move
they complicate even further the lives of the family. "Complicate" seems a gross understatement, as I simply cannot find
the right word in the English language (or, for that matter, in
Hungarian) to describe the chaos this change of countries can
bring into the family unit. I happen to be a victim of such a
move.

And yet, I should in fact rejoice that my child, my Jewish
child, had the good sense, the deep commitment, to practice
being a religious Jew in the most obvious place for a Jew to be
— IN JERUSALEM!

The strange truth of the matter is that I wholeheartedly
sympathize with the idea of living in Israel, especially for religious Jews. Where else but Israel?? Was it not I who wrote the
courageous article in 1978, after my daughter moved to Israel,
the article entitled: "And Now Your Child Wants to Go on
Aliyah," in which I openly indicated my total support for going
on *aliyah* when the time is ripe to do so.

Would I still write the same article today — more than a

decade later, when I have a married, religious daughter with four children, living in Jerusalem and I living in Australia?

I am not the first one to remark that theory is not the same as practice. In theory, I would still state honestly and firmly that, since Israel is our very own country, where else should one live but in Israel? In theory... but in practice it presents an almost unbearable problem: the unbearable problem of being a long-distance mother.

It was in May of 1989 that my own beloved mother was diagnosed as being terminally ill. She turned 88 that month, on the 20th of May, the same date on which Natalie was born, and all at once I recalled vividly what my daughter used to say about this double birthday: "One day this day will be a sad day of remembrance for me."

There was not the slightest suggestion of Natalie flying to Australia. How could she? How could she leave four small children and her husband? Up until this time, the only flying that had been done in emergencies was by us, the grandparents, and in particular, by me. The mother of a B.T. must be ready-set to go at all times. The daughter, on the other hand, living far away by her own choice, is generally immobile, what with her own family obligations.

So, naturally, when I needed my daughter's support during the sad time we were experiencing due to my elderly mother's fatal illness, there was nothing for me to do but FAX long, detailed letters, giving Natalie the latest news. (We both have FAX machines in our homes, something I highly recommend to parents of B.T.s who can afford this unequaled means of communication.) I was amazed to read one day in a return FAX: "Don't you think it is time for me to come and be with you?" Then Natalie added: "I would bring the girls with me." And at the end of the letter there was the magic sentence: "Don't worry about anything — we will manage."

I read and reread this last sentence. Could she mean that in such an emergency she would not be SO meticulous about her usual religious habits? I was certain she had something in mind, as otherwise there was *plenty* to worry about, and managing would be as near to impossible as one could get.

Having read chapter after chapter about the changes I have undergone since my daughter's transformation, how accommodating I have been regarding her religious observances, and how many of these practices I have joyfully taken upon myself over the years, you must be wondering why Natalie's impending visit was a cause for concern. Well, it's really quite simple. Despite all the *kashrut* restrictions we rigorously observe in our Jerusalem home, in Sydney we have remained more or less as we always were — that is, our kitchen is not kosher. This is not to say that it will always be this way, but it certainly was at the time of Mama's illness.

There was a further complication. In our old, huge house in Sydney, we had set up a little kosher kitchen, tucked away from my own non-kosher kitchen, so there had been no need to share kitchen facilities with my "*glatt*" daughter when she visited. In our new, small, cozy place, there is only the one kitchen. I could not imagine, and probably neither can you, how *glatt*-kosher and *non*-kosher could possibly function side by side.

Well, let me enlighten you. It is possible. In retrospect, however, I would say that it would have been simpler by far, and much wiser, had I made my whole kitchen kosher. There would have been a lot less aggravation all around. [We have been talking this matter over with our *Rav* recently, and getting closer and closer to actually doing it. I know in my heart that we should, but somehow it remains a big step for us to take.]

The truth of the matter, though, is that at the time I did not think too seriously about the possibility of real problems coming our way, as I was somehow guided by that one wonderful, important sentence that rang loudly in my ears: "Don't worry... we will manage." Neither did I *want* to think seriously about potential problems.

There was no doubt about it, I told myself, Natalie should come and see her grandmother once more. After all, she was Mama's oldest grandchild. Also, she should show Mama her fourth child, little Ruthi, who so resembles Natalie as a child. If anything could make poor, suffering Mama happy, this reunion could. So without further ado, we arranged for Natalie and her two daughters, aged four-and-a-half and two-and-a-half, to arrive as soon as possible. Time was running out...

I was secretly relieved to know that our grandsons would not be coming. Although we adore them, we realized that at seven and six years old, they would have been more difficult to accommodate in our non-kosher home. They had been attending *Cheder* (religious school) for the previous two years, and would have been greatly troubled and confused witnessing the secular lifestyle we lived when away from Israel (a nagging, uncomfortable thought that stayed with me right through the next three weeks).

For the time being, I pushed this thought and all other concerns aside. I was terribly excited at the prospect of having our daughter home once more. With her promise (which I took at face value) repeating itself in my head — "Don't worry" — I did not worry. Why should I, if she said it was not necessary?

RULE NUMBER 1: Don't ever translate their words into some make-believe promise, as I did. What a B.T. might consider to be "no bother" is as far from your reality as anything you could dream up in your wildest imagination. A good B.T. would never deviate from her religious standards or habits, NEVER. How on earth could I have been so crazy as to think her "Don't worry" even remotely resembled what I had translated it to mean?

In my own hopeful head I had interpreted her "Don't worry" in the following way: "My dearest Mummy, as you are in such a sad situation, our beloved Mama being so terribly ill, I want to come home and share the burden with you. In times like this, my place is with you. And don't worry about all the complications — they're not important."

Let us be honest. Did my daughter say one word about compromising about anything???

I must have been out of my mind to even suppose anything as outrageously impossible as a B.T. compromising on religious observance. I fell into my own self-made trap because I always tend to daydream and interpret things in a way that is convenient for me.

Oh, but I was so happy. I ran around town shopping for winter things for the girls, all three of them, as they were coming from summertime in Israel and it was wintertime in Australia. We waited for them at the airport with the new warm clothes.

The sight of them running towards us was unforgettable. In fact, I commented to my husband: "Look at them, all three of them. Nobody would even notice that they are 'different'." What I really meant was: religious, "black," ultra-Orthodox. After all, we were in Australia now, where we were "normal" and *they* were "different."

Natalie was wearing the most interesting headgear, a rather chic snood which, in our wintry weather in Sydney, could easily have been mistaken for a smart turban. As for the girls, you could almost fool the world with them. As they huddled in their brand new coats, boots and hats, they looked like pink snowballs. Yes, our granddaughters looked like perfectly "normal" little girls. It was so terribly important to me that everyone look normal.

Our oldest, dearest friend was waiting with us at the airport. He too wanted the joy of welcoming them. John has known Natalie from the day she was born. Naturally he hugged and kissed her as though she were his own daughter, and I watched with tears in my eyes.

Then suddenly Natalie broke loose from his embrace and

cried out: "Oh, Johnny, you must never kiss or hug me. It is just not possible anymore."

I certainly knew about the ban against kissing any man other than her husband, father or brother, but really, John was almost like a father to her. Still, my daughter knew better. And she stuck to her principles right through the visit; in fact, she did not even shake hands with some of our oldest friends. She just stepped back, smiled, and shook her head from side to side, indicating: *No; forbidden*.

Natalie had not seen our new house, as we had moved only three years before, just after her last visit. In fact she had been instrumental in our decision to move. When, three years earlier, I had come back from the airport after seeing the family off, I found our large, rambling house unbearably empty without the children. I was overcome by "empty-nest syndrome," and impulsively I turned to my husband and said: "Don't you think it is time we realized that for the two of us this house is far too lonely? Why don't we sell it and buy a much smaller home?" This led to a lot of soul-searching and decision-making, the end result of which was the sale of the big house and our move to this much smaller, cozier one.

I shall never know whether or not we did the right thing by moving, but I did know that gone was the second, small kosher kitchen, gone was the separation from visiting guests or family from Israel.

In advance of their arrival on the coming Thursday, I had prepared everything to the best of my knowledge and experience. First, I had acquired the most important guide: the 1989 Kosher Products Directory, issued by the Sydney *Beth Din*, a little blue booklet which lists a wide choice of kosher products available in Australia.

With this booklet in hand, I had done my shopping for the forthcoming first *Shabbat* meals. My husband, my son Danny and I had convened a family meeting, and in our wisdom (and very obligingly, we thought) we had decided to have only *glatt*-kosher meat for the duration of the visit. In this way, we felt, we would be avoiding any problems as far as meat was concerned.

And so I had gone to the *glatt*-kosher butcher, a very pleasant young South African newcomer, with a black *kippah*. I told him, in a nutshell, my whole life story, mainly about being actually non-kosher at home, but shopping *glatt* for the arrival of my B.T. family. I could see on his face a kind of questioning concern, but after all, I was only his customer buying *glatt* meat, not someone seeking spiritual guidance. Which I must have sounded badly in need of.

But he did do something. Together with the meat, he handed me a small cream-colored booklet and said: "Just follow this, and you will be fine."

I knew at the very moment I was handed THE book that I should follow it scrupulously. But it was at that precise moment that I decided (IN ANGER): "Surely the *Beth Din* booklet is good enough for everybody," and as soon as I got home I put the cream-colored booklet way in the back of the bottom drawer of my desk.

RULE NUMBER 2: Never ignore the "little voice" deep down in your subconscious mind. When you have a choice and you know, deep down, that the first alternative would be the right one, never opt for the second, easier one. You will be proven embarrassingly wrong.

On Friday morning, I rose bright and early, before the children. I rushed out to buy fresh bagels, challahs, and a few last minute things for our first *Shabbat*. By this time I had become a familiar figure in Bondi, our Jewish "ghetto" district, I with my slacks and uncovered hair, among all the modestly attired religious women. A couple of women who knew me asked, in what I felt was a slightly mocking tone of voice: "Is your daughter coming for a visit, that you are shopping in our stores?" I answered that they were "spot on!"

It was on that morning, after returning home to find Natalie standing in the middle of the kitchen, looking at me, that I started to waver about the meaning of "Don't worry." She stood there with the blue *Beth Din* Kosher Products Directory in her hand, and in a quizzical voice asked me: "Mum, tell me, are you sure this is the only book on kosher products in Australia?"

The great old anger arose in me, the anger I thought no longer existed. Not even trying to hide my feelings, I turned to my daughter and snapped: "I thought you meant what you said, those famous words you wrote — 'Don't worry.' Or have you forgotten about them already??"

Natalie looked at me and answered calmly: "But Mummy, of course I remember having said 'Don't worry,' and I did mean it. *Baruch Hashem* I am here with you, and that is all that matters now. But what has this got to do with my question about the book?" She held the blue booklet in one hand, and embraced me with the other.

My immense anger was now coupled with equally immense shame. Should I admit to her the whereabouts of the obviously *real* book, or should I go on evading the truth???

You see, I had reached a dangerous, new period vis-à-vis my Orthodox daughter. After eleven years of observing and learning the B.T. ways, I thought I knew enough to use my own discretion as to what is right and what is wrong. But I was sadly mistaken.

I slowly walked towards the desk drawer that contained the little booklet of Yeshiva-style kosher products in Australia, retrieved it and handed it over to my daughter.

I could hear Natalie ask the very same question I had asked myself just the other day, when in anger I had hidden the booklet in the back of the drawer. "Whom did you want to hide it from?" she asked, in a warm, friendly tone.

And suddenly the answer was crystal clear: from MYSELF.

Along with that admission came the realization that I was behaving very foolishly. It was time to stop that and start dealing with the situation in a mature and practical fashion.

Fortunately, we did not have to start from scratch. We had a whole carton of kosher dishes, which are in use only when the *glatt* family visits, and a kosher microwave oven just for them. All these things and a few newly purchased ones were set up at one end of my kitchen, ready for inspection.

It was Friday morning, with *Shabbat* due at 4:36 P.M. (I had looked it up in our *Australian Jewish News*), and Natalie surveyed the scene. She approved. I breathed a sigh of relief. Then she said: "Oh, I must run now and '*toivel*' a few new dishes." How lucky is the mother who already knows the meaning of all these funny, "black"-sounding words! What Natalie meant was that she had to take the new things to the *mikveh* (ritual bath) and dip them in the water there, rendering them usable in a kosher home.

By this time it was clear to me how wrong I had been to think for one moment that "Don't worry" had anything to do with Natalie's religious practices. If anything, she was even more stringent than she had been previously, but at the same time more familiar and more at ease with the rules and regulations.

She turned to her father and asked in an affectionate tone: "Dad, could you construct two wooden boards, one for *fleishig* and one for *milchig*, so that I can work in this kitchen?" She knew that her father could do everything and anything with his hands, and she was right. Within a few hours he had made two large plastic-coated wooden boards, one white, one brown (one for dairy and one for meat). He placed them in the corner next to the sink.

My daughter used these two boards for all her needs in the kitchen, interchanging them as required. I doubt if she erred even once. I stood there, that first morning in my kitchen, and watched her setting up her "kosher corner." Then and there I decided that I would not worry. I would let her do whatever she needed and wanted to do, and I would enjoy just having her there with us.

Thus began three weeks of often hilarious, sometimes infuriating, but all in all unforgettable moments connected with a B.T. visiting her secular family.

Mind you, the events of the subsequent three weeks could not have been hilarious or even mildly amusing with B.T.s who are too rigid and unwilling to relax their stringencies *a bit*, for the sake of *shalom bayit* (domestic tranquility). Or parents who lack the sense of humor which must be coupled with an incredible amount of tolerance and love. Without these components, the three weeks would have been a catastrophe.

I cannot deny that I have a double standard. When I am in Givat Dat, I may feel very positive about my daughter's religious observances, but in Sydney, on my home ground, they are sometimes an embarrassment to me. I can't help it. That is the way it is and that is the way I am.

Take for example the matter of my daughter's *sheitel*. Had I not been proudly telling every Moshe, Chayim and Yitzchak that "those days are over," meaning the days when I could not relate to Natalie wearing a wig? Did I not glory in my daughter's beauty, achieved as a result of her wise decision to take off the *tichel* and put on a fashionable *sheitel* instead? It may have taken me a long time, but I have certainly become reconciled to it.

Now, in Israel, in her home in Givat Dat, there is a wig-stand — a styrofoam head, which in Orthodox homes may be found almost anywhere: the living room, the bedroom, the bathroom. Wherever you go, you may bump into these stands with *sheitels* perched on them.

Naturally it bothered me and I found it a bit unnerving at first, but I do not let it bother me anymore. I finally realized that my daughter, my *frum* B.T. daughter, looks more elegant with a *sheitel* than with a *tichel*, and since I like for her to look elegant, and since these wig-stands enable her to keep her *sheitel* tidy-looking, tolerating their presence is the price I must willingly pay. But that was in Givat Dat.

Let my daughter, my frum B.T. daughter, come to my *treif* house in Sydney, Australia, and all my gracious tolerance disappears. All because of the *sheitel*-stand.

Because, you see, I do not own a stand for either wigs or *sheitel*s. I have a very good mop of hair, my very own hair, and I am very happy with it, just as it is, and where it is.

Natalie, after her initial unpacking, looked around the room she was sharing with the girls and said: "I don't think you would like me to keep my *sheitel* in the bathroom. I had better leave it here."

And with one quick move she took an Italian terra-cotta vase off the bookshelves and placed her *sheitel* on it, right smack in the middle of the room — the room that would be visited by all my friends during the coming three weeks. They would certainly all want to see the girls, sleeping, waking, whatever time of the day they might drop in.

I looked at the vase (one of my favorite purchases in Venice about twenty years ago) with the *sheitel* perched on it, and exclaimed: "Please take your 'hair' off that vase. It looks unbearably horrid to me." Without waiting for Natalie to move, I snatched the wig off the vase.

I stood there with the *sheitel* in my hand and glanced around the room, from top to bottom. No place seemed obscure enough. I was really looking for some hiding place, like a closed wardrobe. But this large room had only one couch and two single mattresses on the floor, and no wardrobe. There were only open shelves. That's all.

Finally I, who am at least a head taller than my daughter,

stretched myself to the limit and took down a glass figurine, an ugly sort of half-man, half-beast thing. It is something I must have gotten as a present sometime and hidden from view on the topmost shelf.

Natalie watched me silently. She did not move or say a word. I felt very conscious of every move I made, of the silence in the room, as I stood there with the *sheitel* in my hand.

I put the wig on the figurine. It looked a bit lopsided but I ignored that. Then, with great effort, I replaced it high on the top shelf, behind a vase of dried flowers, and said: "This is a good place, don't you think?"

All I could think was: "If eyes could speak, what would my Natalie's gray eyes be saying to her mother?"

Natalie herself did not say one solitary word. She just took a chair, climbed up on it, and pushed the glass figurine with the *sheitel* on it still further back. It was almost hidden out of sight now.

I could not believe that my daughter would be so helpful, so understanding of my sensitivity. Then I heard the Voice: "Who is kidding whom? Next time when you start telling everybody how proud you are of MY or OUR ways, just remember that you simply could not cope with the mere fact that in your famous house in Sydney someone might get a glimpse of your B.T. daughter's *sheitel*. Mum, tell me, when will you grow up?"

My answer was simple: "I don't know. Maybe never."

It took me two or three days and intense concentration to learn some important rules my daughter outlined with great concern and detail. "Mummy," she said, "these things might seem trivial and silly to you. Don't try to analyze them, or short-cut them, even if you are convinced that they are ridiculous. For us they are part and parcel of our daily existence. What might seem impossible and unnecessary to you, could be very important for us. Do not measure logic with your yard-stick, just accept it and do it our way or not at all."

Wow, I thought, and unfortunately could not help saying: "What on earth would I do without your sermons?" My daughter sadly acknowledged my uncalled-for comment. I bit my lip, and would have liked to take back what I had said.

By the middle of the first week, she had all the necessary tools and implements to conduct her *glatt kashrut* in my *treif* kitchen. I presume this was what she had meant by "Don't worry." I had to memorize the color of cups and dishes for dairy and for meat. There was no room for error with table settings, placemats, and so forth for each meal. Their cutlery and all utensils were divided into red for *fleishig*, and white for *milchig*, so this caused no difficulty. Natalie cooked and warmed everything in the microwave oven, so this part was easy too.

Anyway, the girls knew everything by heart after two days and they prevented me from making any errors. If by any chance Ima was not up yet, or not at home, I had to see to it that they said their *berachot* before meals and on all other appropriate occasions.

It may sound surprising that I, who spends so much time with my family in Jerusalem, still find these things odd. But being in their environment in Givat Dat or even in my apartment in Rehavia, is very different from having my B.T. family staying in my non-kosher home in Australia. Not only is the environment different; *I* am different.

Before the first *Shabbat*, Natalie asked us, straight out: "Mum, Dad, could we have the next three *Shabbat*s my way, as much as is humanly possible?"

"Yes," we replied in unison, and Natalie continued enthusiastically: "Good. Let us pull the phone plugs out — just as we do in Israel — and you will see how nice it is not to have the shrieking bell disturb us." (In retrospect, I must admit that the silence that came with the arrival of *Shabbat* was most welcome, especially after the frenzy that had preceded it.) "And let us have the lights off, with some exceptions." They were.

She continued, smiling: "Now, this might sound hard at first, but I thought it all over and I hope it will be acceptable to you: No cooking from the start of *Shabbat* to the finish." Naturally, this was our practice in Jerusalem, but I wondered how she intended to accomplish this in *my* kitchen in *Sydney*. I restrained myself and let her go on without interrupting. It seemed she had thought of everything! "We must [Dad must] concoct a *blech*," (that is, a piece of metal placed over an even, slow flame, on which the food is kept warm).

I hate to think what happens in a household with similar problems where Dad is not a born genius like ours is. On Friday afternoon, just in time, there was a metal homemade contraption, very suitably called a "*blech*," covering our electric stove. One would have thought this was IT, but no, our daughter continued, somewhat sheepishly. "There is a little cost involved in cooking the *Shabbat* lunch, but I assure you, you will all love it. I would like to buy a 'Crock Pot' [slow cooker] in which I will prepare for you the most delicious *cholent*. This will cook all night and it will be ready for *Shabbat* lunch." It was. Ready and delicious.

That covered the biggest problem — *Shabbat*. The rest was easy...

We were lucky to live close enough to the hospital where Mama was that we could visit her even on *Shabbat* by walking there. But I warned Natalie not to set out rules for visitors who might want to come and see us on *Shabbat*, including her brother.

She was not concerned about "others," but she dearly would have loved her brother to sleep over and spend *Shabbat* with us. This unfortunately did not happen, as this was not in her or our power. Danny has his own very strong views on these matters. But he simply adores the girls and spent as much time with them as he could. He spent every Friday night with us (no questions asked about how he came and went) and each *Shabbat* lunch.

I try not to interfere with my children in matters regarding their contrasting religious beliefs. They are both adults, both intelligent human beings; they must sort things out between themselves.

But one silent doubt cropped up in my mind as I watched my thirty-year-old son with Sarah and Ruthi on his lap, as they recited the "Grace After Meals" *by heart*. At least Sarah did — every single word from beginning to end; Ruthi occasionally uttered a few familiar words. I could not help but look and wonder: "On my highly educated son's lap sit two little pre-school girls, who seem to know something quite beautiful and important as far as Jewish tradition is concerned. Yet he has not mastered a single word of it."

I felt a strange sensation, an awareness of a lack of some-thing; a minus for us, a plus for them. But then, immediately, my thoughts swung to the other extreme, and with a sudden shrug of the shoulders, I said to myself: "We do not need these things. We get along just fine without them" — but do we?

Shabbat was truly well-organized. There was not one minor detail my daughter had not thought of. I was not sur-prised to find neatly cut-up toilet tissue in our bathrooms. I was already familiar with this regulation about not tearing anything on *Shabbat*.

Yet there were still some small, insignificant things to spoil the mood. Even after all these years, some things my daughter does simply drive me out of my mind. So ridiculous and petty they seem to me; so important they are to her. I'll give you an example.

My youngest granddaughter Ruthi hates umbrellas. During the first ten days of their visit, Sydney was drenched in rain. We could not help but use umbrellas and Ruthi kept crying and shrieking "No umbrella, no umbrella" each time we used one. I decided to cure this phobia and went and bought the sweetest little umbrella: white plastic with flowers, birds and butterflies painted on it.

I rushed back home and wanted to show it to her immediately, but it was *erev Shabbat* and I got caught up with the preparations. So I placed the umbrella in the entrance hall to show it to her later on.

After the beautiful Friday night dinner and singing, I said: "Now Ruthi, come and Savta will show you what she bought for her darling." We went outside, just she and I, and just as I was opening the umbrella, a shrill cry stopped me. "No! It's *muktzeh*, it's *muktzeh*! Don't you know this is *muktzeh*?" Natalie was very agitated.

I looked at Ruthi, who had been on the verge of smiling at the open umbrella. She did not cry. Just as I thought I had cured this nasty phobia, I was stopped in my tracks.

I knew very well what "*muktzeh*" meant, and I also knew my daughter's tendency to exaggerate on the subject. I shouted back: "Don't be so overzealous — I am not using a motor. I know what is *muktzeh* and what is not."* Ruthi was holding the umbrella, smiling, when Ima arrived on the scene. Upon seeing her mother's stern expression, she dropped the umbrella and Natalie pushed it aside.

"I don't need you to determine what we call *muktzeh*." She pronounced it "*we*" in a way that clearly indicated that "*you*" was the exact opposite. "Umbrellas are *muktzeh*, and that's that. Now I want you to try to conform to our *Shabbat* rules for these remaining two weeks — *if you can*." She added the last part in a really nasty, threatening voice, and I spat back: "And what if I *can't*??"

The mood was spoiled, and the second *Shabbat* with it. I sulked in my room and my husband did not come to my rescue. In fact he later on reprimanded me: "Must you always

---

*As it turned out, she was right and I was not. *Muktzeh* applies to just about anything you may not move or use on *Shabbat*, umbrellas included.

give your own rendition of *Shabbat* observance? Can't you at least for these few weeks attempt to keep everything her way? After all, she has put her wholehearted trust in you while she is a guest in our home."

I was furious. Such a small matter to cause such a big upheaval. "Oh, they are just fanatics," was my usual comment when I did not agree with or wish to succumb to their ways.

"One less *Shabbat Shalom*," I thought, and suddenly, there was a pang in my heart. I had dreamt about having them with me all year long, and now... I started to cry, an angry, senseless cry. "If only she would not antagonize me so with these really trivial things!" Trivial to *me* and a way of life for *them*. I knew it by heart.

The night was ruined, that much was certain. But I decided to control my anger, and keep the peace for the remaining time.

Another *Shabbat* incident was saved by a happier ending. I was just brushing Ruthi's long, brown, silky hair into two ponytails, when Ima walked into the room.

I immediately overreacted, and in self-defense started to make excuses for my ignorance, for making what the children call "*kukiyot*," with rubber bands and ribbons, on *Shabbat*. "I'm sorry for making *kukiyot*, which must be a real *muktzeh*..." I began, when I heard my daughter laughing.

"Mummy, you are really unpredictable," she said. "Making *kukiyot* is perfectly all right on *Shabbat*." I gave a happy sigh of relief. Natalie, however, added the following words, just in case I got too swell-headed: "But on the other hand, you must make sure first, rather than going ahead and doing something wrong."

She came over and kissed me affectionately. Then to Ruthi she said: "Your Savta always made the best *kukiyot* for your brothers." And turning to me, she continued: "You used to go on and on about having to make the boy's long hair fit under their *kippot*. Remember, Mummy?"

And suddenly I did remember about the boys with their hair uncut till they were three years old. How could I ever forget?

(At that time I had not known about the custom of not cutting a boy's hair until he is three years old. In fact, every time I had seen what I thought was a little girl with "her" hair tucked neatly under a little *kippah*, I had thought to myself, "Now *there* is a weird sight." But then, there are quite a lot of weird sights in Jerusalem.)

Yacov, our firstborn, had the most beautiful blonde hair, and I used to make some fabulous hairdos for him when he was between one and three years of age. I became a grandmaster, arranging my first grandson's — my religious, Orthodox grandson's — long hair. You'd better listen, all you grandmothers of B.T. children! You may very well find yourselves doing this same strange thing when *your* grandsons are this age.

But comes his third birthday, and he will have his long hair lopped off. Or better still, on *Lag Ba'Omer*, the 33rd day of the counting of the *Omer* (which falls about a month after *Pesach*) — a special day when, traditionally, three-year-old boys receive their ceremonial first haircuts, leaving only their sidelocks. This business of sidelocks is a painful subject for parents of B.T.s. I would rather not discuss it now.

While sitting on the floor, trying to make *kukiyot* for my fourth grandchild, my Ruthi, I started to muse. I have actually become a very experienced grandmother over the past few years. I have certainly learned a lot of new things. I looked at my daughter affectionately, this B.T. girl of mine who has changed my whole life in the past eleven years.

Old rules and customs had to be forgotten and replaced with totally unfamiliar new ones. The road was often rough and bewildering and almost impossible to follow. Yet I followed it, sometimes with all my senses screaming loud and clear: "I don't want to do it! I don't want *you* to do it! I don't want to follow these old, antiquated rules! I hate them, I hate them, I hate them!"

But still I went on learning and following. There was always another little voice calling from somewhere within me saying: "Do it, do it, do it — for the sake of love."

I look back with hazy eyes and tender memories to the time I was "doing" the boys' hair. I also remember the happy day when we went to see Natalie after the birth of her second son. I had been alone at home with Yacov, my first grandson, and I had had to do his hair all by myself for the first time. There had been nobody I could turn to for help. I had wanted to do it extra well, as he was to come with us to see his new brother. I remember how excited we were.

We walked into Ima's room, and she took one look at her firstborn and exclaimed: "Oh, how well your Savta has learned to do your hair, Yacov." And I stood there feeling ten feet tall, that's how proud I was.

And now I have become a *kukiyot* specialist, and I feel a warm and happy pride mixed with thanksgiving, that I persevered during those hard years. I remember all the things that seemed impossible then, but today I do them all with relative ease. Some of them have become my greatest joy, like making *kukiyot* for my granddaughters... and *even* for my grandsons.

If you are patient and take one step at a time, you will see: one day you too may be a fine *kukiyot*-maker.

There was another foolish little argument between us, this one over some mints. I had in my bag a little plastic box of Tic-Tac mints, tiny sugar-coated peppermints which I popped in my mouth from time to time. Naturally my little granddaughters noticed this and asked for some. "My darlings," I said, "they are so strong, I don't think you would like them." They tried them and liked them. So I gave them one or two now and then.

On one of these occasions, my daughter asked them: "Sarah, Ruthi, what is Savta giving you to eat?" The question put this way was sufficient to annoy me. Did she not think I knew enough by this time about what to give them? But when she asked me to produce the little box, adding: "Are you sure they are for *us*???" I just could not believe my ears.

"Really, Natalie," I said, "there has got to be a limit to your quiz questions. Of course they are all right for you." I did not give it another thought.

This incident occurred while we were out in the car. When we got home, Natalie opened her cream-colored *glatt* booklet and started to search under the heading "*Sweets.*"

When I heard her asking me: "Mummy, would you show me what you gave them — was it the spearmint, the peppermint or the plain mint?" I was overcome with the fury that was reserved only for interrogations like these.

"Please don't make an utter fool out of me, your mother, in front of the girls," I retorted angrily. "I find this quite embarrassing."

The girls hung on every word, every gesture. They turned their heads from one of us to the other, as if at a tennis match, wondering who would win this argument. This time, I was sure, we were simply wasting our time. I produced the tiny box of peppermints and handed it to her. She took it, examined it closely, referred to her little booklet again, and proclaimed: "Mummy, you will be surprised to hear that you gave the girls a NO-NO. The peppermint flavor is the one *we* must not eat."

With these words, she pushed the booklet under my nose, pointing with her finger to the right place and reading aloud: "Spearmint, mint." Not a word mentioned about my peppermint Tic-Tacs.

The whole thing was like a bad joke. I was not going to let a tiny cream-colored booklet make a complete fool out of me. I was going to prove my innocence!

"There must be a mistake, a printing error," I insisted.

The girls were still watching every move we made, but in a very amiable way. They did not find the ruling out of peppermint to be a punishment of some kind. "Savta, please don't worry about it," I heard their sweet voices saying to me. "It really doesn't matter at all. Ima will buy the ones that are for us."

Fortunately at this point my sense of humor overcame my anger. "Okay," I said, "you will be the mint-and-spearmint persons and I will be the peppermint one." I started to laugh, suddenly realizing the pettiness of the entire argument. The girls joined me, and we all laughed aloud. There was really nothing else to do but laugh.

Then there were the tricky occasions when, in some strange contrary way, I tried to ignore my ignorance. When I was caught out, I would be doubly angry — first, because my ignorance had been exposed, and second, because it was simply unpleasant to be reprimanded. Take this incident:

I went to a park with the girls. Ima had been given the morning off, and she had gone into town. A treat for her, I had said. "Go and enjoy. It is not every day that you can leave your children with their grandmother in Sydney." Natalie had kissed us good-bye and run off happily.

We set out to have a marvelous day. I had decided we would have lunch on the grass near the beach-front, so we went to a nearby deli shop where I knew that I could buy a certain brand of chips, a chocolate drink called *Move*, and some fruit. At the shop, I saw some appetizing, fresh bagels, and for a fleeting moment I wavered: "Should I ask what brand they are?" But the question sounded ridiculous. After all, bagels are bagels, I told myself.

I bought some for the girls, who cried out joyfully: "Oh, we love *bagelahs*." I laughed with them and said: "I call them bagels." Anyway, bagels or *bagelahs*, we ate them and they were delicious.

When we got home, Ima asked the girls what they had

done all morning. They told her about the seagulls, the naughty boys in the park, the sailing boats, and in the end, about eating lunch on the grass. Natalie somehow never misses an opportunity to catch me out in one way or another (or so it seemed at the time. Maybe it's just that I allow myself to fall into these traps). "What did Savta buy for you?" Natalie asked, and the girls shouted in unison: "*Bagelahs!*" I muttered under my breath: "I call them bagels."

To my daughter it did not matter what any of us called them. What mattered was whether or not I had bought the right ones, the ones kosher enough for *her*, the ones listed in the cream-colored booklet.

I knew she would fault me. I was convinced that she was looking for something to find wrong in my morning with the girls. And I said so, too. "Tell me, Natalie, do you want your so-called '*shalom bayit*,' or do you want an argument?"

I already knew before she started to preach to me what she was going to say. It was: "Mum, please try to understand. *Shalom bayit* has nothing to do with discipline and proper *kashrut*. If only you would accept it and learn this much."

"If only you would stop preaching to me *this much*," I retorted angrily. It was really sad that a little matter like what kind of bagels I had bought could come between us and cause unpleasantness. On such a lovely day as we had had...

And then another thought struck me, and my little hidden voice chided me: "Savta, Savta, you knew very well — indeed when you bought the bagels (*bagelahs*) — that all you had to do was ask what brand of bagels they were. But you bought them knowing that they might be the wrong ones. With this purchase it was *you* who rocked the *shalom bayit* boat. So really, Savta, you were wrong, and you had better admit it."

And I did. And *shalom bayit* reigned again.

It had been a tradition in the "good old days" when my children were young, that on Sunday evenings dinner was bought in a nearby shop which sold all kinds of fast foods. This was the only time we ate non-home-cooked meals, but indulged in something like take-out hamburgers or fried chicken.

Remembering this ancient custom, I suggested to Natalie and Saba on Sunday afternoon that we go out to Bondi and buy something ready-made for dinner. The girls squealed with joy and we were off.

As we were leaving the house, Natalie asked me: "Have you any particular place in mind, Mum?"

"Of course I do," I eagerly replied. "We can go to the Hakoach Club." This is a large, popular club established especially for Sydney's Jewish residents.

Natalie looked at me in her ever-doubting way and I knew in advance what she would do next. She went straight to the telephone and dialed her *Rav*. The conversation between them was brief and, obviously, to the point. Then she turned to me and said: "Hakoach is out."*

I counted to ten, knowing it was best to keep quiet rather than explode.

After a few seconds, I went on cheerfully: "Never mind. Let us go to Fiveways instead. It is full of kosher shops and eating places, and we are bound to find something suitable there." The girls started to get a bit excited and a little restless, urging us: "Let's go and buy some felafel!" I caught on fast, and joined them saying: "Let's. I know just the place to eat the best felafel in town, in Bondi."

We arrived at a very clean, light, appetizing place called "Jaffa Felafel," aptly decorated in blue and white, the colors of Israel's flag. It looked almost like any place you might find in Jerusalem on Jaffa Road or in Meah She'arim.

Natalie and I jumped out of the car and entered the restaurant, which was full of Jewish teenagers and Hebrew-speaking

---

* Hakoach, and many other places in Sydney, have since become "*in*," that is, under the Rabbinical supervision of the Yeshiva.

youngsters. I was proud of my find, and I looked it. Natalie, on the other hand, was doing her usual "looking for the *hechsher*" (Rabbinic *kashrut* approval) act. As she was proclaiming: "This is not for *us*," I began counting madly, in two languages — English and Hebrew — to control my rage.

"It's a pity," I managed to say calmly. "It really looked clean and yummy." Natalie did not even react to my comment. Back in the car, the girls were waiting expectantly. "Ima does not like it," was all I could mutter. And there was silence. (They knew better than I when to hold their tongues.)

We circled around in the small district, passing the elegant building which houses the Hakoach Club. I must have uttered a small sigh, as Natalie looked at me pityingly. She must have been thinking: "How can my mother be so childish?"

In the distance we saw a place called "Jewish Vegetarian" and I immediately knew we had hit the jackpot. I could not contain my excitement. "Natalie, look! This *can't* be faulted," I said. "It is Jewish and vegetarian — it must be kosher enough."

To cut a long story short, IT WAS NOT.

But something wonderful happened as she came out of the "Jewish Vegetarian" after her "inspection tour." She met another young woman just like her — the same look, the same everything, except that the other one was pregnant. Natalie exchanged some words with the young woman and came back to the car. She had been a mine of information, Natalie said. "I have the place and the address. It is called "Gershon Glatt." (To me that already spelled trouble, this time trouble as far as MY *hechsher*, not hers, was concerned.)

I was not far off.

The place was badly lit, rather dilapidated looking. A small room with handmade signs advertising the products of the place and "Gershon Glatt" painted all over the windows. Actually, just as "Jaffa Felafel" had reminded me of one of the neat, clean, beautiful places in Meah She'arim, so this place reminded me of a particular smelly little eating place also in Meah She'arim, a hole in the wall.

A young woman with a grubby, dark *tichel* covering her head, altogether not very appetizing looking, was serving at two counters, one *fleishig* and one *milchig*, opposite each other. I was just going to say something when Natalie stopped me in my tracks with: "Mum, *you* don't have to eat here. Just relax."

At this stage we were all cold, tired and hungry, and though I would have opted for scrambled eggs on toast, a thousand times better, all I could say was: "'Gershon Glatt' will do for us all."

I tried to appear cheerful, but obviously my face did not match my voice as Natalie looked at me with a rather critical expression. "Mum, you know, one would think that by now you would *know* what *our* standards are," she said.

"Oh, I know," I muttered, almost under my breath. "Very low." Oh, this stupid tongue of mine — why does it go off so fast?

My daughter, my B.T. daughter, who had come on this important three-week visit to Australia, just looked at me. I felt truly ashamed and sorry, but I also knew it was too late. I was not at all surprised to hear Natalie's hurt voice saying quietly: "Please, Mum, don't play games with me."

And I knew our fun-filled take-away dinner had turned sour for us, all because of me.

Then there were the "*glatt* lunch outing" and the "*treif* lunch outing."

We were having a shopping day in the city, all of us, Ima, the girls and I. Natalie turned to me and said: "Mummy, I don't suppose there is a place in town where *we* could have lunch, is there."

Triumphantly, I exclaimed: "But there is — a genuine *glatt* place. Just leave it to me."

It did annoy me when she asked suspiciously over and over again, as we wandered around in the gigantic city of Sydney, "Mummy, how *glatt* is this place you want to take us to?"

"So *glatt*," I replied with an air of superiority, "that it will suit even you, my darling *rebbetzin* daughter."

We turned in at a massive, beautiful, old building, no less than the Great Synagogue of Sydney. It is an elegant, stately structure which houses not only the synagogue itself, but a large Jewish library and the new Holocaust museum. A significant Jewish landmark in the middle of this metropolis.

I had remembered reading in the *Australian Jewish News* a few weeks earlier a news item that had interested me because of the pending visit of my daughter. "Orthodox Jews can now have delicious snacks and meals at reasonable prices under Rabbinical supervision, in the building of the Great Synagogue," it had read. And now, as we entered the small, immaculately clean, neatly appointed restaurant, I was rightly proud of my find.

The tables were covered with white tablecloths, and a young man in a black *kippah* was serving. There was simply no doubt that this place was Orthodox, and very much what we had hoped it would be.

At least, very much what *I* had hoped it would be. My daughter (who questions a number of kosher restaurants in Jerusalem as well, and often asks the managers to produce their *kashrut* certificates) was not yet totally convinced. She had the audacity to turn to the young man in the black *kippah* and ask about the *hechsher*. I held my breath, and quietly mumbled my own prayer, as I and the girls were very tired, thirsty and hungry, and just dying to sit down at last.

It is at moments like these that I could just *strangle* my daughter for being so rigidly, stubbornly, fanatic. I was getting really hot under the collar. But then, to my great relief, the *hechsher* was approved.

We took off our coats and gloves, and sat with the girls in great anticipation of a nice lunch in the city, for *all* of us, *baruch Hashem*.

The place started to fill up and, interestingly enough, everyone who entered, I knew vaguely from somewhere. We greeted and smiled and were observed by every single person in the restaurant. At least my two beautiful granddaughters were — Sarah with her golden-blond hair and great blue eyes, and Ruthi with her brown ponytails tied with bright pink ribbons, her tiny nose, and huge gray eyes and long eyelashes, both dressed in identical skirts and sweaters, looking just adorable, even if I say so myself. I was beaming with obvious joy, watching my daughter and my granddaughters having lunch in the Great Synagogue in Sydney.

Not for one moment did I think of the numerous exciting places other people go to at lunchtime in Sydney. Who cares to eat Japanese, Italian, Chinese or Hungarian, when after all I can eat *glatt*, right in the middle of the city, with my family from Jerusalem.

Next to us sat a fine-looking lady and her husband, obviously getting great pleasure just from looking at us. She turned to me and said: "It is not every day in Sydney that one sees so beautiful a sight as your family." And I too enjoyed the sight of Ima and the girls washing their hands and saying *berachot* before breaking bread. It is like second nature to them, just doing what comes naturally...

Lunch was a great success. Naturally, they *bentched* silently, while I looked around aimlessly. By then the whole restaurant had come to talk to Sarah and Ruthi, who in turn told them their whole life story — apparently a very interesting one — in a cute mixture of Hebrew and English. Our table became the center of attraction.

Just before leaving, a woman came in and sat a few tables away from us. Natalie whispered to me that this was the mother of one of her old classmates from Sunday school. She went over to her and they engaged in an animated conversation. In the meantime, I paid our check and started getting the girls into their warm outer clothing. They said enthusiastic good-byes to their newly-acquired admirers in the restaurant. Some of the diners even called out an emotional "*Shalom*" to them. I must say, nowhere in Sydney could we have had a nicer time and better lunch or a more memorable experience.

As we were preparing to go, the woman Natalie had been talking to turned to me and, with genuine friendliness, declared: "I must say, I envy you. You are truly a lucky lady to have a family like yours."

In the future, at some lunches in Sydney, when I am feeling lonely, left out, and terribly distant from my beloved family in Jerusalem, I will have to remember and repeat these words, the words of a mother whose thirty-six-year-old daughter is still unmarried and probably far from being as fulfilled as my daughter obviously is. I must remember and repeat: "You are truly a lucky lady..."

Our "*treif* lunch outing" also left a lasting impression. It all started with the fact that Natalie knows me so frightfully well. She knew that deep down in my heart I would like nothing better than to show off my grandchildren at a place where "my kind of people" go.

I had been lucky to meet people I knew in the Great Synagogue restaurant, but there is one place in Sydney where "everybody who matters," in our secular Hungarian-Australian world, goes. It is called "The 21," a small cafe-cum-expresso eating place, owned by a dear friend of ours named Jancsi. Jancsi has known Natalie from the age of three, and in fact he used to give her the same kind of lollipops then as he now gives to the third generation of his customers. His cafe is in the heart of a very elegant shopping center, and it is a favorite meeting-place for young and old alike.

With the three-week visit coming to an end, I kept thinking how much I would have liked to sit in the window seat of "The 21" and show off with my gorgeous girls. Secretly, I admitted to myself that having only the girls here made it sheer joy to go out with my family, whereas in past visits, the boys, with their obviously unusual (in Sydney) outward signs of Orthodoxy, had caused quite a stir. "The 21" is certainly *not* a place for little boys with *payot, tzitzit* and black *kippot.* It is as *treif* as can be — its food, its clientele, its whole atmosphere.

It was therefore all the more surprising when, in the last days of their visit, Natalie said to me smilingly: "Mummy, I know you so well. Would it not be your dream to go with me and the girls to 'The 21' for lunch today?"

I looked at her, aghast. "Would this be at all possible?" I asked hopefully.

Natalie smiled and replied: "I will try to make it possible." And we left it at that.

She phoned Jancsi and had an amusing, hearty talk with him, ending with: "Please make sure we can sit at the front table, near the window to the street. This is Mummy's lunch party, you know."

We got dressed in fine clothes, the girls in plaid skirts and tights matching the color of their sweaters and the ribbons in their hair, and off we went to "The 21" for a family lunch party.

On the way, Natalie stopped for a moment and with a slight frown turned to me and said: "You know I am doing this only to make you happy, as I am a bit worried about 'Morris Ein.'"

I stopped too, and with great surprise asked: "Who is he?" wondering just who this was whom she did not want to meet after all these years.

"Oh, it is one of those 'too hard, too-complicated-for-you-to-handle' kind of things," she replied.

[After she left Australia, I managed to get a satisfactory

explanation of this famous "Morris Ein." It goes something like this: If, while my *frum* daughter and her children are sitting in the window seat of a *treif* eating place, another Jew should walk by, he might, upon seeing her, suspect that she is eating *treif* food, or — even worse — knowing her religious status, jump to the conclusion that "The 21" had become kosher, and decide to eat there too. "*Morris Ein*" is their way of pronouncing "*mar'it ayin*" — the Hebrew term meaning "a semblance." It is an inadvertant deception, something that should be avoided at all times.

When I finally understood this concept, I thought of my daughter, and in retrospect appreciated her gesture even more than when it had actually occurred. What a loving B.T. would not do for her mother's sake! was all I could think. And I say this with all sincerity.]

We entered the place and Jancsi, our host, was naturally ready to kiss and hug Natalie, when suddenly he remembered the prohibition from the last visit, and withdrew in time. He asked if he could kiss the girls and permission was granted.

Our table at the window was waiting for us, all set, and very beautifully, at that. The first thing Natalie did was take off the setting for the three of them and replace it — rather conspicuously, I thought — with paper plates and plastic cutlery from her large bag. (I later learned that the conspicuousness was an important part of the deal: she had to make it obvious to any casual observer that she was definitely not using the *treif* utensils.) Jancsi, who is famous for his sharp but warm sense of humor, was standing by, watching. When the waitress approached our table, he waved her away, saying: "This customer is mine."

Natalie smiled her broadest smile at her old friend and asked: "Where can we wash our hands, please?" Jancsi indicated the ladies' room. "Would you have a cup or a jug in there?" she asked. I was frightened of the possibility of a rude reply, but Jancsi was at his best. Realizing that there must be a reason for it, he handed her a cup from one of the shelves.

When the girls returned from the ritual washing of hands before eating bread, Natalie produced from the bag in her lap three large crunchy bread rolls, apparently bought at the kosher bakery.

Jancsi stood there with a pencil and paper ready to take any orders. When Natalie asked for some salads for the girls, Jancsi ran to the kitchen and returned within seconds with a large portion of fresh, crisp lettuce, served on the paper plate Natalie had given to him earlier. Till then I had sat completely speechless, just sitting back and letting Natalie arrange everything. After all, I was there only to enjoy.

The crisp, green lettuce was unfortunately not suitable, for reasons again too hard to explain and too hard for *us* to comprehend. (Lettuce is one of those vegetables that require extra-special care in cleaning and checking for bugs.)

The order was finally given: "Salmon, tomatoes, and margarine, please," and we finally sat back to relax. The place was full of lunchtime guests, all of whom smiled and waved to us. We Hungarians who move in this circle, our very own, chic, secular circle, all know one another.

Jancsi returned to us with the order, and sat down to join us at our table. With a particularly long, searching look at Natalie, he said: "You look really beautiful. So much better than when you wore that '*shmatteh*' on your head." Natalie graciously acknowledged the compliment.

I thought to myself: "Should I tell him, or should I not?" Finally I decided.

Surprised by my own boldness, I asked him: "Would you like to know why my daughter is looking so much more beautiful?" I didn't wait for his reply. "Because she is wearing a *sheitel*!" Jancsi looked at me as if I had said something entirely unthinkable. In almost a whisper, he asked: "A *what*?! A *sheitel*??? Your daughter is wearing a *sheitel*???"

"Yes," I said, almost defiantly. "And doesn't she look

positively beautiful?"

Our lunch arrived and it was delicious. We ate, we laughed, we socialized with old acquaintances, some waving to us even from the street. Natalie seemed to really enjoy giving me this special treat.

After lunch, just as the girls and Natalie were quietly, totally unobtrusively *bentching*, Jancsi was back again to ask them something. He realized they were busy. He turned to me, asking in gestures: "What next? What are they doing now?" and I tried to explain it to him. "Now I have seen and heard everything," he exclaimed. "*Bentching* in 'The 21' — never before!" Natalie flashed a warm smile towards him, while silently still reciting Grace.

At a last attempt, Jancsi returned to the table with two round, red lollipops, one for each of the girls. They were reaching out for them when Natalie softly but firmly told them: "No." The girls stopped reaching out, and to top it all, said to Jancsi: "Thank you very much, but we cannot eat *those*." And with this, the subject of lollies was closed.

Jancsi threw his arms up in the air and roared: "This is unreal! I have never seen children like these." He wasn't angry or hurt; he meant he had never seen children as well-behaved, as obedient and as disciplined. And on this note, our *treif* lunch outing at "The 21" ended.

In this rather long chapter, I have attempted to describe highlights of my B.T. daughter's visit with her daughters to Australia. My intention was to show you how this was actually possible. But now, rereading it, I feel slightly troubled. Why, after all these years and my so-called total acceptance of their ways, do I still have so much room for hostility?

Were I to paint for you, my readers, a picture which is all rosy, I would not be doing you any service in the long run. I would like for you to trust me, follow me through my good and bad experiences and eventually learn from them how to get the most out of a situation which you may still consider impossible.

I don't hesitate to admit that even after years of trial and error I still come across a lot of situations where I lose my temper, as I am sure you have done. Time and time again, your B.T. children will come out with what seem to you the most outrageous, senseless, petty actions. But, as I have learned, you must at all times try to give them the benefit of the doubt. Whatever it is, it is very important to them. Let them do things their way, conform whenever you can, and don't give them a hard time. You will all be much happier for it. And if you open your mind to learning new things, you will discover new dimensions added to your life, as I have.

Natalie's short three-week visit showed me once again how much discipline is needed in a B.T. lifestyle. I remember how sorry I felt for my grandchildren and how angry I was at my "severe" daughter for not letting them accept the lollipops that she considered unsuitable for them to eat. And then, the other day, I read something in a feature article by a rabbi-columnist in *The Jerusalem Post* that I think makes an appropriate closing note for this chapter:

> In the father's "giving charity" to his child, he does not supply the actual spiritual sustenance, but only the preparation for it. He pays their teacher, and the teacher instructs the child. On the other hand, the mother provides the spiritual nourishment itself. For even a child who studies in a *Cheder*, yeshiva or day-school might frustrate all his teachers' efforts by neglecting to implement at home the Judaism he has absorbed in school.
>
> *It is the mother who must guard and train the child in correct Torah conduct. She earns the "rains" of blessing and success for her entire family.*

I realized then that Natalie was not being "severe" with the children. She was simply fulfilling her duty as a religious mother, training her daughters to lovingly accept the discipline that is so important in their life.

My father, ca. 1918, when he was a "banker"
with the English-Hungarian Bank.

My parents
on their honeymoon
in Venice.

▲
At my grandparents' summer place in Svabhegy, 1926. (L. to r.) My beloved Uncle Eugene (standing); my father's youngest brother Arpad (who somehow got to Israel after WWII but his entire family, his wife and his only daughter Eva perished in the Holocaust); my brother Pista on the lap of his *Fräulein* — his German nanny; my mother and father, with my one and only cousin George, who sent us our Australian landing permits in 1949.

►
Pista and I, not long after our father's demise. I still think he looks like Robert Taylor.

Can you imagine being at your one and only daughter's
wedding and taking part in it as though you were split right
down the middle, as if you were two people? That was
how I felt, like two people. One was the loving Jewish
mother, whose heart beat with every step her daughter
took through the wedding. And the other was the observer,
the spectator, at a most exotic, never-before-seen-or-heard
spectacular: a Jewish Orthodox "glatt" wedding. Here the
Rav is completing the marriage contract (ketubah).

Some of those energetic, athletic yeshiva *bachurs*, entertaining us and rejoicing before the bride and groom.

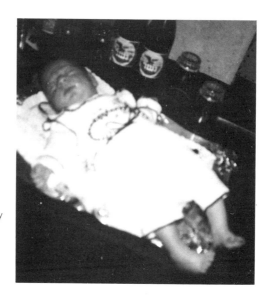

Our *bechor*, adorned with jewelry
and presented on a silver tray,
at his *Pidyon Haben* ceremony.

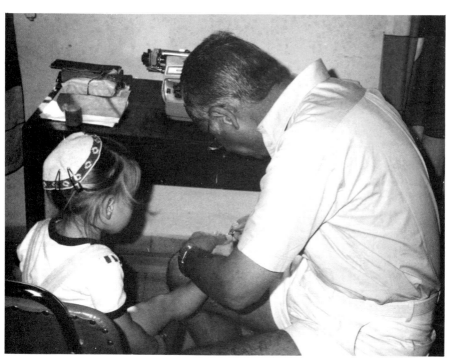

Saba Steven with his still long-haired grandson in our
"quaint" Rehavia apartment.

The two most unforgettable lunch outings I have ever had with my daughter were at "The 21" and at the Great Synagogue restaurant in Sydney.

When we revisited Budapest in
the winter of 1989, my son
could only stare in wonder at
Andrassy Ut 9. "You never told
us you had lived in such a
mansion!" he exclaimed.

On that same visit, we stopped
at my summer villa. This tiny
lane was all that separated my
family from the Weinbergers,
but in truth we were a world
apart.

I still can't quite believe that I had the courage to speak at the Hungarian Holocaust Survivors Reunion in 1984. The renowned nuclear physicist Edward Teller is seated to my right. Rebbetzin Esther Jungreis (l.) was in the first row of the audience.

❊   ❊   ❊

There is a most important postscript to be added to "The Visit," concerning my mother. After all, the whole visit was initiated because of Mama's fatal illness.

Before my daughter's arrival and prior to her first visit to the hospital, I tried to prepare my mother for the big reunion. They had not seen each other since the last visit, over three years earlier.

My mother was impassive and showed no sign of joy at the prospect of seeing her granddaughter. At that stage I did not mention the imminent arrival of her two great-granddaughters, as I did not want to overexcite her. Although Mama was mentally alert and understood everything that happened around her and with her, nevertheless from all the medication, she slept a great deal, and she was very weak and unresponsive.

I had warned my daughter that her grandmother might not recognize her, or worse still, she might not want the children to come into her room. She was in terrible pain most of the time, relieved only by strong medication.

Natalie came to the hospital on the first Friday morning. I entered my mother's room alone, and did what I had been doing for the previous four months: I smiled, kissed her, arranged her bed, and put the usual *Shabbat* flowers in a vase near her bed. Then I said: "*Anyukam* [*mother* in Hungarian. We now spoke only Hungarian, our original mother tongue, which was much easier for her], a very special visitor has come to see you." She did not show the slightest emotion, neither in words nor in her facial expression. At this moment the door opened and Natalie came in.

Before I go on, I would like to stress an important point. To have them fly over to Australia, the three of them, was not a negligible matter in terms of money or effort. But seeing my mother's face upon the arrival of her beloved grandchild was worth everything.

I left the room, as Natalie had said she would like to be alone with her grandmother.

In the afternoon of that same Friday, Natalie brought the two girls to the hospital. I was not present to witness again the visible joy on my mother's face, but the nurses told me about it the following day. They had not thought it possible to see my mother still gaining so much pleasure from something, in the time remaining to her.

This continued for the entire three weeks, on a daily basis. Either Natalie went in alone or with one of her daughters, or I with another great-granddaughter, or sometimes even all of us, for short periods. With each visit my mother's face gleamed with pleasure. She was able to eat a little bit more and even asked to be sat up for longer periods, especially when she expected the girls to pop in.

The three Friday-afternoon visits turned out to be sort of *erev Shabbat* concerts, with the girls singing *Shabbat* songs in their adorable voices, not only to their great-grandmother, but sometimes even to other patients in the nearby rooms.

And all this in the Wolper Jewish Hospital, which prides itself on being the only *glatt* Jewish hospital in Sydney. The fact that my mother was in Wolper was an extra bonus for the whole family. It was the only place where the girls could freely nibble from everything that was brought in on the neat food trays.

These Friday afternoon choir sessions became a very special time for my gravely ill mother. One could see clearly on her face what joy she experienced hearing the Hebrew songs sung by her great-granddaughters at her bedside in Sydney. My mother's critical condition improved dramatically during their visit. We were all — doctors, nurses and family alike — exalted at the fact that the visit had such a marvelous effect on Mama.

Natalie, who was a graduate in Social Work at Sydney University and had specialized in working with dying patients, had some very serious and honest talks with her grandmother. She touched on the possibility of her pending death and even mentioned the eventual "meeting" at last with her beloved husband, deceased over 45 years ago. It was Natalie's strong belief in Hashem's way that gave her the strength to talk openly about a subject we did not dare to touch.

But no matter what they talked about in their "private sessions," it certainly did not have a negative effect on my mother. If anything, this terminally ill lady seemed to gain tremendous strength from this three-week visit by her grand-daughter and two little great-granddaughters.

The last day of the visit approached, and we were growing very sad with the knowledge that undoubtedly it was the last time my daughter and her beloved grandmother would see each other. But as everything that Natalie does has deeper meanings and motivations stemming from her strong belief, she parted reassuringly from her dying grandmother. After all, it was not the funeral that would result from their visit, but an unforgettable store of memories.

My beloved mother passed away on *Shabbat*, the 18th of the Hebrew month *Av*. Peacefully, with her family close to her.

I phoned Natalie in Jerusalem early Sunday morning. There it was Saturday night, 11:00 P.M. The line was so clear that I could hear her breathing. And then a great sigh. There was silence, total silence, for a brief moment. Then my daughter said: "Mummy, you don't know what this date really means." It was more of a statement than a question. For me, until then, my mother had passed away on Saturday morning, the 19th of August.

But not for my learned, religious family, who find beauty in everything. They try to discover more meaning and gain extra comfort through their knowledge of Judaism.

"I have heard it said that Hashem takes his favorite ones on the *Shabbat*," Natalie told me, "but that it should also be on the 18th!" She paused. "It signifies clearly," she continued, her voice getting really excited, "that our Mama was an *Aishet Chayil* [a woman of valor]. The number 18 is the symbol for *chai*, which is Hebrew for LIFE."

I found this information from my *frum* daughter very comforting.

On the day of the funeral, we were as closely connected with our Jerusalem family as is humanly possible. We lit the first *Yahrtzeit* candle for my mother at exactly the same time — "together" — Natalie in Jerusalem and I in Sydney. It really was as if we were united, heart and soul.

The following morning, the second day of my *shivah* (the period of mourning), the most beautiful FAX was waiting. Natalie wrote: "Dad, I will be eternally grateful for the opportunity you gave me and the girls, to say our good-bye forever to our grandmother."

In the following days we exchanged notes often. It was marvelous to retain the closeness. Natalie said that the four children had been told about their great-grandmother's passing, which they took seriously and without comments. But four-and-a-half-year-old Sarah asked an interesting question. In the preceding months, the children had prayed every single night, after reciting the *Shema*, for a *refuah shelemah* — a complete recovery — for Mama.

"Ima," Sarah asked, "does this mean that we should not *daven* for Mama anymore?"

Natalie told us that all four children had become so accustomed to praying for Mama, that each night following her death, one had to remind the others to leave out that special prayer for Mama's recovery.

I think nothing can demonstrate more how beautiful and how caring is the upbringing of children in religious families.

22   *One of "Those" Moments*

Life is really made up of those rare moments. The rest is all hard, hard work. But some of "those" moments make it all worthwhile. Let me tell you about one of them.

The occasion itself was rare, as for once I had arrived in Jerusalem not on my own but together with my husband. Those days of my visiting alone and having to cope by myself with the *balagan* were over. The seemingly endless cycle of births, *brits*, and births, again and again, was behind us and our "*glatt*" family was on the road back to what we considered "culture."

The four children (*baruch Hashem*) were perfectly spaced: the boys, now seven and six years old, and the girls four-and-a-half and two-and-a-half. Quite civilized ages.

We congratulated ourselves: our children are not after all living in the dark ages; they know what is good for them, for their family, and, last but not least, for us. Natalie and Avi are not that young anymore, both in their late thirties. Not old, but not so young.

Being with them for the first time for the High Holidays*

---

* Please see the next chapter for highlights of the Holidays.

and spending a lot of time in their home in Givat Dat, we felt that at last we were reaping the fruits of having B.T. children. No more diapers, no more babies being sick at the table, no more spilling and burping and fussing. There was no irritating high chair anymore, no perpetual car-cot. All that was over. Now there was only *naches* — and *naches* galore. The children were growing up and we were one big, happy family.

Now we could talk, all of us, together and separately. The children were able to speak English and Hebrew; the boys and Sarah could write. They could all help out in the house, even little Ruthi. They would set the table for *Shabbat* and do any other little chore Ima or Abba asked them to do.

Saba and I had discussed it and we were convinced that our children could see how good it was this way, for them and for us. Natalie was even working again, in her profession. When I had heard about this, I said: "Steven, you see? I told you one day she would take her degree out from somewhere, hidden under all those diapers, and would go out into the world, earn money and be like all other normal Israeli women. She would work, enjoy her family and enjoy life a little."

I thought that we could at last plan some family holidays, go to a hotel for a week, all of us. We would not have to worry about prams and diapers and all those bags and bags full of things that one has to take for babies.

Oh, the marvel of it all! To have four grown-up grandchildren!

I had brought with me a lot of things for my daughter this time. It was so easy to shop for a daughter who had a constant, unchanging waist measurement and dress size. Not like before, when I did not like buying her lovely things because one never knew...

I had searched high and low for a chic denim skirt, as this was what she had asked for a few months before, and I eventually found a beauty in Singapore on our way to Israel. There was also a whole stack of pretty things she hadn't asked for but I knew she would love.

When I went over to her house with the presents, Natalie looked at the skirt and, without even trying it on, said: "Mum, this skirt will be too tight."

"But my darling," I protested, "this is your regular size. This is what you wear, this is what you asked for, remember?"

I must have missed her reply.

I showed her the other things, delicate items in black and white and silver gray that I had bought for her in a beautiful store in Singapore, but she hardly glanced at them. She merely repeated the same words she had used when she saw the skirt: "They will be too tight."

"Well, my darling," I said archly, "to tell you the honest truth, you could lose a few kilograms and you would once more be the same old Natalie with the small waistline." She was not amused.

And I still did not attach any special significance to the matter, perhaps because as the mother of a B.T., I have a sort of built-in self-preservation device. I never want to face the truth when it is presented to me in dribs and drabs. I wait until it is said loud and clear.

It was *erev* Yom Kippur. Not the real *erev* Yom Kippur, but in religious circles *erev* can be almost any length of time preceding a holiday, depending upon the holiday and the extent of the preparations necessary for it. In this case, it was the night before real *erev* Yom Kippur and we had just had a beautiful *Shabbat*. Things were all working out so well between us and Natalie. Why had we been so worried before? We really could hardly remember the difficult times; they were behind us now.

The children could all dress themselves alone, although Ruthi might sometimes put her left shoe on her right foot. They were all becoming responsible little people. It was wonderfully relaxing.

We had walked a lot on this past *Shabbat* with our grandchildren, all of us holding hands in one straight line, marching right down the middle of the street, as there rarely are any cars on the streets of Givat Dat on *Shabbat*. I thought we had made a lovely picture: Saba and Savta and their four grown-up grandchildren, aged two-and-a-half to seven. We had walked, skipped, laughed, and had what I had always envisaged: "grown-up" family fun.

When we had returned, Avi was out attending evening services, and the kids went off to their rooms to play. We sat with Natalie in the living room which previously had housed a playpen, a high chair, and baby toys and had always been in a mess. But now it looked almost as tidy as my own living room, or "lounge-room," as we call it in Australia.

I think I will never learn to keep my mouth shut. I started telling Natalie about the apartment upstairs where we were staying for *Shabbat*. (Whenever possible Natalie would find a vacant apartment somewhere in her building for us to stay in.) The two-bedroom apartment had previously been owned by our very good friends, the Schoens, who have six children, and since it was vacant for the Holiday Natalie had arranged for us to use it temporarily. "You know, Natalie," I said, "I will never cease to be amazed how some of these religious families can live in such a small space and yet the children all look so clean and well-dressed. The Schoens and their six children actually lived in only three rooms."

It was I, stupid me, who actually pointed to the fact that one does not have to have only two children to a room. It was I who started to explain to my B.T. daughter how well-organized a family could still be while living in a small apartment.

Natalie looked triumphant and nodded eagerly in total agreement with me. Then she said: "Dad [she always says Dad first] and Mummy [she always says Mummy when she wants to be nice to me], please listen to me. Tomorrow is *erev* Yom Kippur and I want you two to know what all of us here know already, that our little grown-up family will still be growing and there will be a new little person coming into our family..."

We looked at each other, my husband and I, and our faces could not hide our feelings. We were shocked. We had not expected this to happen to *us*. We really thought we had enough grandchildren; we really thought everything was perfect as it was.

You will never believe what went through my mind at that very moment. Despite my dismay, I suddenly remembered all the beautiful, wonderful families that I knew who had not four, but five children, five beautiful, healthy, grown-up children. But I did not say a word about what I was thinking — I don't know why.

A picture flashed in my head, a picture of me and Natalie packing away the children's outgrown clothing along with Natalie's old maternity outfits. Natalie was standing on a ladder and I was handing things up to her. With each bundle of Sarah's clothing I passed to her, we would say, "This will be for Ruthi," and with each of Yacov's things, we would say, "This will be for Zevi." But when I handed her a bundle of Ruthi's outgrown baby clothes, I would say, "And this will be for nobody," and she would say, "This will be for somebody." We went on like that, telling ourselves our own little stories.

Each tiny outfit I folded gave me heart palpitations. I knew even then, despite my "little stories," that it was not possible at all that I might one day find myself taking down these bundles of newborn baby things for further use in our own family. The thought was too much for me. I felt I could not continue to play this game and that I should tell Natalie outright that I simply could not cope with any more babies.

I stopped myself just in time. I knew exactly what her answer would have been: "But Mummy, they will not be *your* babies. They will be *my* babies." I did not want to hear this often-repeated saying of hers, as I really do know — and she knows that I know — that her babies are *her* babies and *my* baby is SHE!!

So instead of aggravating her and getting into a whole argument on the subject, I said: "Natalie, I think I am getting quite accustomed to the idea of your having more children in the future, but I think I could only cope if you would first have a few years' rest." There, I had said it!

My daughter actually nodded, and told me that she had been thinking along the same lines, for health reasons.

No, she had never said that she would not be having any more children. So why, on this *motza'ei Shabbat*, was I in such a state over her announcement about the expected addition to the family? Because I had really and truly wanted to believe that we had a "meeting of minds" on the subject. I was wrong.

We did not say "*Mazal tov.*" We just walked out of the room. We pretended we had heard nothing. We took the kids and went for another walk.

When we brought the children back, we went up to "our" apartment and packed our things. We knew *Shabbat* was out, but we did not want to wait for *Havdalah*, as we wanted to show that we could not simply be informed about a new grandchild on the way and go on as if nothing had happened.

I must admit, with a feeling of guilt, that we were angry. That old, great anger was back. For all sorts of reasons that made perfectly good sense (to us), we just could not accept this piece of news. We felt betrayed.

We came downstairs and they were all standing around the table finishing the *Havdalah* ceremony. I felt sad that we had not joined them. We told them we were going home. The children looked disappointed and held out their cheeks to be kissed.

I went to each one of them and kissed them passionately, telling them jokingly to "have a good fast" (jokingly, because they were all far too young to be required to fast). And they laughed and said: "You too, Savta." And Saba looked on, a bit surprised that I seemed anything but angry. Yet I most certainly was angry.

And then I came to Natalie, and I did not waver even for a moment. I stooped down and kissed her on both cheeks and said: "Have a good fast or whatever you decide to do in your condition."

What can I say — a mother is always a mother, if she is a *mensch*, that is! And suddenly I was worried that maybe my pregnant daughter should not fast all day.

We were still angry when we got home to Rehavia but we decided not to talk about it. We were planning to attend services in the Great Synagogue for Yom Kippur — this was to be our very first Yom Kippur in Jerusalem, so Steven had bought us tickets. We knew this was no time to be angry. We knew it, yet we were.

Somehow, we could not face the "threat" of another baby, and all it entailed. "You know," I said, "they are going backwards, instead of forwards." I thought that was rather clever at the time. But a few days later, I realized it did not make sense. Having another child is going forwards, in anybody's book.

We went to the Wailing Wall on *erev* Yom Kippur, and there I once more felt very close to Hashem, a feeling hard to describe. When I stand there at the Wall, touching it — even if only with a finger but being in contact — I feel close to *something*, to *Someone*.

I prayed for our daughter to have a healthy baby, and that all should go well. And then I had the strangest sensation: I was standing at the *Kotel*, but my heart and my mind were miles away in the distant past.

I had not thought about "*kapparot*"* since childhood. This

Kapparot literally means "substitutes." The custom represents the symbolic transfer of one's transgressions to the live chicken. The bird is then ritually slaughtered as "punishment" for what are now its "sins," and its flesh donated to the needy. The expression "*Ah kapparah*" is used idiomatically as solace when, for example, a precious possession is destroyed or lost, meaning that its loss should be a "substitute" for a greater, more terrible loss.

Jewish custom, which my father observed all his life, I had forgotten about. How could I? Perhaps because I had always had a sort of love-hate relationship with the whole ritual. Each year I would wait anxiously for my father to hold the live chicken above my head and circle it around — why he did this, I never knew — and, at the same time, I would tremble with fear. I recalled my mother saying to my father: "Dezsokem, you frighten the children with the chicken, be careful," and my father answering each time without fail: "Let them be frightened, but I must do this just as my father did it to me. It is most important to do this before Yom Kippur."

And I had never asked why, and never — until that day in Jerusalem —thought about this strange custom we kept so religiously in our house when I was a child.

Standing near the Wall with my eyes closed, some 45 years after the last time that I associated my father with *kapparot*, and praying as I pray only there, I suddenly felt as if my father were holding the live chicken above my head once more and making those same circling movements, and I could hear my mother saying, "Dezsokem..." I had the sensation that a great weight was lifted off me.

But my story is not yet finished.

You might think that I had stopped being angry altogether and was running to say "*Mazal tov*" to my daughter. Not at all. I was still angry, we were still angry. We still thought they were "doing it" to us again, as if the main reason for having another baby was to shock us with their fanaticism.

We did not say a word on the subject to either of them, not before Yom Kippur or even after the fast. The following morning I was going to mention something to Natalie over the phone about the "unexpected baby," but when I started to tell her about our anger, she asked me to stop as she wanted to say something to me first.

"Mummy," she said, "you know you are really great."

I was taken aback. "Why am I great?" I asked in real surprise.

"Well, I know how shocked you were when you heard the news on *motza'ei Shabbat*, and yet you came and kissed all the children warmly and told them to fast well, which they loved hearing, as you treated them like grown-ups." She paused for a moment and then continued, her voice choked with emotion. "And then you came to me, you bent down, and you kissed me on both cheeks and you said what only you could say: 'Have a good fast or whatever you decide to do in your condition'."

Then we both laughed and cried together, and as always, after every shock (and may Hashem spare us from any *real* shocks!), we understood each other, as only a mother and a daughter can.

So what shall I tell you... Would you believe that I hoped she'd have a girl? Up until that moment I had been saying: "What can be more beautiful than two boys and two girls?" But suddenly I began thinking, What could be more beautiful than two older boys and three little girls?

23   *Our "First" Chaggim*

It was almost the end of *Elul* 5749, and the beginning of a new decade was only a few days away: Rosh Hashanah 5750. Our very first Rosh Hashanah in Israel with our B.T. family.

To me this was nothing short of a miracle, a sort of two-thousand-year-old dream come true.

In fact, Steven and I were to celebrate the entire month of *Tishrei*, which contains not only Rosh Hashanah and Yom Kippur but also the joyful Festivals of *Sukkot* and *Simchat Torah*, together with the whole country, in the Land of the Jews. The feeling was overwhelming!

From my early childhood, the Festivals have meant a great deal to me. There was nothing new about knowingly and wholeheartedly observing them, just as we had done in Hungary in our own traditional way,* and later in Australia. For over 41 years in our home there, we had gathered at our family table, to duly observe the beautiful customs of each Festival.

* I have belatedly learned that my understanding of "traditional" differed from that of other people. More details about my upbringing, which I think will interest you, appear in the chapters entitled "Legacy" and "Full Circle."

My table on *erev* Rosh Hashanah, that I set first under my mother's supervision and later on with my daughter's help, was noted for its traditional splendor, replete with the special dishes of honey to make the coming year sweet; the round, sweet challah; the apples my husband would peel and slice in his orderly manner, then dip in the honey and hand to each of us.

I had a set Rosh Hashanah menu consisting of all the traditional foods, excluding only the rather Yiddish-sounding gefilte fish. We somehow never ever thought of making or even buying it. We just did not relate to that sort of food.

But I did incorporate in my menu two new additions: a huge bowl of prunes, apples and dried apricots, and *tzimmes* — a sweet cooked-carrot dish. I had learned to prepare these from my new South African Jewish friends, who knew of and routinely prepared many more Jewish dishes than we Hungarian Jews did. My dear mother, may she rest in peace, never failed to comment in a slightly disapproving tone of voice: "In Budapest we never had these Yiddish dishes. Where did you get the idea to cook them?"

Out of respect for my mother and because of my son and my brother's family, I could not abandon the tradition of cooking and baking and setting the table for Rosh Hashanah. As long as I had my family in Australia, I knew where my place was.

With each year the thought of being with my ever-growing family in the Orthodox environment of Givat Dat became more tempting. I often moaned: "I wish I could be in Jerusalem for the *Chaggim.*" And as we prayed in the big Central Synagogue in Sydney, where hundreds of grandparents stood proudly alongside their elegantly dressed (overdressed) grandsons or granddaughters, my thoughts wandered to my religious family in Jerusalem. Often, with tears of envy in my eyes, I stood there thinking: "If only I could stand in the synagogue holding hands with my two grandsons and two granddaughters, if only..."

Sometimes wishes are granted, and mine was. I had finally made it to Israel for the High Holidays. The reason for this was that structurally our family had changed. My dear mother had died a few weeks before, my brother and his family had travel plans, and last but not least, my son was in Frankfurt doing a year of research towards his Ph.D. in philosophy. And so my husband and I had made great haste to join our family in Israel. At last!

The previous weeks had been truly hectic and I was exhausted as always from the long journey, so I decided I would take it easy for a good few days. For the first time in my married life, I would not have to set the festive table, I would not be the hostess of numerous guests. We would be celebrating in Givat Dat, as guests of Natalie and her family.

I basked in this glorious, luxurious feeling of nothingness as we awoke on the first Friday morning, without any worries about the coming Rosh Hashanah festivities.

My daughter had found accommodation for us during the Holidays in the building where they live. The apartment we were to stay in belonged to a family that would be away for the Holiday, and it was fully furnished. All we had to do was bring our few personal belongings. Natalie would arrange everything else. She had even written to us to tell us not to bother about our own prayer books. She would get for us the same kind we always used, with English translation.

Naturally we had agreed to everything. After all, what could be better? We had earned our keep; now it was our daughter's turn to do something for us.

We were really pampered from the first moment on. Natalie suggested that we take it easy over the first *Shabbat* and not come out to Givat Dat. There would be plenty of time for us to be together, she said, and we were overjoyed at her consideration. Although we adore being with them and our grandchildren for *Shabbat*, we do prefer to sleep in our own good, comfortable, king-size beds, especially just after the long journey from Australia.

Natalie supplied all the food for us for our first *Shabbat*. She cooked, baked and brought all the things over to our place, and even lent us their (our) car in order to drive to Givat Dat on *motza'ei Shabbat*.

The car was really our car, but as we were not in Israel most of the time to use it, we naturally "lent" it to them. This was gradually becoming a bit of a problem, as they had come to need it so much that it was difficult for them to get along without it. So we, in our wisdom, usually rented a car for ourselves for the duration of our stay — our contribution to *shalom bayit*.

The children were most unhappy that we were not coming to stay with them, but our understanding daughter explained to them with great patience how tired their Saba and Savta were and how much they needed this rest on their first *Shabbat*.

What glorious times were waiting for us! we told ourselves. We had finally made it: our child considered our needs, understood them and even catered to them. Had we ever doubted that such times would come? Had we ever doubted that after the initial struggle, we parents of B.T.s would receive our rewards, at last?

Well, if we had, we were soon to be proven wrong. Deliciously wrong.

Our *Shabbat* was marvelously restful. We strolled about, we slept in the afternoon, and our best friends from Tel Aviv arrived, unexpectedly, to spend *motza'ei Shabbat* with us in Jerusalem. We told them that as soon as *Shabbat* was over, we were going to see the children. And also to return THE car. They laughed and said they would go with us and drive us back home.

We naturally left not a minute sooner than 6:12 P.M., when *Shabbat* officially ended. We hoped we had timed it well so as to reach Givat Dat in time for *Havdalah*.

As we drove up to their building and got out of the car, I

noticed Natalie at the window watching out for our arrival. I knocked on the door and the children asked in chorus: "*Mi zeh?*" ("Who's there?")

"It is Saba and Savta!" I replied, and the door flew open and they were kissing us, hugging us, obviously overjoyed to see us.

They love our Tel Aviv friends like family. In fact they call the husband Saba Bulu, a very original and well-chosen name given him by our own grandson, and the wife they call simply "Agi" as she too possesses the same rather unoriginal Hungarian name as I do. The welcome to all four of us was great.

We entered the house. After a few minutes and still no sign of Natalie, I turned to the children and asked: "Was it not Ima looking out of the kitchen window just now?"

The children replied: "Yes, it was."

I felt a bit strange asking: "So where is she now?" In place of an answer, Natalie came out of the bedroom and without any emotional signs of welcome, she smile-lessly greeted us. All of us in one bunch.

I might be oversensitive, but somehow I expected a happier welcome on our first *motza'ei Shabbat* in their house. I hid my disappointment and immediately adopted my happy tone of voice: "Isn't it marvelous to come into the house and be welcomed with so much love from the children!"

Natalie did not react. I looked at her and again I had this nagging thought: "What does not please her, why does she look unfriendly already — the very first time we enter the house?"

Avi returned from evening services. He at least seemed happy to see us all, I observed with a sigh of relief. Natalie walked in and out of the kitchen and dining room, and still not a word or a question escaped her lips.

Then she looked at us and, deliberately over-pronouncing each word, she asked: "Are you ready to hear *Havdalah* with us now?"

I, in my oversensitivity, felt a certain cutting edge in her tone of questioning but Saba and the others all seemed unaware of it and just happy to be there and to do whatever was next on the agenda. I had a definite feeling that something was the matter with my daughter. But what could it be? I mean, we had not been there long enough to have done or said something, *anything*, wrong. Why did I feel an atmosphere of resentment towards us?

I tried to smile and hoped I did not reveal my true feelings of anxiety. We all joined in *Havdalah*, sniffing the spice-box and wishing one another a loud and enthusiastic "*Shavua tov.*" I turned to Natalie and repeated this beautiful wish for a good week to come, but again there was no response from her at all. By then, I knew something was the matter, but what?

She offered cakes and drinks, to which I replied: "Oh, don't worry about us. We just wanted to see you and the children for a few minutes and hear *Havdalah*, but we are going back to our place for supper." Then I added: "We knew the children had to go to bed soon after *Shabbat*; that is why we hurried to catch them."

No matter what I said, I felt it was the wrong thing. I was quite distressed at the hostility in my daughter's behavior, but decided I must not let my feelings show. I would remain composed and just hope it would pass.

We kissed the children good night and walked towards the door. Natalie was standing firmly at a distance. There was no hope of her running towards me and maybe kissing me good night, something I would have welcomed dearly on that first visit to her home, seeing them all once more. But she did not move, she did not kiss me or her father or our friends. I left most discontented, but did not say a word about it. Not then or later on that night.

The next day was Sunday, which to me at first always feels like Monday, since in Israel it is a regular weekday. I was ready to start a most energetic day of cleaning and getting my own house in order.

Around nine o'clock the phone rang and it was Natalie. She had been working since eight o'clock in the morning, in her wonderful new job as a supervisor of kindergarten teachers.

Over the telephone, she sounded exactly like a supervisor should: stern, serious and unemotional — with me, her mother, on this long-awaited visit in Israel. But I was determined not to take any notice of her "professional" voice. I spoke to her as one speaks to one's own child. "Good morning, my darling," I said. "How are you? Are you in a better mood this morning than you were last night?"

If I had tried, I could not have started the conversation more stupidly. It was an open invitation for further, continued unpleasantness. I was just going to take it all back, when Natalie said in a humorless voice: "Mum, I am not in any better or worse mood than I was last night. As you know, with you [and she pronounced this *you* as if it were something terrible] one never knows where one stands."

I was speechless. What on earth was she talking about? I simply had to ask: "My darling, what do you mean?"

The reply came fast. "You know very well what I mean. Just think a bit harder."

I was really at a loss as I had no idea what she meant. So I asked her again. "Natalie, I *don't* know what you mean. Have we done something to upset you, I or Daddy?" knowing that we certainly had done nothing of the kind.

"Oh Mum, come *on*," she groaned into the telephone. "You arrived last night without calling beforehand to say you were bringing friends, just walked in on us, all four of you, without our knowing where you were coming from or... anything."

Now I understood. Well, I was ready with an answer this time! She was not going to start off like that with me, not when I was really innocent and had actually been so considerate of her needs. This time my tone of voice was sharp.

"Now you listen to me for once," I said. "The days are over when you can attack me like this. You should know by now that I would not come from anywhere else but from home, or at any other time but after *Shabbat* was over. I felt no need to call you in advance and ask for a gold-rimmed invitation to come and kiss our grandchildren on our first *motza'ei Shabbat.* You knew we were coming. Neither do I need your permission to bring our and your best friends along. I would appreciate it very much if you would from now on just think before you start accusing me of things that are only in your imagination. You must trust me just as much as I trust you."

There was a silence on the line, and then something wonderful happened. Natalie's voice became soft and tender as she said: "Mummy, you must understand me. I still worry so much about the things you are used to doing when you are not with us. I thought, and wrongly so, that you might have driven down to Tel Aviv, maybe even to the beach with them, and had just returned for the evening. But I am sorry. I was wrong. I should have known that you would not do things like that anymore."

Oh, how marvelous, how truly wonderful, when one can talk like a mother with one's child. Mother and daughter, B.T. daughter and a mother who has learned to do things acceptable to her child. This was an important moment in our lives, both our lives: we had declared our mutual trust.

Natalie and I were now on equal terms with each other. We could communicate as mature adults and treat one another as equals. We could accept and respect each other, with all our differences. But I must warn you, my readers, that this can only be achieved successfully when you have a clear conscience and are fully aware of what is expected of you, as by now, *baruch Hashem*, I am.

It was good to put the phone down with no hostility left between us.

Later in the day Natalie called again, this time from home, and asked me politely if I would mind going over the coming big week's program with her. "Not at all," I said, and pulled over a chair to seat myself in comfort, as it sounded as though I was in for something lengthy.

I was not far wrong. Natalie came straight to the point. "Mummy, you do feel rested enough to swing into action during the coming week, don't you?" she asked, already assuming my positive reply. What use would it be even to consider replying in the negative when I knew, deep down, that my daughter expected me to be swinging into action as of that very *moment*?

My answer was also to the point. "*Ein brerah*," I said. "There is no choice. I am ready."

And Natalie shifted into her drill-sergeant mode. "So we will do the usual," she said (not asking anymore). "I make the soup and the cakes and you cook the middle part of the meals."

I had no time to start calculating how many "middle parts" there would be in the next days with *erev* Rosh Hashanah included, but I dared at least to ask: "How many will there be for each middle-part of the meals?"

Natalie laughed, a hearty and friendly laugh. "Good question, Mummy."

I was so pleased that she agreed that my curiosity was not unreasonable. I laughed with her and asked again: "So, how many people are expected for *erev* Rosh Hashanah, and how many for each lunch and dinner? I hope you won't have any living-in guests as well, will you?" The answer to the last question was a definite no, but to the one about how many, she was not quite sure yet. We were going to be a big, happy family.

Was it not I who had run away from Australia, out of sheer loneliness? Was it not I who had dreamed about our "family *Chaggim*"? "Okay, my girl," I told myself, "just shut up and take the orders as they come, and in between you can thank Hashem for giving you the *naches* of planning, cooking and working for a big family holiday."

And that is exactly what I did.

I really had to hold myself back from laughing as my daughter lectured me on the "*simanim*" — the special symbolic dishes served at the Rosh Hashanah meal. She spoke in her highly instructive voice about things that *I* had taught *her* all about. After all, it was at home in Australia, on our dining room table, that she had observed for years the beautiful preparations for the Rosh Hashanah festivities. I knew that there was no comparison between our traditional observance and her Orthodox observance, but she could not take away the credit which was due initially to me, her mother, who had carefully set the table each year with (I thought) all the "*simanim*" that there should be for Rosh Hashanah. Maybe we did not say the *berachot* as diligently and properly, but "*simanim*" there were plenty of.

I did not want to interrupt the flow of her speech, so I sat and listened and held back my laughter. But in the end I could not let it go completely unremarked. When Natalie's lecture was exhausted, and she paused after the long teaching session, I quietly mentioned: "You know, my darling, in our home we too celebrated all the Rosh Hashanah festivities, with exactly the same '*simanim*'."

Natalie was quiet for a moment and then said, to my great surprise and joy, "You know, Mummy, you may be right!" And again there was total harmony between us.

I gave a short run-down on the shops where I was going to buy the food, just in case, as in the old *shemittah* days, I might run into serious troubles. But all was accepted. When I said I would buy all the fruit and vegetables at my local greengrocer on Aza Street, I heard a quiet murmur on the line, something Natalie was saying to herself. I asked: "You're sure this will be all right with you?" And I heard the murmuring voice again, this time saying: "Yes, yes, it will be. I just have to '*miser*' it, that's all."

I knew this word. Of course I knew it, but I was not quite on the ball yet, so I repeated it and asked: "What were you going to do with it? Would you say it and spell it for me?" I was actually trying to memorize this word, so as to use it properly in my book. I confess this was my ulterior motive.

Suddenly my daughter became impatient, angry with me. "Look, Mum, would you mind not writing your book just now, certainly not before the *Chaggim*? There are just too many much more important things to concentrate on now than your famous book."

I must say I had to agree with her on this point, but still I did not want to be controlled all the time. And besides, I did want to jot down the word she had used.

I tried again: "I understand this is not the time for writing the book, but first, during the time it took you to reprimand me, you could have given me the word. And second, I thought you would love for me to finish the book as soon as possible. So you must understand me, I don't let good words pass me by, no matter what."

I must tell you that Natalie is actually very keen on my writing this book. She inspires me and motivates me all the time. It is she who says how proud she will be when my book is published. In Jerusalem, and especially to her friends in Givat Dat — where I have over the years become a sort of strange landmark that comes and goes, does not change very much from visit to visit but certainly does not ever offend anybody or anything as far as religious standards are concerned — she will, when introducing me, say: "This is my mother — you know, the woman who wrote THAT BOOK!"

So Natalie controlled her impatience long enough to explain that to "*miser*," which is *their* way of pronouncing the Hebrew word *ma'aser*, means "to tithe." Produce of the Land of Israel must be tithed as a symbolic reminder of the days when the Holy Temple stood. The major produce growers' as-sociations and supermarket chains have Rabbinic supervisors who see to this, but many Orthodox Jews do not rely on this tithing and prefer to do it themselves.

All I can say is that it was the most beautiful and unforget-table Rosh Hashanah of my life. It was all worth waiting for, I can assure you! Absolutely marvelous — we, our B.T. family, our grandchildren, and the atmosphere around us. I would not, could not, add or take away a thing from it. It was just perfect.

Forget your own traditional Rosh Hashanah, as I must too. I might have boasted about how we observed Rosh Hashanah in our home in Australia, with "simanim" and all, but how wrong I was! We hardly touched the surface of it all. Just listen and eat your hearts out, all you parents of B.T.s who think you want to miss out on all this fun. Yes, I said FUN, as this is what it was.

Did I say we knew all about the symbolic dishes? Not only did we have at least four new "simanim" but we had a gold-printed chart from the local yeshiva bearing very best wishes to us personally for Rosh Hashanah from the Rosh Yeshivah himself, and a detailed program of how to conduct a "glatt" Rosh Hashanah Festival.

Did I think we had it all when I said honey, apples, and the ceremonial challah at the meal? Well, listen to this!

Not only was the challah sweet, round and delicious, but it was baked by my very own daughter! I have never in my whole life tasted anything as sweet and delicious as the challah my daughter's hands produced. You should have heard the children praising their Ima. And I thought: I might have consid-ered myself a very good mother, but how do I compare with my daughter? Would it ever have entered my head to bake my own challah? Never.

Then, in addition to the honey and the apple slices, there

were black-eye beans on one plate (delicious!), and leeks on another, each with its own special prayer, invoking Hashem's blessing for the coming year.

Then there was spinach, which luckily I love, and the *berachah* for this was: "May it be Your will that our enemies disappear." I was amazed at how very topical this prayer still is, and especially in Israel. Then came dates, and a gourd, which did not taste very good, but the *berachah* made up for it: "May it be Your will to tear up our bad verdict, and may our good merits be called out before You."*

Here I must stop and tell you something: Eating these "*simanim*" and reciting the *berachot*, I felt a kind of pride, a humble gratitude, to be able to take part in this Festival. With each *berachah* I felt better. And I felt very sorry about having missed all this, the very essence of it, in all our previous Rosh Hashanah dinners.

Next came the fish. The head of the fish, with eyeballs and all, I could have done without, but again the blessing made up for it.

"Natalie," I said, "eating all these '*simanim*' and your fantastic challah dipped in honey, I feel as if I have already eaten a whole meal."

She smiled back and said: "We have not even scratched the surface yet!" And she wasn't kidding.

It was a long, memorable meal. The children participated in everything. They did not leave the table. They loved having us there — you could see it in their shining eyes and in the way they kept looking at us. Oh, how lucky is the parent who does not miss out on all of this. But for our "*glatt*" daughter, *we* could have missed out on it all. And I mean every word of this.

I do not want to write in chronological order about how we spent the next three weeks of Festivals in Jerusalem, in Givat

*The blessings are each a play on the Hebrew names of the various symbolic foods.

Dat and with our B.T. family. I will only write about the high points of joy and new discoveries. Apparently, it does not matter how old one is: there is always room for learning.

The weather was perfect. In fact it reminded me a bit of my childhood Rosh Hashanahs in Hungary, as there too it was early autumn and not early spring as it is in Australia. This was an additional new-found pleasure: being back at last to what we ex-Europeans think of as normal seasons.

The quietness of the streets, the feeling that we all — each and every one of us — were celebrating Rosh Hashanah, was the most exciting new experience. When we celebrated it every previous year in the *Galut* (the Diaspora), the cars roaring around us, our neighbor probably mowing his lawn while we walked to the synagogue all dressed up for the occasion, people stared at us, probably wondering: "What are all these people doing so elegantly dressed on an ordinary weekday?"

We were always a minority, outsiders, on every one of my previous Rosh Hashanahs. Now, for the first time in my life, I felt that I belonged. And not only did I belong, but I belonged to a religious family, an Orthodox, learned family: my own family. I cannot emphasize enough to you, my perhaps still skeptical reader, what a GREAT feeling this can be. At least it was for me. The greatest!

Across the way from my daughter's apartment building there are beautiful villas, one of which belongs to a Rabbi with a large family. On the lower level of his house, he built himself a private synagogue, a small *"daven*ing place," as my daughter calls it.

You cannot imagine what this can mean to a family like ours. Here I include every member of the family. Take Avi. Though he usually *daven*s at the big yeshiva a few blocks away, if by any chance he oversleeps or arrives home a little bit late, all he has to do is go across the road for services. To Natalie the little synagogue is a constant source of spiritual stimulation as she can just "tune in" to all the praying while standing in her kitchen doing whatever she has to do. For the children it is the best, as they can sit in the window seat and sing every song together with the congregation.

And last, but not least, it was very convenient for Saba and Savta, still a bit tired from the long trip and also from the *erev* Rosh Hashanah preparations. Our lodging was on the second floor of Natalie's building and directly opposite this prayer house. All we had to do was open the window wide, stand with our prayer books in our hands and follow every word of one of the most meaningful prayers: "*Avinu Malkenu*." I stood there at the window, and my tears just kept on falling...

Now I must tell you something strange about myself. I never had a *sukkah* — not in Hungary, where I vaguely remember having heard the expression "*satoros unnep*," meaning a Festival connected with tents, but I never knew why or what it represented. Neither did we have one in Australia. Although there we were much more conscious of this Festival, we were never involved in it enough to either go to synagogue on this day or have our own *sukkah*. In retrospect I realize how easy it would have been in our tropical garden in Sydney. But we did not think of building one.

Possibly the children did go to the synagogue once or twice and did see a *sukkah*, but they were never impressed enough to ask: "Could we have our own, please?" But I know these things stem from the atmosphere in the home, and from the mother. Obviously I was far removed from "old-fashioned" things such as building one's own *sukkah*.

But — and this is interesting — in the past few years, since my daughter became a B.T., I have tried (sometimes quite desperately) to get invited to the home of friends who might have a *sukkah* (not that there were many of these). I never knew much about the actual Festival itself; only the outward things, the ones the eyes could take in. No more.

So imagine how this woman, this Savta, felt upon entering

our own family *sukkah* for the very first time in her life. I simply cannot put it into words, it was so moving. It made up for every past *Sukkot* Festival when I was ignorant and uninterested. But, as they say, it is never too late! *Baruch Hashem*.

There was tremendous excitement in my daughter's house for days before, but I thought they were probably exaggerating, as they often did. I can still fall into my nasty old habit of thinking that they overreact.

Well, maybe they did, but on a *chag* like *Sukkot* there is nothing better than to go to extremes — to want to be extremely happy. That is the name of the game. It is a *commandment* to rejoice on this holiday.

The day before the Festival, Natalie said to me: "Avi and I want you to come for all the meals, to spend as much time as possible with us in our *sukkah*." I must admit that in my ignorance I did not know that one is supposed to have every meal in the *sukkah*!

"Mummy," she continued, "you are in for a great surprise, as you have never seen what *Sukkot* is really all about."

I was more than surprised; I was ecstatic!

The *sukkah* was in the small garden just outside Natalie's apartment. That year, *Shabbat* and *Sukkot* coincided, so preholiday excitement was even greater than usual.

We arrived an hour before *Shabbat*. It was still light outside and a gentle autumn breeze was blowing. Pleasant, mild weather. The children, all four of them, were outside on the street awaiting our arrival, all dressed elegantly; the boys in their navy outfits, and the girls wearing identical pink dresses, their hair tied back with *Shabbat* ribbons and fancy, lacy hairclips. They looked just beautiful.

Arriving and seeing them was already "*dayenu*" (enough) for me, and we had not yet entered the *sukkah*. Driving through Givat Dat had given us an interesting preview, as there were literally *thousands* of sukkahs — on balconies, in gardens, on the sidewalks. Everybody had one.

On the street in front of our family's building was a huge *sukkah*, and our eyes were drawn to it. The children, all four of them, were now clutching our hands and pulling us, saying: "Come on, don't look at other *sukkahs*. Come and see *ours!*" We walked with them the few steps down into the garden, and I can tell you, they were right! I had not seen anything until I saw OURS!

I was completely overwhelmed as we walked into it with our grandchildren squealing with joy and excitement, thrilled to be showing their *sukkah* to their Saba and Savta.

Our *sukkah* was like a small self-contained apartment. It had everything you needed for comfort, at least for the seven days. There were walls and a proper "door," which could be opened and shut in an ingenious way, all made of colorful cotton materials. The roof was made of leafy branches.

The walls were covered with pictures, artwork of all kinds, made by our grandchildren in *Cheder* and *gan*, all done with their own little hands. This was really the most fantastic sight. They did not know which one to show me first and I certainly could not have looked on with more amazement. Everything had a symbolic meaning and I listened in wonder at all the things these children knew, things I had never even heard about before.

The "room" contained the dining-room table, a sort of buffet, lots of chairs, two armchairs, a narrow sofa bed in the corner with colorful cushions on it, and a high table covered with a tablecloth. On this the candles were set up, one large candelabrum for Natalie to light and one small one for me.

And then I noticed the tablecloth under the candlesticks, and for a moment I felt quite faint. My heart started to beat so fast that I had to force myself to stay calm. Well, as calm as I am capable of being.

I looked at the faded white, hand-embroidered tablecloth and I had to close my eyes in order to really capture the memory that this old cloth evoked. Svabhegy, our summer place, in 1939 or perhaps a bit later on. The good old times, our beautiful summer days. Our magnificent garden with tables and chairs everywhere, to sit, to rest, to lounge about.

I think it was under the huge walnut tree that we had a square table and on it, this fine linen tablecloth. My father would be dozing on a deck chair, and I would wait in anticipation for a nut to fall from the tree (as often happened) and wake him up. And when this happened we always laughed and laughed so happily... A lifetime ago, but I could see it so clearly as I stood with my eyes closed and the thoughts went zig-zagging in my brain. Oh, these beautiful memories! I so loved to recapture them.

But the children were impatient and cried: "Savta, Savta, don't close your eyes. Look, Ruthi made this drawing all by herself in her *gan*." And they showed me this artwork, a drawing entitled "Our *Sukkah*" and Ruthi ran to me and translated for me what her drawing meant. Just two-and-a-half years old, and already she knows so much.

Suddenly I felt quite dizzy. It was too much for the moment. I could not contain it in myself and I looked around for Natalie. Our eyes met and she came over and put her arms around me, saying: "Yes, I know. It is the tablecloth your grandmother made with her own hands, for your 'Svabhegyi Villa'. You often told me about it, and I knew you would like it used today in our *sukkah*."

I was not ashamed to cry openly upon entering my first *sukkah*. The children were a bit bewildered and asked: "Why is Savta crying? Does she not like our *sukkah*?"

But Ima assured them: "Oh no, children, Savta loves our *sukkah* very much. She is crying only from happiness. Sometimes it is the most wonderful feeling to cry from happiness."

And this was exactly what I was doing.

How to Be a Pro

Three major events made it possible for me to spend more time in Israel during the past year than I did in Australia. First, the sad, but not unexpected passing of my mother. It made me realize how strongly she had kept our family together, especially during the Jewish holidays. Once she was no longer there, we had even more reason to spend all the Jewish Festivals in Israel.

The second major event, as I mentioned earlier, was our son's studies abroad. His presence so far from Australia and yet so close to Israel provided a marvelous opportunity to bring the whole family together for the first time in Jerusalem for *Pesach*.

And last but not least, the impending birth of our fifth grandchild: Natalie was entering her eighth month of pregnancy and I longed to be with her to help out in any way I could.

After a lot of persuasion, my husband acceded to my plea to arrive in Jerusalem in time for *Purim*, and not wait until *Pesach*. The children had asked on the phone in their most irresistable voices: "Savta, if you miss us so much, why don't you just come?" And I discovered that I really had no excuse at all. So I came.

There had never been such a small span of time between my visits as there was this time. Only two months since our previous visit, and I was on a plane again, headed for Jerusalem. As I get older (and I sometimes do feel the years not creeping but running ahead), I become increasingly aware of the importance of being healthy, mobile and enthusiastic. These are a treasure we must make the most of while we can.

My son-in-law picked me up at the airport alone. It was a stormy day so Natalie had decided to wait for me at home. This in itself was no cause for concern, but when I saw her at last I was taken aback by her appearance. Although I had seen her during her previous pregnancies, I had never seen her looking so heavy and big.

I made no comment and tried to conceal my dismay.

Natalie's living room was in a chaotic state, with numerous pieces of fabric and ribbons all over the place, and a sewing machine on the table. "Mummy, look — your dream has come true!" Natalie proudly explained. "At last I am putting the sewing machine to good use, and I love it! Look at all the marvelous things that I made for the children for *Purim*. You will be so proud. I too will be one of those pregnant, happy mothers with lots of children, displaying none other but homemade *Purim* costumes. Remember last year, the lovely chemist lady you were so impressed with, the one with lots of children and all the homemade costumes? Well, listen to this: she has just had her tenth baby!"

That was all I needed to be greeted with as an arrival booster. After all the speeches my husband and I had rehearsed! How we would, after the birth of Number Five (and naturally not a minute before), propound our very valid and serious arguments to make them see that five children are the very maximum for anybody, and certainly for our family. We knew this and they must know it too.

My husband and I were determined to explain to them that

there simply should not be another baby after this round figure of five, and that to have five healthy wonderful children was really the most any parent could wish for. But I had not even arrived at my own front door, when those well-rehearsed speeches disappeared with the wind, out, superseded, finished. Why else would my daughter be so terribly impressed with the lovely chemist lady (whom I do remember, of course) who had just had her tenth baby and was probably already sitting up in her hospital bed and sewing *Purim* costumes while feeding Number Ten.

There was certainly no sense in even thinking of saying anything on that first night, but somehow I knew all future nights or days could also be excluded. There is simply nothing we parents can say or do regarding the number of offspring our B.T. children will produce. We have to get this into our heads once and for all.

I was not ready, physically or emotionally, for a Givat Dat *Shabbat* after my very long and exhausting flight from Australia, so Avi drove me to Rehavia.

And so there I was once more, in my own place in Jerusalem, which seemed with each visit to be more tatty, more run down, and more in need of a good all-round overhaul. Maybe after the baby!

That is what we had been saying for the past nine years — that we should do some renovating, so that I won't have to break my back washing our dishes in the solitary, very low, tiny sink. And maybe we could put in another bathroom, for when the children visit...

One glance around the apartment convinced me that the day had come. I decided, with so much time on my hands this visit, there was no sense postponing the renovations. We would rent a small apartment nearby for us to live in while the work was under way. And I would schedule the move from our place to the rental for the day after Natalie's due date. My decision made, I went to bed and slept 'round the clock.

Natalie called on Sunday morning, her voice cheerful, to suggest we meet in town and that I go with her to the doctor and see the ultrasound examination. I must say, my daughter really does know what would make her mother jump out of bed on a cold Sunday morning. No invitation could have been sweeter to me than this one from my heavily pregnant daughter.

We arranged to meet at 11:15 and I hurried to arrive at the appointed spot before she did. I love waiting for my daughter. In fact, one of the many things that I miss so painfully in Sydney is meeting Natalie and having the kind of mother-and-daughter outing that we have in Jerusalem.

Natalie appeared on the dot at 11:15, and she looked radiantly happy to see me standing there waiting for her. She put her arm in mine, kissed me, and we proceeded to the doctor. As we walked I could not help but notice this very strange sight: my daughter was wearing slippers — blue flannel, backless slippers. "Darling, why are you wearing slippers on the street?" I asked automatically.

She smiled and replied matter-of-factly that they were not slippers; they were the only kind of comfortable thing she could walk in.

I realized immediately that if in the days, weeks, months to come I was to have peace and love, arm-in-arm kissing reunions, a harmonious *Pesach* and a happy Number Five delivery, I would have to watch every single word I uttered. I would have to think before I made a single sound, as one unfortunate comment, one reminder of something that was relevant last year, but obviously is not anymore, would wreck everything for the rest of the time. I knew this, and decided to act accordingly.

I squeezed her arm in mine, and said: "But of course you should wear whatever is most comfortable for you. After all we were warned already last time that your varicose veins would play havoc with you in your next pregnancy. How could I forget?"

And though I felt positively sick at the thought that my once glamorous daughter now walked in heavy elastic stockings in the most impossible shade of brown, and in blue flannel slippers, for an outing in the city to the doctor, I did not add one solitary negative remark.

Though I am aware that the rules I made for myself apply equally to all mothers of married daughters, I feel they are more applicable to mothers of sensitive B.T.s.

This ban on comments prevailed right through the following days. I was constantly aware that this pregnancy was causing quite of lot of discomfort to my daughter, who was still holding down a part-time job, had her four children to dress, feed and send off to school, kindergarten and preschool, ran a reasonable household and still remained pretty cheerful.

And what could I — this Savta with her so-called Australian civilization, a foreigner with outdated habits and ideas about hygiene and do's and don'ts about how people should look, dress, live — say? As if I were such an authority! Well, I am certainly no authority in the B.T. world, and I have learned that the less I say, the better off I am, as after all, who needs my opinions, when there is the whole Circle, with their know-how, to consult?

Who is to say, for example, that children should not bathe together, in perfect hilarious harmony? I, with my old-fashioned notions of one child to a bathtub? I did not say a word or blink an eye when I was asked to give the four children baths — the two girls together and the two boys together — and to let them wash each other while I just sat there and had family fun with them. What was I to gain by saying: "But my darling, I would gladly bathe them all separately"?

All my preconceived notions were kept to myself. And it was so that we glided through the first week without a bad word between us. But let me tell you, I was exhausted from the sheer frustration of it!

The supreme test came when Natalie went to the obstetrician one evening and came home pretty downhearted. "Is everything all right?" I asked.

At first Natalie just sat and stared at the collection of *Purim* costumes for her children. I thought she might be worried about something and was hesitating to tell me. I waited. "Well, Mum," she said at last, "my legs are very swollen, and I must elevate them for twenty minutes three times a day."

You might think that a mother would take advantage of the opportunity to say: "Did I not warn you during your last pregnancy that you would have a bad time if you considered another baby?" But not I. Not a word came out of my sealed lips. I was in fact hanging on every word and waiting for those she was yet to utter, as I sensed with a mother's intuition that this was not all the bad news.

It was not. She had also been told that her blood pressure was high. She was to be very careful, or she might have to remain in bed for a while. She did not tell me this so that I would know I would be working double shifts; I already knew this for myself. She told me about it simply because I am her mother. And because she trusted me not to say: "I told you so."

As I had been proven right, I could stupidly have opened my mouth and lost my B.T. daughter. You should know, mothers, that your B.T. daughters know all about the risks in advance and it still does not deter them from pregnancies. Words will not make it any less uncomfortable for them or influence the possibility of further pregnancies.

Learn this, and you will be well on the road to becoming a professional mother of a B.T., like me. Your B.T. knows all the pros and cons. And still goes on having babies...

Healthy, beautiful, clever, babies — with Hashem's help (and yours).

25   *"This Year in Yerushalayim"*

We had never before been in Israel at Passover time. It was the only Festival left that we had never celebrated with Natalie and her family.

Passover seems to me to be the one Jewish holiday enjoyed even by secular people who still want to preserve some Jewish traditions. Even if they do not go to the synagogue as well, *Seder* night is something that takes them right back to their grandparents' home, where this beautiful Festival was most likely observed one way or another — just as was the case with my family in Hungary, and later with our family in Sydney.

In all our years in Australia, from the first to the forty-first, we celebrated *Seder* night in our own inimitable fashion, with our family around our dining room table.

And now, at last, I was to have the tremendous privilege of celebrating *Pesach* in Jerusalem. For 2,000 years the Jewish people have prayed for this, so it was not to be taken lightly.

The pre-*Pesach* mood in Israel is contagious. There is no set date for what religious people call "*erev Pesach*," as preparations may commence even months in advance, but certainly any time right after *Purim* qualifies. The whole city, in fact the whole country, was anticipating *Pesach* — shopping, cleaning, more shopping, more cleaning. That thought gave me a marvelous feeling.

So much did the local mood affect me too, that I wrote to my husband who was due to arrive six days before the holiday: "I wish you could come a few days earlier, as you will be arriving right on *erev Pesach*."

My husband, very much surprised, immediately wrote back, asking: "Do I have the dates wrong? I was under the impression that *erev Pesach* is on Monday night, and my arrival date is on the previous Thursday. Please advise urgently."

I laughed and replied: "Your arrival date is okay as *Seder* night is on Monday, but here everything is *already erev Pesach!*" Only after his arrival in Jerusalem did he understand what I had meant.

I have a very wise friend here in Israel. She herself is secular, but she respects my daughter's religious ways totally. She has often been an effective intermediary between Natalie and me. She called me a few days before *Pesach* and gave me the following advice: "Do *everything* that your daughter suggests, no matter how ridiculous it might sound or seem to you. There is no use arguing about anything."

Little did I know that her advice would become immeasurably valuable within twenty-four hours, when Natalie arrived at my place, sat down opposite me in the kitchen, and said: "Mummy, we would like to sell your kitchen. Clean all the surfaces and tape all the cabinets closed, as your kitchen, for the entire week of *Pesach*, will be a forbidden zone. You must not enter it at all."

I immediately thought of my friend's words. Though totally bewildered by my daughter's suggestion, as it did not make any sense whatsoever to me, I nodded half-heartedly and quietly said: "All right."

I knew my kitchen was very old and tatty, and wondered how she could sell it. But I thought that this might possibly be a symbolic sale only. Well, it turned out to be a sale only of the *chametz*. Once more I was grateful for my friend's advice.

The greatest excitement for me, to top all the other excitement, was the arrival of Saba and our son Danny. For the first time ever, we were a complete family together in Jerusalem, awaiting *Pesach*. I was ecstatic.

I did not worry about the week-long ban on our kitchen and my good old motto "We will see" prevailed successfully. Natalie allowed us to have a new electric kettle, some new cups and plastic utensils, so we could at least have breakfast (consisting of coffee and matzah) on the entrance room table. That pleased me, and as for the other meals, Natalie insisted we eat at her house. "Besides," she added, "you will be invited out a lot anyway."

I have learned from past years that whatever Natalie plans for us turns out, in the long run, to be successful and very pleasant, and so it was with our *Pesach* meals all through the week. We had no need at all to use our kitchen.

Although my pregnant daughter was still working at her eight-to-one job every day, she also managed to clean every corner of her house before *Pesach*, working until late at night. The children all helped, and did a lot of the cleaning in their own rooms by themselves. In Givat Dat this entire procedure was far from unique, but for me it certainly was!

Natalie's *Pesach* household became a constant source of amazement to me and to my family. We had never experienced anything like it. Her kitchen took on a different color, shape, mood. Everything old was put away, and the utensils that replaced them were new, or at least new to me. I was astonished at the abundance of beautiful things she had set aside all the year 'round to take out only for the week of Passover — cutlery, soup tureens, sets of dishes, crockery, pots and pans, and more. And the list of things that had to be "Kosher for *Pesach*" was seemingly endless: from toothpaste to soap, from face cream to washing powder, even medicine, not to mention all food items — and I do mean ALL.

Finally *erev Pesach* arrived. The real *erev Pesach*. The children napped in the afternoon so that they would be able to stay up till the very end of the *Seder* — at 2:00 in the morning. Although Natalie's *Seder* table had many items that were new to me, I still felt very proud and happy in the knowledge that we too had always had a nice *Seder* night back home in Australia.

Avi and Saba took turns reading the *Haggadah*, and Natalie said something about this that touched my heart. While Saba was reading aloud from the *Haggadah* that he had brought with him from Australia, a treasured gift from Natalie, she said: "I love hearing my father's voice at our first-ever family *Seder* night in *Yerushalayim!*" I could not agree with her more.

The best, the most joyful part of all, was when our clever grandchildren asked their father some very clever questions, and when three-year-old Ruthi stood on her chair and recited the whole of the *Mah Nishtanah* BY HEART. My thirty-one-year-old son Danny exclaimed happily: "Oh, at last someone else can take over my old job — and how much better she does it, too!" The children sang songs I had never heard before, and our first *Seder* night in Jerusalem, with the whole family together, was unforgettable, especially the closing words of the *Haggadah*: "Next year in Jerusalem."

Danny had brought a friend with him, a secular Australian young man, who was invited to stay the night and naturally the first day as well, as leaving Givat Dat would not be permitted by Natalie and Avi. One either came and stayed for the entire *chag*, or one did not come at all. That was their house rule, and it was extended with warmth to Danny's friend.

He told me privately that he could not imagine himself being "locked away" in Givat Dat for an evening and a whole day. I told him he might change his mind, as a Festival in my daughter's home was rather beautiful and a treat for a visitor, but he insisted that he would walk out of Givat Dat after breakfast, unnoticed. I gave up trying to persuade him, yet I knew in my heart he would have a wonderful time if he stayed on.

Not only did our visitor not leave in the morning, or at any other time during the first day of *Pesach*, but he asked to go to the *Shul* with Avi and the boys. He enjoyed the services very much, ate the heartiest lunch of all of us, and in the afternoon played a most exciting board game with Danny, with all four children joining in.

I could not resist commenting. "Peter," I said, "I am happy to see that you survived the night and the day in 'black, stifling' Givat Dat." He only beamed at me with laughing eyes and continued to play with the kids. It was a heartwarming sight indeed.

The following day, the second day of *Pesach*, was not observed in a strict way as it would be abroad, since in Israel only the first and last days are observed as full holidays. The in-between days are half-holidays. Schools are closed as well as many businesses, and there is a general holiday mood in the whole country. An extremely great, new feeling for me.

On one of those in-between days, Natalie and I were sitting in the kitchen, preparing a meal, when she looked at me and asked: "Would you like to hear a most beautiful tune?"

When was the last time that Natalie had asked me something like that? I could not remember, but I replied very quickly: "Yes, of course."

She put on a cassette and said: "Listen — it is so beautiful. It's called 'Little Neshamah' [little soul]." I listened and it *was* beautiful, and the two of us sat there, in real harmony. It was one of those special moments worth capturing...

When it came to the last day of *Pesach*, we all felt a bit sad. It had been an especially marvelous holiday, with all of us together in Jerusalem. That night, when *Pesach* was over, Natalie asked her father to help pack and put away the cartons of Passover dishes and utensils. They worked feverishly together, Saba standing on a ladder and Natalie handing the packed boxes up to him and to Avi to be stored away for the next year, each carton marked to indicate its contents.

Natalie looked at her father and said: "It is wonderful to see your handwriting on my *Pesach* boxes." When I heard this I felt choked, holding back my tears. Happy, very happy tears.

I simply could not get this sentence out of my head, out of my heart: "I love seeing your handwriting on my *Pesach* boxes." I translated it to myself in the following way:

"NEXT YEAR IN YERUSHALAYIM!"

26   *Just a Simple Haircut*

With *Purim* and *Pesach* behind us, we were now ready for the next major event: the birth of our fifth grandchild. Of somewhat lesser importance, but scheduled for the same week, was the start of renovations on our Rehavia apartment.

For ten years we had been waiting patiently for a peaceful time in our family and in the country to start these major renovations, but in the life of a B.T. (and her parents) no time is all that peaceful. There is always *something* happening.

So now it was Friday, the day before Natalie was due to give birth and two days before our scheduled move to temporary quarters — an apartment around the corner from our place, where we would stay throughout the renovations — and I was packing up our belongings.

The phone rang and I ran to answer it, thinking as I did with each phone call, "This is *it*. The baby is coming. Forget about our moving on Sunday morning."

But no. Though it was Natalie, her voice was happy and warm. She had phoned to ask if we would be able to pick up the four children for lunch, take them to the park, maybe bathe them in our havoc of a place and dress them in their *Shabbat* clothes. "Darling, we will fetch them *after* lunch," I said, "as Daddy and I are going for haircuts before lunch."

Deadly silence on the other end. After a moment, Natalie composed herself and asked: "Do you mean to say you are both having a haircut *davka* today, today of all days?"

I wondered briefly what was wrong with having a simple haircut, which was overdue anyhow, and quietly answered: "Yes." The voice on the other end was surprisingly agitated. "Could you not possibly wait another week? After all, next Sunday is *Lag Ba'Omer*."

And I suddenly remembered. How utterly stupid of me to have forgotten, I who had noticed during the past weeks how "old" all Avi's friends had once again become, with their unshaven, graying beards, just as it was in the weeks before *Tisha B'Av*. I knew about *Lag Ba'Omer* but it had simply slipped my mind in all the chaos. *Lag Ba'Omer* is the 33rd day of the "Counting of the *Omer*," a seven-week semi-mourning period between *Pesach* and *Shavuot* — the Festival of Pentecost. It is customary during this period not to shave or cut one's hair until the 33rd day.

My mind started working overtime. On the one hand, we did not routinely observe all these *minhagim* (customs) of the Orthodox. But, on the other hand, with our daughter about to give birth, with Number Five due to arrive at any moment, and with our renovations about to commence — with all this pending, how could we willingly, knowingly, do something against *Halachah*, Jewish Law?

We are mortals, humans who want all the good things to happen to us, who want Hashem to do everything for us. How could we just ignore His Laws? These thoughts went whirling around in my dazed brain, while I contemplated the simple act of having a haircut that day or waiting till *Lag Ba'Omer*.

I made my calculations, my *cheshbon*, and suddenly I knew there was no other alternative for us, absolutely no other thought but to cancel all appointments for haircuts.

Who ever heard of having a haircut DAVKA one week before *Lag Ba'Omer*? Certainly not I.

Epilogue

Balancing the Books

As I wrote this book, I was tempted to soften the retelling of painful events, as they do not show me or my daughter in a very good light. But I quickly realized that if I were to paint a pretty face on these events, you, who quite possibly are living through similarly difficult times, would not be able to identify with me, to empathize with me, and as a result, would not learn what I have learned: that in the present all the painful events become past history, and the present becomes a continuous string of joyful new experiences.

How ignorant, how hostile I was in the early years. Only now, after ten years of learning, adjusting, and enjoying the full benefits of having a B.T. child, do I really know how the good can cancel out all the bad.

Nothing could illustrate this better than the gratifying story about our number five grandchild, our third grandson, and his beautiful *Brit Milah* celebration on the 15th of May, the 20th of *Iyar*, in Givat Dat. The contrast between this event and "The Birth of Our *Bechor*" is, I think, striking.

The last days of Natalie's pregnancy were nothing short of a small miracle. It was, as she said (and I conceded in full knowledge of the meaning of the term) "*min ha-Shamayim*" —

straight from Heaven Above.

It was Sunday, and everything was going according to plan — except for our grandchild's birth, which was now one day late. But we had successfully moved all our belongings to the apartment that would be our home for the next three months while our renovations were being carried out. As the moving truck delivered our last piece of furniture and the last heavy box was carted into our small lodging, I turned to Steven and exclaimed: "*Baruch Hashem*, so far so good."

The timing was perfect, as at this moment our phone rang for the first time in our new, temporary place. It was Natalie. She quietly informed me that she thought her labor pains had started. I said with enthusiasm: "It could not have happened a minute earlier — we have just finished moving in and I can be ready to go to your house right away."

Natalie said that that was not necessary yet, but that I should just stay in and be ready. Merrily we began to unpack.

The whole day was one long expectation, filled with many phone calls back and forth. But it was not until I was almost collapsing from exhaustion in our new place, having unpacked almost everything, that the call came through: "Mum, I think this is it. COME!"

I took an emotional leave of Saba, who said I must try and sleep, as he himself was falling off his feet. I nodded half-heartedly, and we parted.

Natalie and Avi had decided that they would go to the hospital by themselves, while I would stay with the children. I was to lie in their bed and just take it easy. The children were all sleeping except for Sarah, who decided to "babysit" me, as she was not feeling sleepy at all. About one hour later Natalie and Avi returned: false alarm. They had been told that the baby's arrival could be still a few days away.

I was too tired for lengthy discussions, and, half asleep, I wandered down to our "luxury *machsan*" where I slept like a log until morning, when I was gently awakened. It was Saba, coming to take me home.

Suddenly I was not quite sure of the meaning of the word "home." I was certainly not "home" in Australia; we were out of our own "home" in Jerusalem; we were not quite in our temporary one; and I really only felt happy and at *home* in Givat Dat, where I knew I was needed most.

We arrived back in Rehavia and strolled over to our abandoned home that was to be demolished that day — a strangely eerie thought coupled with the expectation of birth. I stood there and felt quite faint with a longing for everything to be normal again. But this was not to be for quite a while, I knew.

We still had the phone working at our old place and when it rang, I knew who it must be. "Mum, I'm starting to have stronger pains," Natalie said. "The children are all in school and kindergarten, and I wish you would come over."

Suddenly I had an idea. "Darling, since it might be quite a while yet," I said, "why don't you get in a taxi and come over to us. There is so much still to be done and arranged here. You can stay with us, and whatever happens we will take it from here." She agreed.

Our architect, our builder and his foreman were all at our place to discuss the final plans when Natalie waddled through the door, obviously experiencing some discomfort, to say the least. There was no place for her to sit or lie down so she stood with us for a while and then said, "I'll just go out to the cafe around the corner. When you're done here, you can come and join me."

Somehow I got so involved that I completely forgot about her for almost an hour! And then suddenly I realized that for all that time my daughter had been sitting and waiting in a cafe, having labor pains — and I was not with her. In a panic, I ran outside and around to the cafe on Aza Street. There, at the lone table smack on the sidewalk, very near to the bustling traffic, sat my daughter, calmly sipping a tall ice coffee and looking as cool as a cucumber, as though she did not have a worry or care.

I took one look at her and we both burst out laughing. We just laughed and laughed. It was a most hilarious moment.

I wiped the laughter tears from my eyes and suggested we go back home to her house and I would wait it out with her. We did just that.

By the time Natalie was really ready to go to the hospital, it was nighttime again and the two boys were already asleep. The girls were awake and they kissed their Ima good-bye, and asked me at the same time if they could sleep in the bed with me. I would have said yes to anything at this stage. Natalie kissed me and her parting words were: "Mummy, get some rest and *keep calm.*" The girls did move in with me on the bed, and they fell asleep without protest.

I know I've already said it, but I simply cannot get over how well-behaved religiously-raised children are. There is a secret bond, a unity between them, that is quite outstanding. And it is I who must admit that this is mainly because of the number of children so close in age. It creates a unique relationship between brothers and sisters.

I was secretly very proud of how the girls stayed with me without a moment's hesitation. They had total trust in their Savta, who they know adores them. They felt secure with me, and I was very grateful for this trusting love between myself and my grandchildren. Happily I watched them sleeping peacefully, my two beautiful girls, light-blonde Sarah and brown-haired Ruthi, sprawled on the big bed close to me.

It was after two in the morning when the phone rang. "*Mazal tov,* Savta!" Avi's voice shouted cheerfully. "We have another boy!"

"A boy?" I exclaimed with surprise (as if there were so many choices!), and the girls suddenly awoke and burst out crying bitterly: "But we wanted a little sister!"

At this moment the boys arrived on the scene, shouting happily: "We have a little brother!" And then our wise *bechor* turned to Ruthi and cuddled her like a grandfather. "Don't cry, Ruthi," he crooned. "You will still be our own *bubah*, our little doll, the youngest girl."

This was really all Ruthi had needed. Her tears seemed to reverse direction, to be replaced by a most engaging smile as she repeated the wise words: "I will still be the *bubah*."

We sat around the kitchen table drinking hot cocoa and toasting "*L'chayim*" to our new little family member until Abba returned from the hospital, happily exhausted. He chased us all back to bed.

The next few days passed like a hazy dream as all the jigsaw puzzle pieces fell into place. Somehow Natalie, from her faraway hospital bed, was still cleverly running her family. With the children so well-disciplined, life just continued at its regular pace. I spent each afternoon at her house, to be there when the children came home from school. Abba saw them off each morning and then went to his office, and the only wonderful disturbance of the day was visiting Ima in the hospital.

Natalie shared her room with five other religious women, something that would have upset us to no end in previous years, when we had only known about private, elegant rooms in Australia. It is quite amazing how one gets used to everything. We knew that the care she would be getting in this kosher Israeli hospital, with its staff of dedicated doctors and nurses, would be superb.

Natalie was in a glorious mood. She looked radiant, and she said I did too. I felt happy and totally relaxed. She asked me to pull my chair close to her bed and she produced long lists of things for me to do while she stayed in hospital.

Then she asked hesitantly: "Would you mind looking after the *Shalom Zachar* and *Shabbat*, as I would love to go for two or three days to a convalescent home with the baby."

I could not quite believe my ears. I was delighted that she would be taking it easy for a while, but incredulous that she would actually leave all these religious duties to me, to arrange everything, to welcome — together with Avi — their Orthodox friends on Friday night and to prepare for *Shabbat!*

I felt gloriously proud. "Natalie," I said with tears in my eyes, "I have come a long way since your first son was born." We looked at each other and embraced, and we both cried happy, grateful tears. This was a moment I wanted to keep and treasure for as long as I lived. This was the moment I had been waiting years for. My B.T. daughter, my religious, observant daughter, was at last satisfied and trusting enough to leave the most important duties to me.

I composed myself and started to write down everything she wanted me to do.

Natalie made it easy for me, as she had thought of everything. The trust and love that came from her to me made me feel very strong and capable, enabling me to carry out my responsibilities joyfully and, I might add, successfully.

The *Shalom Zachar* turned out to be a huge event. The people of Givat Dat, who have grown to know and like me, thought nothing of it when I welcomed them together with Avi and Saba into Natalie's home. The living room was full of religious men. Some even brought their wives along, as they knew I would be there, and the women wanted to say a special *Mazal tov* to "the grandparents who are always there for *simchahs*." This is how they think of us. This is how we want it. This is who we have become: the grandparents who are always there...

The *brit* took place on Tuesday morning, and one of Natalie's friends gave me a very special greeting. "How marvelous, to have a *brit* on Tuesday," she said, "as Tuesday is special. When Hashem created Tuesday, the third day, He was so pleased that He said, 'It is good' not once but twice, so Tuesday is considered a day doubly blessed." I will never cease to learn more and more interesting things from these religious, learned young people.

The fact that we were so relaxed and familiar with everything and everybody made it the most beautiful *simchah* we ever had. Natalie and Avi were totally at ease, the children were gorgeous and deliriously happy — and helpful, all four of them very much a part of the celebration. It was a most delightful morning.

There was nothing that Natalie had to advise me about. I knew for myself what was expected of me. I did not do anything out of a sense of duty but out of joy. I who never covered my head, wore a white beret for the occasion, a modest outfit, and stockings. I knew where to be, what to do, and when to do it.

I stood back, knowing I must not shake the hand of the *Rav*, who wished a hearty *Mazal tov* to me, the Savta, whose third grandson was about to be accepted into the Jewish world.

I felt Natalie's glance from the other end of the hall. We smiled at one another, expressing our total satisfaction and pleasure in the occasion. Our smiles said: "Well done!"

Suddenly I looked around me and stopped to gather the thoughts that zig-zagged in my head. My ever-present inner voice asked: "Look around and tell me — what do you see?"

It was the same environment — an Orthodox yeshiva, full of black-coated, ultra-Orthodox Rabbis and *bachurim* — that had terrified me so at our first *brit*, and had made us feel so alienated from them. There was the same separation between women and men which had been unbearable to me eight years earlier. The same renowned *mohel* performed this circumcision too. Our daughter and son-in-law, who I had thought had separated themselves from our culture, our world, purposely to turn against us, their parents — they were the same. And last but not least, we were the same Saba and the same me. Or were we?!

What miracle has happened to us? I wondered. Or did it happen to them? Or has time, love, and more love erased the differences?

It was after the announcement of the baby's name that

Natalie, standing in front of me hand-in-hand with her two daughters, looked back, searching for me. Her laughing gray eyes spelled out all there was to say, all I wanted to hear:

"Mummy, you see? It was worth it. All the early pain, all the hostility is gone, forever. Here we are, together, all one very happy and grateful family."

This was what her eyes said, and this was precisely how I felt.

I also felt, somehow, that Hashem was keeping a great ledger of good and bad, and that from here on, the good times would easily outweigh the bad times — everything would be in the "plus" column. I believed that at last Hashem had balanced our books.

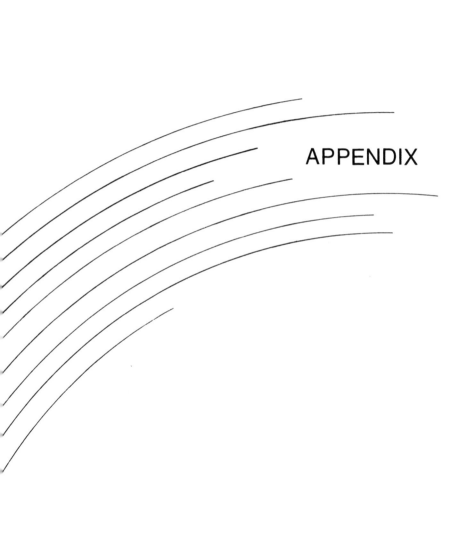

APPENDIX

Appendix I

Bashert — Now I Know!

Despite my objections, my publisher chose to call this part of my book the "Appendix," which to me sounds like something that should be taken *out*, whereas I felt strongly that these chapters should be put *in*. Although my story is really done (or really just beginning, depending on one's point of view), I still have more important things to tell you.

The first is about "*bashert*." In an earlier chapter, I described my skepticism upon hearing and understanding this term for the first time. But today, when I look back over ten years of experiences as the mother of a B.T., I can honestly say that I have become a firm believer in this concept. It is true: Everything is *bashert*.

I would call my whole love affair with Yerushalayim *bashert*, as one would have thought it more characteristic of me to have chosen New York, London or Rome for a second home. But the "something" that happened to me as I walked down the steps of the plane at Ben Gurion Airport way back in 1969 was certainly the work of the Upper Hand, that held me then and has held me ever since.

My decision to buy an apartment in Jerusalem was a crucial one — financially, emotionally and psychologically. I felt that by buying a foothold in Israel, where our daughter could live in a wholesome environment, I was also doing something for the needs of my own soul.

I had come to Israel to spend some time with my newly-religious daughter and we were sharing a small, rented apartment in what was for me a very alien part of Jerusalem — Armon Hanatziv. My small room overlooked an Arab village, and I had an incredibly stunning view of the Judean desert from my window. I think I could even see the Dead Sea. I awoke each morning to the sound of Arab Moslems in the village being called to prayer — an eerie, yet exciting new sound to my European ears, something I certainly could never wake up to in our suburban home back in Australia. As lovely as it was, this area was not for me.

Steven and I discussed the subject at length on the telephone. I asked his consent to buy a modest apartment in Rehavia, which I told him was a suburb very similar to our own Bellevue Hill in Sydney, a tree-lined, beautiful neighborhood very close to the heart of Jerusalem.

"But you must be very careful," he warned me, "and you must try to find a good, honest lawyer, preferably English-speaking." Then, as an afterthought, he added: "I am afraid there are a lot of '*ganefs*' who might try to take advantage of a woman ignorant in such matters as purchasing an apartment in a place as foreign as Jerusalem."

I thought to myself: "Neither is Jerusalem foreign to me, nor have I found people to be '*ganefs*,' but I will not argue and I will try to be very, very careful indeed." Natalie was pleased with our decision and the prospect of living in Rehavia in the not-too-distant future. She even recommended a lawyer.

It was July and that meant heat in Jerusalem. By the time I found my way to the address Natalie had given me, I was practically dehydrated. Although the temperature often got just as high in Australia in the summer, the sun had never felt as hot as it did in Israel. And to add to my misery the secretary at the law firm informed me that the lawyer Natalie had recommended was no longer in their employ.

"Would you care to see the senior partner, Mr. L, perhaps?"

I did not know what to do. I was afraid of making a wrong decision and, remembering my husband's words, thought: "What if I am falling into some *ganef*'s hands?"

Finally, I decided to see for myself whether or not this Mr. L was a *ganef*. I walked into his sunny office to find, seated behind the desk, an unusually warm and friendly man of about 60 or so, with twinkling eyes and a suntanned face. His voice was a laughing, chuckling voice, as warm and friendly as his face. And he seemed genuinely pleased that right in the midst of his terribly busy morning, in the heat of the day, I, a complete stranger, had burst in upon him practically unannounced.

"Before we do anything else, you must sit down and have a large, cold glass of water and just rest a while," he said, "and then you tell me what I can do for you." His words were music to my ears.

Mr. L's accent (which I later learned was Russian) was strong, but his English was very good. I thought to myself: "This lawyer looks anything but a *ganef*."

I had barely opened my mouth to speak when Mr. L chuckled and said: "Ah, you are a Hungarian, a Magyar. I'll bet you make a good paprika chicken." And I beamed back at him and replied: "Yes, I was born in Hungary; yes, I was a Magyar; and yes, I do make an excellent paprika chicken."

Then Mr. L did something strange. He arose, told his secretary he did not want to be disturbed, nor did he want to take any phone calls for a while, sat back behind his desk and asked: "So tell me, what makes you want to buy an apartment in our beautiful Yerushalayim?"

I, after another long gulp of water, wiped the perspiration off my face, sat back in my small armchair and asked: "Do you really want to hear it all, right from the beginning?" And not

even waiting for his reply — as I *knew* he *did* want to hear it
— I started to tell this total stranger my entire life story.

When I at last ran out of steam, Mr. L waved his hands excitedly and said: "So you are really nothing short of a 'wild,
Hungarian Zionist'?"

Suddenly my eyes filled with tears. This total stranger had
expressed in one concise phrase something that I had never
been able to fit into a short sentence. And I added: "Yes, that
is exactly what I am, and I am also the mother of a wonderful
young woman — a *Baalat Teshuvah.*"

"*Beseder gamur,*" Mr. L said, using a term that would
become my byword — the equivalent of "A-O.K." And we went
to work.

Later on, I was convinced that *everything* that had
transpired — from my first step on Israeli soil, to finding a
lawyer/friend like Mr. L and his elegant, witty, delightful wife
Doris (a perfect English lady, who also became my dear friend),
to discovering the ideal apartment for us in Jerusalem — was
all the work of the Upper Hand, that it was all *bashert.* Especially when Doris, who not only has a law degree and was a
practicing lawyer, but also holds a degree in mathematics and
has authored several books and many articles, decided to help
me prepare my manuscript for publishing. This happened nearly ten years after our first encounter, and during that time our
friendship had grown.

Doris's involvement meant more to me than words can
express, as I had never even shown my notes to anyone
before. But when Doris read them (while I paced nervously and
fidgeted, my heart beating wildly), she uttered the words every
aspiring author longs to hear: "I love your writing," she said.
And then *she* went to work.

But that was only the beginning.

Natalie and I had planned a rendezvous in town, though it
was 34° Centigrade in the shade. This time I wanted her to

look at something I was going to buy, as she has marvelous and very sophisticated taste. I waited for her at a bus stop on Straus Street, near Meah She'arim, where I had seen a perfect garden chair.

As the bus approached, I could see her lovely covered head at the window. In her arms was the current baby. I grabbed my grandchild from her and helped with the bags and folding stroller as she got off, and we headed for the shops.

After making our purchase, we decided to have our usual "*glatt*" Meah She'arim coffee-and-cake-time. We have a favorite coffee shop, where they serve a colossal cappuccino and cheese blintzes that are out of this world. The shop is always full of the most interesting looking Orthodox women — women originally from many different countries, speaking many different languages (French, Spanish, even the Queen's English), fine, very well-dressed religious women out on a morning stroll with their smallest children and friends. And I must tell you that I no longer feel at all alien sitting there among them, with my beautiful family.

I know that it may seem that I am sidetracking the story about what *bashert* means to me, but this is all connected. So, let me tell you about something that I remembered as I sat with my daughter in that cafe. It was an incident that occurred more than ten years ago when Natalie was still unmarried. After her first visit back to Sydney, we were traveling back to Jerusalem with her.

As my husband had close business contacts in the United States, we always traveled via New York, a stopover I simply loved. This time I had the additional joy of traveling with my daughter, for the first time in New York. What a marvelous time awaited us!

We certainly did have a good time, but not at all the kind I had expected. Being with my B.T. daughter can always turn even the dullest event into something exciting.

I must admit that my husband and I have a weakness for

staying in good hotels. Some people prefer more travel time; we prefer to do with less but to stay in good places. Nothing is more important than staying on a good street when you are in New York, as it is a jungle of a place — but I love it. So we were booked into the Park Lane Hotel, which is just about the best place to be in New York: opposite Central Park, on the corner of Fifth Avenue.

We knew we would have some problems eating out with our newly religious daughter. Gone were the times when we could run to a deli before going to the theater, or grab a bite anywhere afterwards. On this trip, our meals were to be eaten in places I had never known existed before, such as a *glatt*-kosher Chinese restaurant — where the food was delicious. The restaurant was full of very religious and very interesting people. I could have gone without food; I was full with the excitement of the place. But no matter what *glatt* restaurant we went to, and there are more than a few in New York, none surpassed the cafe on the Lower East Side where we had our "*glatt*" breakfast.

I had been in New York at least ten times previously, but I had not known there was such a thing as the Lower East Side. And had it not been for my daughter, I would have missed out on some real fun (I who loves fun).

Natalie asked me one morning if I would like to come with her to downtown New York. After her explanation, I said "No, thank you," and headed for Saks Fifth Avenue while she went somewhere downtown on her own. I really don't have to know about all those horrid places she has started going to, I told myself.

I returned from my day's outing. Just as I was about to enter the elevator to go up to the suite we shared with Natalie, I saw someone in the lobby carrying a huge black roasting pan, large enough, it seemed, to hold a whole lamb.

After my initial shock, I realized that it was *my daughter* who had walked into this elegant place (where they knew us well) carrying this thing, this indescribably huge black *thing*. I felt ashamed as the porter opened the door for Natalie with his usual courtesy.

As I rode up with Natalie, I asked her why she had had to embarrass her parents, and especially her father, who saw important business associates in the hotel. Natalie was indignant about my complaints, and said: "You know, you don't really know what you are missing by not coming with me to the Lower East Side."

To cut a long story short, we were sitting in a taxi at 9:00 sharp the next morning and Natalie said: "Mummy, I know you — you will love it."

We arrived at a street which was as foreign to me as anything can be. It reminded me more of Jerusalem or Jaffa than of my elegant New York, and I made this plain: "If I want to be in downtown Jaffa, I go to downtown Jaffa. But I can certainly do without *this*."

We were supposed to have breakfast there. This was part of the deal Natalie had made with me, saying: "You have not had breakfast in New York until you have eaten at least once on the Lower East Side." When we got out of the taxi, she put her arm in mine and guided me into a place which was empty except for the proprietor, a man with a long black beard and all the necessary accouterments of Orthodoxy. As if that weren't enough, the only language he appeared to speak was my native tongue: Hungarian.

The place was tiled white, not quite my idea of elegance. The floor was a bit dirty, the tables were bare but the counter was FULL, full of the most fantastic looking food I had ever seen before, even in Israel.

Natalie did not take her eyes off me. She wanted to savor every moment of her triumph over her mother's "Palm Court in the Plaza Hotel" (where my husband and I sometimes had breakfast).

But triumph was slow to come. "Natalie," I said, "I simply

cannot eat in a place like this. And there is not another soul here at this hour of the day. How can you do this to me?" She smiled and answered: "Just wait."

I did not have to wait long. The place quickly filled and, still reluctantly, I began to eat. To my surprise, the breakfast was rather exotic, with all kinds of tasty foods I was not familar with, but enjoyed fully. The Hungarian Jew was entertaining, and Natalie did not miss a trick. She told him (in Hungarian, which she can speak fluently) that her cosmopolitan, Budapest-born mother, a seasoned traveler, was not used to places like this. To which the owner replied, as if I were not present:

"Tell your dear mother, that she has not lived if she has not been to the Lower East Side, especially to this place, for breakfast," virtually reiterating Natalie's words to me. Then he produced photographs of some very famous Hollywood celebrities who regularly patronized his place for breakfast, lunch or dinner.

I smiled and answered, in my mother tongue, that I would cherish the memory of this breakfast.

There is no point in going on with the story of how we spent the whole of the morning on the crowded, dizzying, yet fantastic Lower East Side, except to add that the following day, together with Natalie's father, we were sitting in the same place, at the same time, with the same happy Hungarian Jew serving us an even better breakfast, and we shopped and shopped until we had filled the taxi which took us back to boring Park Lane Hotel.

I remembered this episode while telling you about my garden chair and our lovely Meah She'arim coffee break. As we walked back toward the bus stop again, Natalie stopped for a moment, hesitating over going into what I call her regular "*glatt*" bookshop, which she never fails to visit when in town. Anticipating my remarks, she muttered something and pulled me on, past the bookshop.

But it was I who walked towards the shop, my attention

captured by something in the window. It was a children's book with a title that contained the word "Savta," and as I am so very much a Savta in my heart, I entered the shop to examine it. Natalie tugged on my arm and quietly whispered in my ear: "But you said you hated this shop."

"I did not say I hated it, I only mentioned how much I would like for you to read something other than religious books."

She went on: "But I told you, they are not just religious books. They are English books from all over the world, including history books, cookbooks, children's books and everything related to Jewish subjects." Then with a very sweet chuckle she added: "In fact, Mummy, if you really do write your book, it would be in this very shop that your book would be sold. It is this window you would see filled with copies of your books." Her eyes sparkled with mischievous joy.

Some months after this episode, on a subsequent visit, I was to go to the Jerusalem Book Fair with my Tel Aviv friends. The Book Fair was most impressive. I had never before been in Jerusalem at the time of the Fair and I looked with great interest at all the famous, international publishers represented. There was a huge Hungarian booth, where I bought a beautiful book called *A Shema Yisrael* — the *Shema* in Hungarian — to take back to my ailing mother in Australia.

My friends stopped at various stands that did not interest me particularly and I just strolled by myself from display to display, quite nonchalantly, certainly not like somebody who is writing a book and is looking for a publisher, as maybe I should have been doing.

Among all the large book stands, one caught my eye and made me gasp for air. It was not the booth itself that was impressive, but the sign above it, identical to the sign over Natalie's favorite bookshop: Feldheim.

I felt drawn to it as though somebody were leading me, guiding my steps to this spot among the many hundreds of stands. Quite by coincidence, *one might say*, Feldheim's edit-or-in-chief was present at the time, and when I told her about the book I was writing, her eyes lit up with interest.

When I rejoined my friends, who were still at the Hungarian pavilion, I said quietly: "You will get special mention in my book, as it was you who brought me today to the Book Fair and it was thanks to you that I have finally made contact with my publisher."

And so, I thought then, all of this — my love affair with Israel, my meeting the Ls, my B.T. daughter's bookshop, my Book Fair encounter — all of this added up to a clear case of "*bashert*." But then I did not know what I know *now*.

I think I was carrying too far my own interpretations of "*bashert*." What I so proudly called "*bashert*" was really only my own way of expressing my appreciation of all that I would have missed if not for my daughter's influence in my life.

But now I believe I understand for the first time the FULL meaning of this beautiful new word.

I might allow myself to use the word *bashert*, with humble pride, if one day a mother writes to me and lets me know that she has carefully read my book, she has followed some of my suggestions, and she is starting to gain similar joy and fulfill-ment from *her* B.T. child.

If this happens, if my words reach a mother in distress and help her — only then may I use the word *bashert*, only *then* can it be said that what I set out to do was with the grace of God, that it was fruitful and beneficial not only to *me*, but to others.

Appendix II

Legacy

How are we to know as children how events will influence our lives in the future, how our feelings for loved ones will play a role in the pattern of our existence?

Looking back, reflecting on my youth and even later years, I am aware that I came face to face not once, but a number of times, with something close to a miracle. This realization provides all the more reason to take notice of events and try to preserve them.

I think that the greatest influence in my life has been my father. Everything I can remember about him — our brief private talks, a nod, a wave, even the smallest gesture, are stamped deeply in my memory.

My father was a handsome, beautiful man. My favorite photograph of him is one that was taken on his fiftieth birthday, only four years before I lost him. This picture is framed and travels with me wherever I go. But there are many other dashing photographs of him, (some only in my memory), as a young Hungarian officer in his uniform, or with my mother in a honeymoon snapshot in St. Marks Square (a favorite honeymoon place for bourgeoisie Hungarian Jewish newlyweds). In that photo, he is standing with one arm outstretched in an inviting gesture toward the tourist attraction, the pigeons, and he is dressed with immaculate elegance, in a suit and an expensive overcoat — most likely purchased in the most exclusive menswear shop in Budapest, where he was a regular customer. And a hat, oh yes, I must not forget the hat, as my father wore elegant hats during all seasons of the year.

He was a big man, tall and broad, with a big chest and wide shoulders. An impressive person. His face was what I would call today a face where everything is in the right place: a perfect oval shape with a high forehead, a strong straight nose, gray-blue eyes, bushy eyebrows, and a strong chin. His hands were the most beautiful hands, with long, slender fingers. On his right hand, he wore a ring, a ring that was called in Hungary a "*pecset gyuru*" (a signet or seal-ring) — the ring that has been on my second finger for the past 46 years, ever since it fell off his hand towards the end of his illness, sometime in June 1945.

I remember the day it fell off. I had not moved from his bedside for months, as I knew that his days were numbered. Time had stopped for me, and nothing mattered, only he. When the ring fell onto the floor I picked it up and said: "I will put it away until you can wear it once more," though I knew this would never be.

"My Agi," he replied, "till that time, you must wear my ring and may it guard you, keep you, as long as you live." I have never removed the ring from my hand. I have had many arguments over keeping it on when giving birth, or having an operation, when doctors and nurses insisted the ring must come off, but I won each time.

Memories of my father and his great influence on me have occupied me very much in recent years, since my daughter's return to our ancient roots, her *teshuvah*. And especially since what I recognize to be my own *teshuvah*. In my youth, I never felt the need to go searching for my ancestors' religious roots. I was quite comfortable with what I knew about both sets of grandparents. I was close to my mother's parents, my only living grandparents, and accepted the fact of their Jewishness without ever feeling any need for anything more.

For all of my pre-war life we celebrated *Seder* night in my grandparents' home, together with the whole family. Each Passover, countless numbers of aunts and uncles appeared together out of nowhere. I never really knew where they were during the rest of the year, but they gathered in my grandparents' spacious home at *Pesach*, and I remember that as a child I was kissed, squeezed and patted all over by these aunts every year. They were always amazed at my having grown taller and taller each year, and I looked forward to being fussed over all night. It was part of my life's rhythmic, normal flow.

I could not, or did not, notice any difference between my grandparents' degree of religious observance and ours. I don't think this question ever came to my mind. I was a rather dreamy, full-of-fantasy child, which kept me quite happily busy. Never did religion cause me the slightest problem or concern. I was completely satisfied being what I was: a Jewish child in a great big non-Jewish world.

But as I now probe more deeply into my memories, I find some interesting recollections vis-à-vis other Jews that must have greatly influenced my thoughts and feelings and my initial reactions to Natalie's *teshuvah*. The "other Jews" were apparently of a totally different kind. I only had my father's word for this, but I certainly did not need more than that. He gave me his views, his thoughts about THEM, and I accepted this without further questioning.

My father was born in a country-district called Dunantul (over the Danube), in the small town of Veszprem, in the western part of Hungary about two hours' train- or car-ride from Budapest. His parents died before I was born, but I felt that I knew them nevertheless, from the large, beautiful photos of them that hung on the wall in my parents' bedroom.

My father went to work every day of the week — except

Sunday — to a huge clothing shop that my mother's father had established. It was one of the largest coat businesses in Budapest, and my father continued to run it. But he had not always intended to be a clothing merchant; in fact, a very different future had been planned for him.

After finishing his schooling in Veszprem, he had come to Budapest, as was customary in those days, to build his future in the big city. His parents had owned a big inn-*cum*-tavern, and had apparently worked very hard in order to provide their four sons with a good education and bring them up like gentlemen.

My father was by far the handsomest of the four and I think also the most ambitious. When he came to Budapest, he started to work in the English-Hungarian Bank. He was slowly but surely working his way up the ladder of success, when he was introduced to my mother.

In those days, the fact that a dashing, young, eligible Jew had come to Budapest was quickly (I don't know how) brought to the attention of the wealthy Jewish families with marriageable daughters. Working in a prestigious bank, my father was considered a "good match" for an intelligent, serious, elegant young lady like my mother, so a meeting was arranged, and marriage was the natural, eventual outcome. I never directly questioned my father's happiness over being the owner (which he became soon after marrying my mother) of the well-known coat business, but I did have a vague suspicion about it.

The business was located in an area that was known as a Jewish commercial district, and, interestingly enough, although the businesses there were owned largely by Jews, the clientele were mostly middle-class gentiles. The store was at the corner of Kiraly and Loudon Utca, and I was always unpleasantly conscious and embarrassed at the Jewish connotation of these street names.

Because of this, I often tried to avoid mentioning the address of our business. It is likely that the "shame" I felt was the same kind that my father must have struggled with all his life: the fact that he, the dashing Hungarian officer, he, the promising banker, did not become after all the Director of the English-Hungarian Bank, but instead became heir to a very well-established and flourishing clothing business in a Jewish commercial district of Budapest.

My father compensated for this "defect" in his image in many ways. For one thing, he moved to the most elegant street in Budapest, which, although it happened to be only a stone's throw from the corner where his store was, was in fact a world away, and the small distance made a vast difference. Andrassy Ut, where we lived, was the broadest, longest, most high-priced street in Budapest, with the famous Budapest Opera House only a short distance from us, on the opposite side of the street. Whenever I gave my address to people, I knew it represented wealth. This was what my father wanted, and this was what I was born into.

The corner building which housed the business belonged to my grandparents, and they actually lived on the first floor, in a huge apartment with a beautiful balcony. My grandfather also owned several other large buildings in Budapest, but this fact was only mentioned as an aside, in a faint whisper about their wealth.

I never gave it much thought. All my young life I knew that I need never worry about going without anything; I was never in need of anything. I knew that I *had* everything.

Though he worked quite hard from morning till late afternoon, my father always came home for a big midday meal, when the whole family sat around the beautifully set dining room table. My parents, my brother, my *Fräulein* and I, were served by the maid, who cooked substantial, delicious meals for us. But always, either before, after, or in the midst of our midday meal, there was the familiar and exciting exchange of numerous phone calls between my father and his younger brother, my beloved Uncle Eugene, who was a member of the stock exchange. During these daily phone calls my father discussed financial transactions, using expressions I learned by heart.

They evidently discussed the sale or purchase of stocks and bonds, and this daily interruption of our midday meal was not at all to my mother's liking. But my father's strong, authoritarian ways were not to be overruled by anyone, not even by my mother. This much I knew too. He was the boss.

Sometimes, when other children asked me what my father's profession was, I would invent a nice little story, in order to make the picture compatible with my own image of my father (and possibly of my father's image of himself as well). "My father was a banker," I often said, "and he is now a businessman. He is also on the stock exchange." This white lie was a marvelous cover that enabled me to avoid openly admitting that he was associated with a *shop*, albeit a large one, but a shop nevertheless, in the wrong part of town, in the middle of the *Jewish* part of town, in the Jewish world.

What did I mean by "Jewish world"? Were there *two* Jewish worlds? *Was I living in one while others lived in a different one?*

I was never aware of being different from anybody around me. My family, my friends, my parents' friends all had quite similar lifestyles. We lived in similar circumstances, we ate the same kind of food. All the children went to good private schools, as I did. I went to the Evangelical School in my neighborhood, which lots of other nice Jewish children attended.

Some of my most precious memories are of my father taking me for a special treat. He would pick me up unexpectedly from my afternoon gymnastics class, or my piano lesson, or maybe from my English teacher's house. Suddenly, there he would be, waiting to take me home. It was those times, when there was only my father and me, the two of us, strolling arm-in-arm, talking, stopping at every chocolate shop we passed (and there were several) and buying a piece of marzipan, that I loved so much. I can still hear my mother's voice saying: "Dezsokem, you spoil her terribly!" to which Dezso always, without fail, replied: "I know I do, and I love doing it." Oh, how much those words meant to me!

We also stopped in front of windows of shops which sold clothing or furniture, or pets — my favorite. We rarely spoke about the people around us, but once or twice, during our walks, we came face-to-face with strangely clad, black-clothed, bearded men. These men wore large black hats and had terribly weird-looking hairstyles, horrible looking ringlets hanging on either side of their face, which my father told me were called "*payess.*" They also had mysterious strings dangling from their belts, and altogether they looked to me (and I am sure to my father too) ugly, unwashed, and very alien indeed.

They were, my father told me, Orthodox Jews. Actually, if they had not been Orthodox, they would only have been called Jews. But this was impossible, as *we* were the Jews.

My father said that they were *Galicianer,* or Polish Jews, which meant nothing to me. But obviously they came from other places, and not from Budapest, my beautiful Budapest — though they did *live* in Budapest. They lived in the so-called ghetto, consisting of small, narrow, crowded streets that were not far from where our business was located and where my grandparents lived. But it was certainly a different *world* from where we lived.

The Jewish ghetto was crowded, noisy, full of dirty-nosed children — thousands of children, or so it seemed to me — and the always-hurrying weird-looking young men.

Our street, by contrast, was the wide, tree-lined, elegant boulevard that housed only *our* kind of sophisticated families. We too were Jewish, but we were *Hungarian* Jews. As we looked completely different from the "Orthodox Jews," we were probably *un*-Orthodox Jews, or whatever was the opposite of those "black" Jews.

My father told me that they even ate totally different food than we did and that their diet consisted of a lot of onions. He thought they would probably smell of onion as well. I noticed once or twice that he would take me by my arm and gently steer me across to the other side of the street, to avoid walking too close to those strange "black" Jews.

It didn't worry me too much; I didn't think about them too often. I knew that we were as far from them as "Mako from Jerusalem" — an old Hungarian expression implying a really great distance; Mako, a small town in Hungary, was as far as one could be from unreachable Jerusalem.

In those days in Hungary, we were aware that we intelligent, sophisticated Jews were still Jews nonetheless, with a special look about us. Narrowed down, I realized that it amounted to larger noses than our gentile fellow countrymen, dark curly hair, and, what I personally found very attractive, fiery, dark eyes, with a certain special bright look.

I do not recall any unpleasant experiences as a result of my being a Jewish child. Although the school I attended was Evangelical, in my class alone there were at least a dozen Jewish children. I had no problems at all about living in a predominantly gentile society. I was neither ashamed of being Jewish, nor particularly proud of it. I accepted it as a normal part of my very pleasant life.

As I mentioned in Chapter 2, in early May, while we children were still in school, my family would move to our summer home in Svabhegy, a very lovely mountainous area, about half an hour's cable-car ride from the city. This was part of my beautiful childhood, and it really was a privilege to have a summer place as luxurious as ours was. But my father had a special affinity for the "good life" (something I must have inherited from him), and he also had the talent for providing his family with the high standard of living he loved so.

We would stay in Svabhegy from May through the entire summer vacation until late September, when school had already reopened. This created some difficulties for my parents, but for me it was sheer joy. I had the incredible delight of traveling to the city in the mornings together with my father, first on the little cable-train and then on the bus.

We schoolchildren returned home to Svabhegy at midday, although my father did not. As he worked till late afternoon, often into the evening (the shops stayed open till seven o'clock), he would arrive home late and very tired.

I loved running out to the station where the little train stopped — it was only a minute from our house — to wait for my father and walk back home with him. I often helped him carry the packages he had brought. They most probably were shares or stock certificates of some sort, the kind he dealt with on the phone with my Uncle Eugene. September brought the High Holidays, and I always looked forward to them. Except for one thing: the perpetual anxiety that my father would arrive home late, far too late to get to synagogue in time. This happened every year. It never failed to worry me in advance. I would have so loved it if my father had not gone to work that day, and we could all have eaten a leisurely festive meal and walked together to synagogue.

I must clarify this. Our "synagogue" was not a real synagogue. It was a large room in a dilapidated hotel in the middle of the main square. We had a so-called Rabbi (he may have been merely a Cantor) and a congregation of about fifty families who either owned or rented homes in the area. We all attended this synagogue in Svabhegy during the High Holidays each year.

It was a festive time that we all would have enjoyed, if only my father had not spoiled it for us. I wished with all my heart that he would be on time just once. But he never was. He was always late and there was always a messy, argumentative and overexcited evening, on both Rosh Hashanah and Yom Kippur. And this from a man who was normally so punctual! It was almost unforgivable. Not once did I enjoy a High Holiday in peace. Little did I know how short-lived even the agitated ones were to be!

But there was one day of the year when everything stopped for my father. On this day nothing else mattered, no business, no stock exchange, no private life. One day of the year my father dedicated to the most sacred memory of his parents, the *Yahrtzeit* of the death of his beloved father and mother, the grandparents I never knew. I think I can say that this was the most solemn day in my father's calendar.

It was a ritual that belonged to my life also, from early childhood for as long as we were together.

My father and his three brothers would hire a car to go down to Veszprem, to their parents' grave site. On this combined *Yahrtzeit* day, I was regularly taken along each year, together with one or more of the other children, my brother or a cousin.

We would arise at dawn. My father was in a frenzy, as he preferred to arrive earlier rather than later. The drive was through a lovely rural part of Hungary, filled with tall cornfields and quaint-looking peasant houses that we passed on the way. I was not familiar with the countryside; I had been brought up very much as a city dweller, the child of real Budapest "city people."

I remember the whole ritual of arriving at the entrance to the cemetery, where the caretaker was already waiting for us. My father always took the lead, speaking to everybody and arranging for everything.

We would stand for a long time (or so it felt to me) in front of the old grayish-black gravestone that had my grandparents' names inscribed on it, in Hungarian and in Hebrew. My middle name is Laura, after my grandmother. I sometimes wished they had given me the name Laura, such a romantic name, as a first name instead of Agnes.

My father and uncles would pray from some tatty old prayer book, in Hebrew. It always amazed me on this day how well my father could pray in Hebrew, the only time I ever heard him utter Hebrew words.

I recall now, with great surprise, that on the night before the visit to my grandparents' grave, my father would also light a special kind of *Yahrtzeit mecses* (candle) in a glass holder. He would do this with great care and attention. I can still hear his words, as he lit the candle. On this occasion he would speak only German: "*Ich zunde die fur meine Eltern,*" and then he would utter some names that included the word "*ben*" or "*bat.*"*

I did not know as a child what his words meant. I would just stand there near my father, watching and listening to him and filled with a deep love for him, for the son who remembered his parents with such humility and devotion.

Childhood impressions of our parents are some of our most precious legacies, and we retain them for a lifetime. I, for instance, have said, ever since my father's death, each year on his *Yahrtzeit* and on Yom Kippur as well, when I light my *mecses*, "*Ich zunde die...*" and I add his Hebrew name.

This is one of the rare bits of Jewish observance — of *Yiddishkeit* — that I received in my parents' home. But what I did not learn from my parents, I have learned from my daughter. This is a precious gift from Hashem and one for which I am very grateful.

I am trying to remember almost forgotten yet vitally important memories — including those few which were connected to what we called our "Jewishness." And the deeper I probe the more I find; small, almost invisible threads, stretching from

* "Son of..." or "daughter of..." On all occasions pertaining to religious observance, Jews are identified by their Hebrew first name, the son of (or daughter of) so-and-so. (E.g. "Yitzchak ben Avraham" — Isaac, the son of Abraham.)

childhood to adulthood. No matter how insignificant they might have seemed then, they are invaluable to me now, in my new, deep consciousness as a Jew. They all represent the strength of my love for my beloved father and his strong influence on my life. No matter how long ago those threads were woven, today they help to make me the strong, thinking and feeling Jew that I have become.

I remember the autumn of 1943 especially clearly. I was then already a teenager, as I had turned fourteen in January 1943. My days as a happy, lighthearted child were over, as I could sense and feel the tension in our home, particularly in my father. All he ever did in those days, in his spare time, was listen to the English news on the radio. I knew that catastrophe threatened us Jews, but I tried to block the ugliness out as much as I could. I was still a dreamy young girl, and I tried to spin my own fantasy world.

In the summer of 1943 I was tall, thin, with long chestnut brown hair and an oval, intense face that resembled my father's. I remember that this year, school did not start in September as usual. Because of the lack of fuel for heating the schools, we were to start only in November.

We were still in our summer place in the mountains, and I started taking tennis lessons twice a week. There was a sports center very close by, in the so-called "Svabhegyi Sanatorium." In some of the adjacent buildings Hungarian officers were billeted. There was a short-cut through these barracks to my tennis school, which I preferred to the longer, regular road. I also had a secret admirer among the officers stationed there. This filled my days with anticipation.

It was the perfect hideaway from the ugliness that surrounded my whole existence at the time. I was trying to escape to another world, through my romantic adventure. I kept the existence of my officer a secret from everybody, as there really was very little to tell about him. We had only noticed each other, smiled, and maybe waved, but we had exchanged not a single, solitary word.

But it was enough to enable me to shut my ears to the noise of the loud, yelling voices blaring from our radio. My father was suddenly lost for me; he only lived for this horrible radio. I was so angry that I decided to do something, which deep in my heart I knew I should not do. But I was lonely, and very angry at the whole world.

One day, walking back from tennis, the officer approached me and we at last introduced ourselves and started to talk. He knew on which days I went to tennis, and urged me to come just one more day in the week, only to talk and maybe walk together with him. I thought this a splendid idea and we actually made a date.

Boys as such were part of my normal everyday life, as my brother, who was four years older than me, almost always had a houseful of friends coming and going, especially in our summer place. I was used to having boys around me to bicycle with, and play jazz records with.

I had one favorite: he was my brother's best friend — a quiet, gray-eyed, serious boy, who never took any notice of me. I decided I wanted him to wait for me, until I grew up, which I was in no great hurry to do. After all, I had my dream-life, which was more exciting than any real-life story ever could be.

My Hungarian officer and I met a few times and I even let him walk me home from tennis. On one of these occasions, almost at the end of summer — how was I to know that it was really the end of all summers? — we came upon my father.

He was in our garden, where the gardener's small house was, and he was instructing the gardener, probably about some flowers, trees or shrubs to be planted or replanted now, as summer was ending. Father was already planning for the next summer, the summer of 1944 — the summer that never came, the summer that brought the deepest tragedy in Jewish history, and in my own life.

Father saw me walking alongside the Hungarian officer. He stood there distant, yet so close, and looked only at me. I knew I was doing something wrong, something of which my father disapproved. In fact I saw on my father's face an expression that I had never seen before or since.

He gestured toward me, as if to call me into the house. Only me. He ignored the officer. I took leave of my officer, and let go of my fantasy. I ran into the house.

My father followed me into my room, sat down beside me on my sofa-bed and reached for my hand. Gladly I placed it in his, and suddenly I knew that whatever I had done, could not have been so bad. I felt an overwhelming sensation of love and trust from my father. I knew that everything would be all right.

He embraced me and, calmly and softly, said: "My Agi, you are growing up and the world is growing crazy around us. I am so sorry that you cannot have the good time and the fun that you should be having. But the times before us are dark and unpromising. I really don't want to reprimand you, but I must. You see, you are a Jewish young lady and I do not want you to go out with non-Jewish young men."

He stopped for a moment, and we just sat there together, motionless. He sighed and continued: "It is hard for me to explain this all to you, especially when times are so bad and nothing is like it was anymore. But more so now than ever before, we Jews must stick together, as we are facing terrible times. I would like for you to obey me, and not go out with this officer anymore. I do not want you to go out with non-Jewish boys at all. Please take note of what I am saying to you, as we don't know what the future holds for us." And then he kissed me, and let go of my hand.

I sat there for a long time, huddled up on my sofa-bed gazing at nothing at all, rethinking every word my father had said to me. I heard those words over and over in my head, until they penetrated into my heart. In fact, I can still hear them now, today.

From that day on, I stopped going to tennis. I never walked the short-cut to the tennis school again. I never saw my Hungarian officer again. And I never went out with a non-Jewish boy, ever again.

I never had another beautiful moment with my father in my room in our summer place in Svabhegy. I never again did anything my father could have objected to. Our days together were numbered. But on one last occasion my father gave me the greatest legacy, the one that would serve as a basis for my whole future life.

On the 19th of March 1944, just as winter was coming to an end, the Germans marched into Budapest. And everything came to an end. For me, life stopped altogether, but not for fear of the Germans. I suddenly realized all too clearly that we were no longer Hungarians. This illusion disappeared, vanished. Now we were Jews only, nothing more and nothing less; and to be Jews in Hungary in 1944 was like being dirt or vermin, or worse.

There was only one aim for the Germans, and most of the Hungarians as well: to destroy all the Jews, as quickly as possible. Already too much time had been wasted in dilly-dallying. The Jews had to be packed up in one big bundle and their fate settled by the "final solution."

But for me this was only incidental, as if I were a by-stander. For me the real tragedy, the real end, was the fact that my father was dying of cancer. My mother and I were told, bluntly, honestly, by our doctor friend that Father had only a few months to live. What more was there to lose when I was to lose my father?

It was almost eerie how little everything else mattered. It was as if for me there was only my private hell to burn in. Everything around me seemed blurred and I walked into danger undaunted. I wore my yellow star sometimes, but took it off when I felt like it. I had no fear of the Germans. I hated them fiercely, but I hated the sickness that was killing my father even more.

My father underwent surgery (hoping against hope) in the middle of a very severe bombing raid. And while Jews were being rounded up and taken in freight cars to concentration camps, I sat with my father in the hospital, undisturbed by the horrors around me. My mother was in the same state as I was, but I felt only my own pain. After the operation my father's condition improved slightly and his pain diminished for a while. He was able to return home. But "home" was now a different place altogether. Our house in 9 Andrassy Ut had been declared a "Jewish House," which enabled us to remain there, but in one room only. At least we were still in our own beds. This was something to rejoice about in those days. Every room in our large apartment was now occupied by other families. We had become one huge family sharing the premises of this "Jewish House" that had once been my home.

The one room allotted to us had been my parents' bedroom and I ended up sleeping on the beautiful couch there, with its deep-red Persian rug cover. In the "good old days" it had been on this very couch that my father had rested every afternoon after the midday meal. He had often called me in to sit with him, "just for a moment, until I fall asleep," and when he would, I would quietly tiptoe out of the room, happy for the private moment we'd had together.

My brother had been taken to a "labor camp" months previously. We heard from him at first, and then we heard nothing at all. We worried and talked about him often, but our own immediate fate became our primary concern.

I spent many sleepless nights wondering about the future and our lives without my father. The large sepia photos of my father's parents, the grandparents that I only knew from pictures, talked to me sometimes, in the bleak, empty nights filled only with fear, anxiety and sadness.

Often, there was the sound of wailing sirens, when the bombing of Budapest was carried out. But we Jews had a totally different attitude from the Hungarians towards the bombing. We were not at all frightened of the bombs. We welcomed them! For us they were our only salvation. My father rejoiced in the sound of planes hovering noisily above us. He would say: "Come, come, come!" and often would add quietly something that stirred me greatly: "Let them come and finish us here, together." It was really a time when death was our companion and maybe our secret hope. For the death that awaited us from the Nazis was worse than any other death, this much we knew.

I often only pretended to eat, as food was terribly scarce and I wanted Father to have as much as possible of our meager rations. It was then that I started to smoke. It was a good substitute for food. I chain-smoked, trying to satisfy my appetite. Maybe it did help, as it certainly made me feel sick rather than hungry.

Human nature is a fascinatingly complex thing. In our miserable and desperate condition, crowded, hungry, lacking everything that was necessary for existence, cold — as winter was approaching and we had nothing to heat with or warm up water to wash in — we, a group of doomed Jews whose fate mattered to no one, still felt driven to find enjoyment in whatever there was left for us to enjoy.

There were now two pianos in what had been the spacious living room of our once magnificent home. One was my beloved piano, on which I had learned to play jazz, the music I adored. The other belonged to my famous teacher and her even more famous son, Gyuri Feyer. They were one of the many families that had moved into our "Jewish House." It was my idea to have some musical evenings whenever Gyuri appeared (I really did not know from where) for a few hours to visit his mother.

On such evenings, we asked him to play for us. He would sit at his piano and play Gershwin's "Rhapsody in Blue." It was unforgettably beautiful, and for a few minutes we Jews, gathered in our home, felt almost human. We experienced something close to enjoyment. But we knew this could not last.

Our final musical evening was not long in coming. The so-called "*hazmester*" (janitor), the menace, the anti-Semite whose word could mean life or death for us, decided that we did not deserve to have such fun. We were not to have any fun at all anymore. That night, the pianos were silenced.

My father occasionally ventured out onto the streets without the yellow star on his coat. We would beg him not to go, as he was not only in danger of being picked up and sent straight to a concentration camp, but he was becoming so weak that he could hardly drag himself about. But even in his sickness he remained such a strong, forceful personality that one could not argue with him. His will was unbending.

On one of these days, as he was putting on his coat without the yellow star, he said to us: "I have something terribly important still to arrange," and in great distress we watched him go. This must have been in late October or early November of 1944. We knew that time was our only ally, as the Germans were being beaten on all fronts and the Russians were moving closer and closer towards Hungary. But the Nazis were in a frantic hurry to round up all the Jews still left in Budapest, not only in the ghetto, but in the "Jewish Houses" as well. The end was getting terrifyingly near.

Father returned home tired, limp and pale. It was one of those days when every Jew found wandering the streets was sent straight to the freight cars. His looks, his non-Jewish looks, were his protection.

Father rested for a while, and then called us in, my mother and me. He sat us down, very near to him on the couch and we waited for him to speak. His skin was chalk-white. His long, slender fingers were so thin that I could not take my eyes off them. Then I heard his voice, sad, but still strong, and ever so loving.

"My Agi," he said, "I have something very important to

give you and to say to you. Listen carefully, please, to every word I have to say, as I don't know what fate has in store for us. We possibly will be separated soon. You are young and you still have your whole life before you. Your life must be saved. Now listen to me and listen carefully. I purchased something today, for an awful lot of money, all the money we have left. I bought some Christian identification papers for you. Under this name, you will live with a Hungarian family and you will try to hide from the bombs in the shelter. You will be safe from the Nazis under this false name."

My father stopped speaking and wiped his forehead. He paused for a long time. I could hardly breathe from the anxiety that I felt. Not anxiety for my own safety, but at the terrible possibility of being separated from my father, who I felt needed me so much!

But I did not dare to interrupt. I waited for him to continue. He raised his voice, and his face was terribly sad. He had tears in his eyes. I had never seen tears in my father's eyes before. He turned to me and held my hand and said: "One thing you must never forget. This is the most important thing that I have to say to you, that I want to leave you with. When this is all over, and you are safe, you must tear this paper to shreds. *We are Jews as long as we live. Don't ever forget that*."

I did not know then that this was going to be my last day with my parents in Andrassy Ut 9. The next day, very early, before dawn, the Nazis took every able man, woman and child from our house. They left my father behind as he was too sick to be dragged along. We were chased down Andrassy Ut. I barely managed to turn back quickly to look at our windows, hoping my father would be watching us. The windows were empty and my heart felt the same.

We were marched towards the brick factory — somewhere I had never been before. There we were to be "selected" and sent to concentration camps.

But that is another story....

Appendix III

Full Circle

Looking back, remembering my childhood, reminiscing about the life I once had is one of the most exciting things for me. To me *that* life seems almost as if it might have been in another time, on another planet — something so faintly resembling the second part of my life that it seems almost like a dream. A dream that keeps coming back, sometimes in dreams, yet sometimes in reality — but even then, it still seems to be only a dream.

There was one aspect of my childhood days, that had an incredibly strong impact on my adult life. The memory had stored itself in the windmill of my mind, and although it occurred so long ago, my recollection of it remains sharp. All I have to do is think of it, and it appears right before me in its entirety.

I will set the scene for you, so that you might relive this experience along with me: our summer house on Normafa Ut in Svabhegy, my beloved garden filled with flowers and fruit trees, different scents of the different seasons, each one with its special flavor and fragrance. In the late spring, when we would take up residence there, it was still lilac time, and the heavy lilac bushes hung over the tall fence that stood between our house and the one next door.

Well, not quite next door, as a little narrow lane — you could not call it a street, yet it had a name, Jeno Utca — separated the two houses. This lane is very important in describing the relationship between us and the next-door neighbors: though we were separated by a narrow little track, a tiny cobblestone lane, in reality there was a *world* dividing us.

I've already told you about my father and his feelings vis-à-vis the "black" Orthodox Jews. So just imagine how he must have felt when *right next door* to his dream house, his beloved summer villa, there lived none other than a "black" Orthodox family. Not that he had anything at all to do with them; it was lucky for him that there was that little narrow lane between us, as otherwise we would have had a common fence with them.

I do not remember my parents ever being invited over to that family's home, or the other way around. They may have been our immediate neighbors, but socially we were very far removed from them. At least my parents were.

But my brother and I could not resist being drawn to that house, as there were children our age living there, and even though the difference between their parents and ours was quite obvious (the mother wore a black *tichel* practically all the time, and what was probably a *sheitel* on *Shabbat*), this did not matter to us. The father always wore a hat, but I don't remember ever seeing his son Gyuri wearing a *kippah*. (This seems strange to me now, because he *must* have worn one, but perhaps only at meals.) To me Gyuri was just like any other boy, just like any other friend of my older brother.

I had a rough time keeping up with my brother's friends, as I was always the youngest among them, but I adored being part of his circle. He was terribly handsome, and to me he was my "ideal," the yardstick against whom I measured all boys. He looked like Robert Taylor (my girlfriends said so); he was strong (I knew he would always protect me); he was the fastest on his bicycle (although I was not far behind him); and he played the drums!

My youth was filled with jazz, the music my brother and I loved, and we constantly played, exchanged, and borrowed records from our friends. At some stage my brother organized a small band, and those days when we had a real live orchestra playing on our huge verandah at Svabhegy were the happiest I can remember. It was good to be the younger sister of an older brother who did such exciting things. All I had to do was follow him, if he let me.

Of course the girls he went out with were older than me, and it was this that created complications in my life. Because of it, I hated the girls and preferred the boys in my brother's circle of friends. I certainly did not count as a "girl" like the girls with whom they walked, danced and played tennis. I was just my brother's sister. I had no name. I was merely the sister who was always around. And I was happy with my status.

Gyuri Weinberger was in our home much more often than we were in his. I don't know why this was the case, but I can think of several possible reasons. First, our parents were more modern, and maybe even younger than his, making for a more lighthearted atmosphere at our place. Second, I vaguely recall that his parents were not quite as "Hungarian" as we were, that they came from somewhere else, possibly Poland. And if they were "Polishi" Jews, *Galicianer,* the ones my father could not tolerate, then obviously we would have been discouraged from spending much time at their house.

I particularly liked Gyuri. He was fun to be with, and in spite of everything I occasionally did go over to his house, where, I remember, even the odor of the food was different from the food we ate.

Our kitchen was downstairs. It was called the *suterin* and it had a "dumb waiter" by which our meals were delivered to the dining room upstairs. Can you imagine anything more exciting for a child than having a "lift," which was operated by a heavy cable, that transported the food from downstairs where the maid and the cook were, to upstairs, where we lived?

They would put the hot, cooked food into the lift, then run upstairs to pull it up, and serve it to my parents, my brother, my *Fräulein* and me, seated properly at the dining room table or, if it was warm enough, on the huge terrace.

Thinking back on this, I must smile, as I remember for certain that my mother never moved an inch to bring in the food, but my father often got up from the table and went down to the pantry to fetch the special bread he ate, as he was a diabetic and had to have many special foods.

My mother would say "Dezsokem, why don't you ask the servants to bring it to you?" And he would reply: "Why? Is there something wrong with my legs that I cannot go down and get it myself?" My father was a very "democratic" man in some ways, and I loved him for it.

I decided I would follow in my father's footsteps when I grew up. I would not ring the bell for everything, but instead would either ask very amicably or get up myself from the table and actually go down and bring something up from the kitchen.

Little did I know in my carefree youth that I would not have to worry about problems like this in the future! Life sorted it all out for me.

On Sundays, my parents always entertained guests. It was a marvelous treat for our visitors to board the little train and in a mere half an hour after leaving hot, humid Budapest behind, find themselves suddenly in the mountains, in the fresh air, and enjoying the good hospitality of our home.

On Sunday afternoons, cakes, fruit platters, coffee and cocoa were served continuously. And for Sunday night supper we had, without fail, stuffed cabbage. There was a special reason for this: some family members, mainly my father's brothers and my cousins, usually stayed over for dinner, and, as the old Hungarian saying goes: "Cabbage is only good when warmed up" (a clumsy, but accurate, translation). My mother would have the servants put the huge pot of cabbage on the stove before they left on Sundays, their day off, and all she would have to do was put it in the lift. We children, my brother and I, would take it out and place it on the already set dining room table.

I have not thought about this for years, but right now I can almost smell that wonderful stuffed cabbage as it sat steaming on the table, while the whole family — aunts, uncles, cousins — helped themselves to their Sunday night supper. And of course there was also cherry strudel, our regular Sunday night special.

It was on one of those happy summer Sunday afternoons that I heard my father calling to me: "Agikam, Agikam." I was at the neighbors' house, playing ping-pong with Gyuri. "Apu, I am here," I shouted back. "What do you want?" And I heard his voice, quite stern this time, saying: "I want you home immediately."

Somehow I knew from his voice that he was angry. But why? What had I done?

I rushed back home. My father was standing on the terrace, away from the guests and my mother, and he waved me over to his side with his powerful arm. I ran to him and asked: "Why are you angry?"

He said that there was something he wanted to tell me, but it was not easy to explain, as he himself did not quite know how to put it into words. I stood and waited on every word he uttered. I was mesmerized by him whenever he talked to me; I was never frightened of him, but I really had no reason ever to be frightened.

At last he said: "My Agi, the Weinbergers are very nice people..." and he went on to say that he thought Gyuri was a good boy, but still, for reasons he could not explain very well to me, as I think he himself did not quite know them, he would rather that I did not take the friendship with them too seriously, as they were quite different from us. I heard what he said to me, but I did not understand it in my heart.

I looked up at my father and asked: "How are they different from us?" I think this question was unexpected, as my father looked surprised when I put it to him.

He replied thoughtfully and slowly: "They are Orthodox Jews. They are not even Hungarians; they are actually Polish Jews."

Aha, I knew it! This is what I had thought they were, and now I understood. I understood that my father, who to me was *everything* that was perfection, had this one weakness, which had something to do with Orthodox Jews. He simply did not like the "black," religious Jews. He liked handsome Hungarian Jews, people like us.

All right, I thought, I will not go over to their house, if that is what my father wants, but I will certainly not end my friendship with Gyuri.

And we continued to be friends, and race one another on our bicycles, and listen to records on our beautiful terrace. And we even danced occasionally on a moonlit Saturday evening, in our lovely summer house at Svabhegy. And then, after our last summer at Svabhegy in 1943, I never saw or heard of Gyuri again.

Like dozens of my friends, boys and girls whom I knew, Gyuri disappeared from my life. Perhaps because our connection was just a summer friendship, I thought about him only once or twice in all the intervening years.

Now I must take a huge leap, to 1984, when Steven and I were spending our usual summer vacation in Jerusalem. One morning, I read in *The Jerusalem Post* that there was going to be an international reunion of Hungarian Holocaust survivors in Jerusalem, the first of its kind for Hungarian Jews only. There were to be sessions at several sites, including one at *Yad Vashem*.

I knew as I read, that I *had* to go to this meeting, and I also knew that it would be tough and very emotional, especially for someone like me. My husband had the same thoughts and tried to talk me out of it. "What do you want to achieve by going to such an emotional event as a meeting of Holocaust survivors in, of all places, *Yad Vashem*?" he asked.

We had been to *Yad Vashem*, Israel's Holocaust memorial, on our first visit in 1969, but we never could make ourselves go through it again. If you've never seen this very special museum, with its haunting photographs and artifacts, you cannot imagine how deeply it affects its visitors. For survivors like ourselves, it was a terribly painful experience.

I said to Steven: "Look, who should go there if not us?" But my comment did not satisfy my much more realistic husband. He insisted that I give him a better reason for getting myself all worked up again!

I thought and thought, and suddenly I had it. "You know," I said, "I might run into Gyuri Weinberger there. Who knows, maybe he too will come for this meeting."

My husband waved me away, indicating that I was hopeless, but in the end he gave in, and we went and put our names down for the meeting of the Hungarian Holocaust survivors in Jerusalem.

Natalie at the time was the proud mother of two sons, with a third child on the way. She was very excited about our Hungarian meeting, and she also warned me to not get too emotional, as it really was not good for me. I promised I would do my best.

I had no idea what was in store for me, and quite honestly, if I had read it in a book, I would have said: "Oh come on, you don't expect me to believe this to be true?" But it is all true; it really happened.

The meeting was very well-organized. The opening sessions took place in *Binyanei Ha'Uma*, the Jerusalem convention center. All the participants received name tags (in case we could not recognize one another after 40 or 45 years!). On the walls there were long lists of names from various towns, with the longest list naturally from Budapest.

The first morning was just "look-and-see." Already this was highly emotional for me. You see, I with my intense, mystically oriented nature, was ready for *anything*!

The opening night ceremony alone would have been "*dayenu*" for me, it was so unforgettable. We were all seated in the large concert hall of *Binyanei Ha'Uma*, and on the stage was an orchestra of young Israeli soldiers, boys and girls, in their uniforms.

Already with the first strains of *Hatikva*, my eyes started to fill with tears. I, who never found any significance in either the Hungarian or the Australian national anthems, get teary-eyed and come very close to crying every time I hear *Hatikva*. Especially on this occasion, as the young soldiers were playing for *us*, Hungarian Holocaust survivors. In Jerusalem.

The chairman of the evening was no less than Edward Teller, the world-famous nuclear physicist originally from Budapest, from where he had emigrated to the U.S. before the Second World War. He spoke with a slight accent, very beautifully, in Hungarian, and his presence made the already great event even greater.

Our very best friends from Tel Aviv, naturally also Hungarians, joined us, and we suddenly became the *Yerushalmi* Hungarians, a title that was music to my ears.

The next day was going to be a highly-charged one, and my husband again tried to warn me: "You must look at things in perspective. You cannot allow yourself to relive each day, each minute," he said. But how can one change suddenly from one's own set, emotional self?

Visiting *Yad Vashem* once more, after decades, and this time with the thought of my grandchildren, my Israeli grandchildren, tucked away in my consciousness, made the whole event (as far as I was concerned) even more emotional. In a positive way!

We stood in the darkened hall in *Yad Vashem*, where the names of the concentration camps are engraved in plaques on the floor, each one with the number of people killed, gassed, liquidated there. Adults and children, separately. An Eternal Flame provides the only light in the room. This memorial is devastating, at any time, but filled with only Hungarian Holocaust survivors, it was deeply moving.

I could not quite believe that it was I who was standing there, I the mother of a beautiful, religious daughter and the Savta of my two Israeli grandsons. In Jerusalem. It was overwhelming.

Yes, I was crying, and I could not help it. I was sure I must have looked awful, and I kept my sunglasses on as we walked slowly out of the dark and terribly sad memorial. There were hundreds of us, and we all walked slowly, sadly, rubbing our eyes as we came out into the burning, golden sunlight of Yerushalayim.

I was quietly walking near my husband, but alone, deep in thought, when I saw a man approach him. I was right behind Steven, and I listened to what the man was saying to him.

The man was about 60, with almost-white hair, a good strong mop of hair, and a very smart, stylishly-trimmed beard. I had actually noticed him already at one of the earlier sessions, just as an interesting looking person, not particularly Hungarian looking.

He looked straight at my husband and said in perfect Hungarian: "Tell me, old fellow (öregem), are you not by any chance Steven?" It is easy to recognize my husband as he really looks so young and unchanged.

The white-bearded man wanted to say something more, but my husband burst out laughing: "How did you recognize me, and what is your name?" I stood quite close behind them now, but still separately, and I thought: It must be one of my husband's old schoolmates.

Then I heard him ask: "If you are Steven, then maybe you will be able to tell me something that I have wanted to know for such a long time, as you were so friendly with Pista. Is he alive, and is his sister, Agi, alive?"

Ah, that old, eternal, agonizing question of one survivor to another!

And my very disciplined and unemotional husband stared at this white-haired man and eagerly asked: "Who are you? What is your name?"

And, as if it might have been the most logical outcome of this whole Holocaust meeting, as if it had been pre-arranged (as it probably was, but obviously by the Upper Hand), the man replied: "Weinberger, Weinberger Gyuri. I lived next door to Agi and her family in Svabhegy."

And my "cool" husband, with tears in his eyes, turned around, pulled me forward, and presented me, saying: "Here is Agi for you. She too hoped to meet you here. In fact, she came only to meet you once again."

But this was only the beginning.

The past 46 years have been filled with the most unbelievable happenings. Survival, reunions — everything that has happened to us since 1944 was a sheer miracle. So why should I have been surprised to see my dear friend Gyuri once more, in Jerusalem, at the Hungarian Holocaust meeting? It was nothing special, nothing to write home about.

But what happened the following day *was* worth writing about, as the story till now has only been the "appetizer." Then came the "main course."

We walked side-by-side the whole day, Gyuri and I and his lovely wife (whom I knew, naturally, from Budapest). My husband trailed after us, with an understanding smile. We tried to fill each other in on everything that had happened since 1943, our last summer in Svabhegy.

The most exciting news (aside from the fact that we were

both alive), was that we both had daughters, almost the same age, and both living in Israel. This was really something to rejoice about. Gyuri's daughter Mary was married to a kibbutznik, and they had two children, a boy and a girl. Gyuri and his wife lived in Canada. Mary was their only child.

Since the Weinbergers were staying at a hotel and would only be in Israel for a few more days, I immediately invited them to come to our home the next day for afternoon drinks, and I suggested that if possible we should try to bring our daughters together.

When I told her about it, Natalie was happy to come, and I asked her to look extra-specially beautiful, because she was going to meet one of my oldest and dearest childhood friends.

I had invited them for five o'clock, and they arrived just a few minutes before. It was marvelous to see them in our own home in Jerusalem, and I really tried to play down the emotional aspect of our meeting, saying to myself that, after all, it was not such an unusual thing to have one's wish come true...

We were sitting in the living room, Gyuri, his wife, his daughter Mary — a very lovely, attractive young woman, about the same age as Natalie — and her two children, and her very, very nice, typical *Hashomer Hatza'ir** kibbutznik husband.

Natalie was a little bit late. Then the doorbell rang and in came my daughter and her two sons. Natalie wore a lovely long-sleeved, summer dress, stockings (naturally), and her hair was covered with one of the pretty *tichels* I had bought for her in Zurich.

She looked the picture of a modern, religious woman-of-the-world. And Yacov and Zevi, blonde, handsome boys, my beloved grandsons, were dressed nicely in shorts, shirts, and their regular everyday *kippot* and *tzitzit*. But why make a point of it; everybody knows that my daughter is a B.T. and that my grandsons always wear these obvious symbols of

---

*An ideologically secular branch of the kibbutz movement in Israel.

Orthodox Judaism.

Everybody but Gyuri.

He was absolutely stunned. He looked at me, and he looked at Natalie, and again at me, and at the boys, and back to me, and it was *then*, it was at *that moment*, that I felt the floor suddenly swaying under me. I, Agi from Normafa Ut, was introducing my beautiful Orthodox daughter and my two Orthodox grandsons, *kippot* and all, to my dear old friend and neighbor, Gyuri.

The rest is nothing else but showing off, but please bear with me. You've had the "appetizer" and the "main course," so you might as well stick around for "dessert":

We stayed on in Jerusalem for another two weeks to be with my family and also to attend the closing ceremony of the Hungarian Holocaust survivors meeting. This was held in a much smaller hall, part of the Great Synagogue on King George Street.

We went together with Gyuri to the ceremony and we sat beside him the whole morning. We kept looking at each other and beaming with joy. The final speech was to be by Teller, and we were going to wait for this. One of the last speakers, one of the organizers from Jerusalem, asked if there was anything anybody would still like to add to what had been said at this very special gathering.

I had never in my life spoken in public, as I am very self-conscious about my accent (no matter how often I am told that it is "charming"). If I've ever had anything to say, I've written it down and let it be published. This has always been my way of communicating with the public.

So what made me raise my hand as if I were signaling that I *did* have something to add to what those clever people had already said???

The organizer, a very nice ex-Hungarian Israeli (Moshe Sanbar), turned to me and said: "*B'vakashah*" (please), and invited me up to the dais, right next to Edward Teller. I, Savta, suddenly had something terribly urgent, something terribly important to say, in a hall in the Jerusalem Great Synagogue, in front of a lot of people.

I had nothing with me, no notes, nothing prepared. I walked up, stood on the dais (next to Teller), and I who usually starts crying at the slightest emotional occurrence, began to tell everybody there, in a strong and firm (and I think proud) voice what I considered the "Full Jewish Circle" to be.

I told them about our meeting, mine and Gyuri's, drew a picture for them to visualize the past and the present, addressed them in a sensible, disciplined tone of voice (not crying — I had already done that at the meeting), and found myself actually explaining to them my own marvelous discovery of how we Jews will always retain our Jewish heritage, no matter what. We might skip one or two generations as far as being religious is concerned, I said, we might think that we would rather assimilate — but, as in my family, we eventually return to our roots.

And I told them that my daughter keeps asking me to try to produce a Rabbi from my family tree, and that I cannot do that, no matter how much I would like to do it for her. I told them that I always end up telling my daughter that she must not worry about the past, but rejoice in the present and think of the future. And I told them that deep down in my heart I think that one of our grandsons has the makings of a *Rav*, maybe one of those big *Ravs*.

I said what I had wanted to; I felt relieved and happy. I heard clapping, some people shook my hand. I even received a note from somebody — I don't know who. The note said:

> *Kol hakavod!* This was the most important speech of the reunion, as you personally represent the "Full Circle" of our great tradition, our great heritage as Jews!

✳

GLOSSARY

Glossary

The following glossary provides a partial explanation of some of the Hebrew, Yiddish, Hungarian and German words and phrases used in this book. The spelling and explanations reflect the way the specific word is used herein. Often there are alternate spellings and meanings for the words.

ABBA: father.

AISHET CHAYIL: a "Woman of Valor."

ALIYAH: immigration to Israel.

ANYUKAM: (Hung.) mother.

AV: the month of the Hebrew calendar that corresponds to July/August.

AVINU MALKENU: "Our Father, our King."

B'LI AYIN HARA: "May [they] be protected from the evil eye."

B'LI: without.

B'SHA'AH TOVAH: "May it be in a good (propitious) hour."

B'VAKASHAH: please.

BAAL(EI) (BAALAT — fem.) TESHUVAH: those who have "returned" to Orthodox Judaism.

BACHUR(IM): yeshiva student(s).

BALAGAN: (colloq.) a state of total chaos.

BARUCH HASHEM: "Thank God."

BASHERT: (Yid.) Divinely predetermined.

BECHER: (Yid.) a wine cup.

BECHOR: a firstborn son.

BEN: son.

BENTCH: (Yid.) to recite Grace after the meal.

BERACHAH (-CHOT): blessing(s).

BETH DIN: a Jewish court of law.

BLECH: (Yid.) a piece of metal placed over an even, slow flame, or an electric food warmer, used for keeping food warm on the Sabbath.

BRIS, BRIT, BRIT MILAH: the ritual circumcision (ceremony) of all Jewish male infants.

BUBAH: doll.

CHAG(GIM): holiday(s); specifically the High Holidays.

CHAI: live.

CHASSUNAH, CHATUNAH: a wedding.

CHEDER: (Yid.) a religious elementary school.

CHESHBON: an accounting.

CHEVREH: (colloq.) group.

CHOLENT: (Yid.) a popular Sabbath stew that cooks overnight.

CHOZER(ET) B'TESHUVAH: see BAAL TESHUVAH.

CHUMRAH: stringency.

CHUPPAH: lit., the wedding canopy; a wedding ceremony.

DATI(YAH): religious (fem.).

DAVEN: (Yid.) to pray.

DAVKA: (colloq.) contrarily; for the sake of being contrary.

DAYENU: enough for us.

EIN BREIRAH: "There is no choice."

ELUL: the month of the Hebrew calendar that corresponds to August/September.

ERETZ YISRAEL: the Land of Israel.

EREV: the eve of (the Sabbath or Festival).

FLEISHIG: (Yid.) pertaining to meat dishes.

FRÄULEIN: (Ger.) a nanny or governess.

FRUM: (Yid.) religiously observant.

GALUT: the Diaspora.

GAN: kindergarten.

GANENET: a kindergarten teacher.

GLATT: (Yid.) extra-strict KASHRUT (of meat).

GOMBOC: (Hung.) a matza ball.

GOOT: (Yid.) good.

HAGGADAH: the text read at the Passover Seder in which the story of the emancipation of the Children of Israel from Egyptian bondage is recounted.

HALACHAH: Jewish Law.

HASHOMER HATZA'IR: an ideologically secular branch of the kibbutz movement in Israel.

HATIKVA: Israel's national anthem.

HAZMESTER: (Hung.) janitor.

HECHSHER: Rabbinic approval of a food product, which determines its suitability for consumption by Jews.

ICH ZUNDE DIE FUR MEINE ELTERN: (Ger.) "I light [these] for my parents."

IMA: mother.

IYAR: the month of the Hebrew calendar that corresponds to April/May.

KAPPAROT: substitutes.

KASHRUT: the Jewish dietary laws.

KETUBAH: the marriage contract.

KIPPAH (-POT): yarmulka(s) or skullcap(s).

KNAIDLACH: matza balls.

KOHEN: a descendant of the Priestly family.

KOL HAKAVOD: "Well done!"

KOTEL: the Western or Wailing Wall.

KUKIYOT: ponytails.

L'CHAYIM: "To life!"

LAG BA'OMER: the 33rd day of the counting of the Omer (the seven week semi-mourning period between Passover and the Shavuot, the Festival of Weeks).

LASHON HA-RA: gossip-mongering.

MA'ASER: tithe.

MACHSAN: a basement storage or utility room.

MAH NISHTANAH: a part of the HAGGADAH traditionally recited by the youngest family member at the Seder.

MAR'IT AYIN: a semblance.

MAZAL TOV: "Congratulations!"

MECHITZAH: a barrier separating the men from the women at a religious affair.

MEGILLAH: the scroll read on Purim recounting the story of the salvation of the Jews of Persia and Media from the evil Haman through the help of the Jewish Queen Esther and her uncle Mordechai.

MENSCH: (Yid., colloq.) a truly decent human being.

MEZUZAH (-ZOT): the parchment scroll(s) placed on the doorposts of Jewish homes and inscribed with the SHEMA.

MI ZEH: "Who's there?"

MIKVEH: a ritual bath.

MILCHIG: (Yid.) pertaining to dairy dishes.

MIN HA-SHAMAYIM: from Heaven, i.e., from God.

MINHAG(GIM): custom(s).

MISHLOACH MANOT: gift packages of food traditionally sent on Purim.

MOHEL: a ritual circumcisor.

MOTZA'EI SHABBAT: the end of the Sabbath.

MUKTZEH: anything that is forbidden to be handled or moved on the Sabbath.

MUNKATABOR: (Hung.) labor camp.

NACHES: (Yid., colloq.) joy.

NESIAH TOVAH: "Have a good trip!"

ÖREGEM: (Hung.) old fellow.

PARASHAH: the weekly Torah portion.

PECSET GYURU: (Hung.) a signet or seal-ring.

PIDYON: redemption.

PIDYON HABEN: the ceremony of the Redemption of the Firstborn Son.

RAV: rabbi.

REBBE: (Yid.) rabbi or teacher.

REBBETZIN: (Yid.) the wife of a rabbi.

REFUAH SHELEMAH: a complete recovery.

ROSH YESHIVAH: the dean of the yeshiva.

SABA: grandfather.

SABRA: (colloq.) someone born in the Holy Land.

SANDAK: the person who has the honor of holding the baby at the BRIT.

SATOROS UNNEP: (Hung.) a Festival connected with tents.

SAVTA: grandmother.

SCHMONTZES: (Yid., colloq.) trivia.

SEUDAH: a festive meal.

SEUDAH SHELISHIT: the third Sabbath meal.

SHABBAT, SHABBOS: the Sabbath.

SHABBAT SHALOM: "Have a peaceful Sabbath."

SHADCHANUT: matchmaking.

SHALACH MANOS: see MISHLOACH MANOT.

SHALOM ZACHAR: lit., "Welcome, male child"; a party usually attended by men and boys only and held on the infant's very first Friday night, his first Shabbat.

SHALOM BAYIT: domestic tranquility.

SHAVUA TOV: "Have a good week."

SHEITEL: (Yid.) a wig.

SHEMA: the central prayer of Judaism declaring the unity of God.

SHEMITTAH: the seventh year in the agricultural cycle during which special regulations for the produce of the Land of Israel are in effect.

SHIDDUCH: an arranged marital match.

SHIUR(IM): lesson(s).

SHMATTEH: (Yid.) a rag.

SHNITZEL: (colloq.) fried chicken breast.

SHOMER SHABBAT: a Sabbath observer.

SIMAN(IM): the symbolic food(s) traditionally eaten on Rosh Hashanah.

SIMCHAH: a joyous occasion.

TALLIT: a prayer shawl.

TEFILLIN: two black leather boxes containing Torah verses which are bound to the head and arm of adult males during morning prayers.

TICHEL(ACH): (Yid.) headscarf(s) or kerchief(s).

TOIVEL: (colloq.) to dip [a new vessel] into the waters of a MIKVEH and thereby render it usable in a Jewish home.

TREIF: (Yid., colloq.) non-kosher.

TREMDEDLI: (Hung.) a spinning-top.

TZADDIK: a righteous, pious man.

TZITZIT: lit., fringe; (colloq.) a four-cornered fringed garment worn by Orthodox Jewish males, usually under their shirts.

UT, UTCA: (Hung.) street, lane.

YERUSHALAYIM: Jerusalem.

YERUSHALMI: a Jerusalemite.